The Collection Program in Schools

Recent Titles in Library and Information Science Text Series

Introduction to Library Public Services, Seventh Edition
G. Edward Evans and Thomas L. Carter

Internet Technologies and Information Services
Joseph B. Miller

The Organization of Information, Third Edition
Arlene G. Taylor and Daniel N. Joudrey

Libraries in the Information Age: An Introduction and Career Exploration, Second Edition
Denise K. Fourie and David R. Dowell

Basic Research Methods for Librarians, Fifth Edition
Lynn Silipigni Connaway and Ronald R. Powell

Public Libraries in the 21st Century
Ann Prentice

Introduction to Technical Services, Eighth Edition
G. Edward Evans, Jean Weihs, and Sheila S. Intner

Science and Technology Resources: A Guide for Information Professionals and Researchers
James E. Bobick and G. Lynn Berard

Reference and Information Services: An Introduction, Fourth Edition
Richard E. Bopp and Linda C. Smith

Collection Management Basics, Sixth Edition
G. Edward Evans and Margaret Zarnosky Saponaro

Library and Information Center Management, Eighth Edition
Barbara B. Moran, Robert D. Stueart, and Claudia J. Morner

Information Resources in the Humanities and Arts, Sixth Edition
Anna H. Perrault and Elizabeth Aversa, with contributing authors Cynthia Miller and Sonia Wolmuth

The Collection Program in Schools

Concepts and Practices

FIFTH EDITION

Kay Bishop

Library and Information Science Text Series

AN IMPRINT OF ABC-CLIO, LLC
Santa Barbara, California • Denver, Colorado • Oxford, England

Library of Congress Cataloging-in-Publication Data

Bishop, Kay, 1942–
The collection program in schools : concepts and practices / Kay Bishop. — Fifth edition.
pages cm. — (Library and information science text series)
Includes bibliographical references and index.
ISBN 978-1-61069-021-8 (hardback) — ISBN 978-1-61069-022-5 (paperback) — ISBN 978-1-61069-372-1 (ebook) 1. School libraries—Collection development—United States. 2. Instructional materials centers—Collection development—United States. I. Title.
Z675.S3V334 2012
025.2'1878—dc23 2012032957

ISBN: 978-1-61069-021-8
978-1-61069-022-5 (pbk)
EISBN: 978-1-61069-372-1

17 16 15 14 13 1 2 3 4 5

This book is also available on the World Wide Web as an eBook.
Visit www.abc-clio.com for details.

Libraries Unlimited
An Imprint of ABC-CLIO, LLC

ABC-CLIO, LLC
130 Cremona Drive, P.O. Box 1911
Santa Barbara, California 93116-1911

This book is printed on acid-free paper ∞

Manufactured in the United States of America

Contents

Illustrations

FIGURES

TABLES

Author's Comments

I would like to thank Jill Warner, graduate student at the University at Buffalo, for locating some of the articles and websites for the "Additional Readings" and "Helpful websites" at the end of each chapter. Jill also revised some figures and tables in the book, as well as added some new figures to the book. Her technology skills and her attention to details during the writing of this book are greatly appreciated.

Dr. Kay Bishop

Introduction

Collection development in school libraries has seen many changes in the past few decades. School libraries are no longer simply repositories for books and other print and audiovisual materials. The addition of new technologies and digital resources has vastly expanded the school library collection. Students can now remotely access the holdings of school libraries (including their digital resources) from classrooms and often from their homes. The collection thus reaches far beyond the walls of the physical library facility.

Many principles and techniques for collection development are applicable to most school library settings; yet the unique characteristics of each school library program generate new and changing demands that require flexibility and creativity. To help school librarians face these challenges, this text:

- describes the learning environment in which the collection exists;
- presents principles, techniques, and common practices of collection development and management;
- raises issues that affect all collections, but that must be resolved in accordance with the goals and needs of a particular collection;
- suggests approaches to handling collection management situations and demands; and
- identifies helpful resources, including suggested readings, websites, and selection aids

This introductory text provides an overview of the processes and procedures associated with developing, maintaining, and evaluating a collection at the building level. The book reflects the opinion that the collection is a key element of the school library program, providing the means for meeting the information and instructional needs of the school population. To serve these needs, school librarians must consider the collection as a physical entity, composed not only of its internal resources, but also of the informational and instructional materials available through the Internet, electronic databases, the community, and resource sharing.

An underlying assumption is that collection development activities interact in a cyclical pattern. Policies and procedures for each of the activities are discussed in detail. Additional important topics and policy statements, such as students' rights, intellectual freedom, copyright and fair use guidelines, and acceptable use of Internet materials are addressed.

Chapter 1 focuses on definitions and characteristics of the collection, while Chapter 2 provides a brief overview of collection development activities. Chapters 3–12 discuss specific collection development activities in more detail, focusing on policies and procedures that need to be addressed for each activity. Chapter 13 deals with issues and ethics related to the development and management of school library collections. The impact of the curriculum on the collection is discussed in Chapter 14. Chapter 15 looks at how the collection can meet the needs of special groups of students, such as autistic students, gay and lesbian students, reluctant readers, minorities, and students with physical disabilities. Fiscal issues that relate to the collection, such as licensing, raising funds, and writing grants, are discussed in Chapter 16. Chapter 17 emphasizes the relationship of the collection to school library facilities and the learning environment. Information related to creating, moving, and closing collections is included in Chapter 18.

The Appendix is an annotated bibliography of resources that can be used for various collection development activities. If resources are mentioned in the text of chapters, they are generally included in the Appendix, with complete ordering information. Items listed in the "Additional Readings" at the end of each chapter are usually not included in the Appendix so readers should also refer to the listings in "Additional Readings" and "Helpful Websites" at the end of each chapter to obtain other valuable information on the topics covered in the chapters. Care was taken to provide a variety of articles in the "Additional Readings," including primarily short practical information, but also (when available) a few articles that discuss research studies relating to the chapter topics. Articles and Websites from other English-speaking countries (especially Canada) are sometimes included, and articles from other types of libraries, such as academic or public libraries, are listed when the information in them also applies to school library settings.

NEW AND UPDATED FEATURES

An obvious change in this edition of *The Collection Program in Schools: Concepts and Practices* is the use of the term *school librarian* to replace *school library media specialist*; this change reflects the American Association of School Librarians (AASL) vote in 2010 to use the official title of *school librarian*. Following the same pattern the author of this book has, for the most part, replaced the term *media center* with *school library.* These changes in no way indicate that other terms may not be as appropriate or useful.

Chapter 17, "Facilities, Digital Resources, and the Learning Environment," is a new addition to this fifth edition of *The Collection Program in Schools*. Additionally, the discussion of new technologies, digital resources, and the use of Web 2.0 tools have been integrated into most other chapters. Many new resources have been added to the text of chapters, particularly in Chapter 14, "The Curriculum." The impact of the Common Core State Standards on the curriculum and collections in school libraries are also included in Chapter 14.

References to the information in AASL's *Standards for the 21st-Century Learner* (2007) and AASL's *Empowering Learners: Guidelines for School Library Media Programs* (2009) are made in many of the book chapters. Additional recent documents, such as the American Library Association's *Minors and Internet Interactivity: An Interpretation of the Library Bill of Rights* (2009), are also discussed in the book. Suggested readings and websites at the end of chapters have been updated with more recent sources. However, this does not indicate that many of the outstanding articles and books from older editions of the book should not be used. In this fifth edition of the book more titles and websites from other countries have also been included.

Most figures and tables in the book have been revised, and some new ones have been added. The appendix has been expanded, with several new titles added.

The author recognizes that the previous editions of this book have been used in many courses for preservice school librarians, as well as by practitioners throughout the United States and in other countries. She always welcomes feedback from instructors of these courses and from practicing school librarians. It is the author's sincere desire that this text will continue to serve as a useful primary source for all readers who are interested in collection development in school libraries.

Dr. Kay Bishop <kgbishop@buffalo.edu>

Chapter

The Collection

What constitutes a school library collection? Before the 1990s, it would have been fairly easy to answer this question. A collection describes the resources (mainly print, but also some audiovisual items) that are housed in a single room of a school, the library. *Tangibility* (the physical presence of an item) and library *ownership* were two basic concepts of a traditional school library collection.

Today, however, it is much more difficult to define a school library collection. Does it include the online databases to which a school library subscribes? Are websites that a school librarian *marks* or *collects* for student use considered to be in the library's collection? If a school librarian provides links to virtual libraries, are the items in the virtual library part of the school library collection? If a librarian can access titles on a union catalog (a catalog combining in one alphabetical series the bibliographic records of more than one library) and obtain those titles for students through interlibrary loan, are they considered part of the school library collection? And if a student can access thousands of websites while seated at a computer in a school library, are all those sites included in a library collection? Few people would argue with the fact that with advances in information technology, the concept of the school library collection has changed significantly and expanded its scope. The collection undoubtedly goes beyond the walls of a single room in a school.

For the purposes of this book, a school library collection is defined as a group of information sources (print, nonprint, and electronic) selected and managed by the school librarian for a defined user community (students, faculty, and sometimes parents in a school). This definition excludes the thousands of websites accessed by students while sitting at school library computers, but does include online databases to which a school subscribes, websites that are selected and managed by a school librarian, materials in virtual libraries that can be accessed by the librarian, and items provided in a union catalog through interlibrary loan. If we ascribe to this definition, which includes viewing school librarians as both collection developers and managers, the concept of collection development policies becomes all-important since one needs guidelines to develop and manage a collection. Writing and implementing collection development policies and procedures for school libraries is a major portion of this book. Several chapters provide tools to assist school librarians in writing and implementing effective collection development policies.

PHYSICAL ENTITY AND ACCESSIBILITY

The collection housed in the school library is a physical entity composed of individual items that collectively create a whole. In collection development and management the value of a single item must be viewed in relation to other items in the collection. When deciding whether to add or withdraw a specific item to one's immediate physical collection, the following questions should be considered:

- Is the same information already in the collection, but in a different format?
- Will an alternative format make the information accessible to more people?
- Is the same or a similar item quickly accessible through a resource sharing network or the Internet?
- Does this item uniquely fill a particular user's need?

Questions like these help identify the relationship of one item to another in the collection.

With access to information through resource sharing and electronic means, school libraries have moved away from a philosophy of ownership to one of accessibility. The immediate physical collection provides only a starting point for students as they begin to search for information. Through online catalogs, students can learn about information resources in other libraries or information centers. The collection as a physical entity provides an initial point for coordinated collection development practices and resource sharing with other school libraries and institutions.

Although answers to students' questions were traditionally found in the collection housed in the school library, the answers today may or may not be. The collection goes beyond the walls of the immediate school library to a far-reaching world of resources and information.

Two types of barriers can limit access to information: physical barriers and a lack of policies and practices that demonstrate a commitment to intellectual freedom. Examples of potential physical barriers are height of shelving, width of aisles, and lack of necessary equipment for using or accessing materials. A small child or short person may not be able to reach an item on a shelf. A person in a wheelchair may not be able to move freely and make needed turns between the shelving. A partially sighted person may not be able to view a document without being able to enlarge the image.

A principle for information access and delivery is that the school library program is founded on the right of intellectual freedom. This commitment is not new; it is part of the profession's history. The position is equally significant today as we help students become critical thinkers and competent problem solvers who can contribute in a democracy.

THE SCHOOL LIBRARY PROGRAM AND THE COLLECTION

In the 2007 guidelines for school library media programs, *Standards for the 21st-Century Learner* (American Association of School Librarians), learners and learning are the main focus. These guidelines emphasize the constructive learning theory and support the belief that the school librarian guides students to becoming critical thinkers, enthusiastic readers, skillful researchers, and ethical users of information (American Association of School Librarians, 2009). A creative, energetic library program incorporates the four information literacy standards for student learning described in *Standards for the 21st-Century Learner* (American Association of School Librarians, 2007): Learners use skills and resources to

- inquire, think critically, and gain knowledge;
- draw conclusions, make informed decisions, apply knowledge to new situations, and create new knowledge;
- share knowledge and participate ethically and productively as members of our democratic society; and
- pursue personal and aesthetic growth.

The school library collection plays an important role in ensuring that the library program is integrated into the overall school program and in providing access to information both inside and outside the school. To meet the school's media needs effectively, the library program should

- be a vital part of the total school program;
- respond to the curricular needs and interests of teachers, administrators, and other staff members;
- consider the multicultural diversity of the student population, the developmental levels and learning styles of students, and the needs of students with disabilities;
- provide guidance in the use of and access to a full range of resources—print, nonprint, and electronic;
- cooperate with other institutions to provide the widest possible access to information, which may involve interlibrary loan, coordinated collection development, and other forms of resource sharing;
- exemplify the total media concept, providing access to materials in a variety of formats, appropriate equipment, trained personnel, and resources housed inside and outside the school library; and
- be managed by a staff that adequately plans and carries out the selection, maintenance, and evaluation of resources.

The school librarian is the person responsible for ensuring that these conditions exist and these functions take place.

The responsible school librarian supports the philosophy, goals, and objectives of the school in which the school library program functions. This person collaborates with teachers and administrators in the planning process to ensure that the library program is an integral part of the school program, manages the library program's operations, selects materials and other resources (including electronic formats), and instructs students and teachers. The school librarian who understands the value of the library program acts as its chief advocate by (a) offering informational, instructional, consultative, and production services, (b) evaluating the services and collection, and (c) promoting the program through public relations activities.

All members of the school faculty share responsibility for the library program. A school librarian cannot run an effective, integrated program alone. The leadership and human relations skills of the school librarian are called upon to involve others in the program. It is necessary for the school librarian to collaborate with teachers in curricular planning, and, in turn, teachers should collaborate with the librarian in planning and evaluating the library program.

A school librarian may find it difficult to involve administrators, teachers, and students in planning, implementing, and evaluating the library media program or collection. However, collection-related activities provide a range of opportunities for involvement. The librarian can increase participation in collection development by

- identifying the characteristics of the school library users and the demands of the curriculum;
- taking steps to involve administrators, teachers, and students in the development of school library policies;
- inviting others to participate in the selection of materials and online resources for the collection;
- facilitating interagency borrowing and lending of materials; and
- involving teachers, students, and administrators in the evaluation of the materials and policies.

The school librarian makes many decisions about the collection: what to add, what to access online or through resource sharing, and what to remove. While others can help with these decisions, it is the school librarian who must develop an overview of the total program, take responsibility for the decisions, and manage a responsive collection while involving others in the planning and evaluation process.

ROLES OF THE SCHOOL LIBRARIAN AND THE COLLECTION

Information Power: Building Partnerships for Learning (American Association of School Librarians & Association for Educational Communications and Technology, 1998) identified the following key roles of the school librarian as they relate to the total learning program: teacher, instructional partner, information specialist, and program administrator. These four roles are essential to the 21st-century school library program. In addition, leadership has been discussed as an important factor that contributes to a successful school library media program. Increased professional commitment and active participation in local, state, and national organizations not only strengthen the skills of the school librarian, but also help advance the profession (American Association of School Librarians, 2009).

The collection can be viewed as one element in the school's library program. From this perspective, the collection is a tool that supports the roles and activities of the school librarian. The school librarian's roles can be characterized as direct or indirect. The roles operate in a cyclical pattern as shown in Figure 1.1. Direct roles involve interaction with patrons and include professional services as teacher, instructional partner, and information specialist for students, teachers, staff, parents, and community members. The role of helping students evaluate the information they find is increasingly important as students face the multiple and varied information sources available through the Internet. The school librarian's *indirect* roles provide the means for carrying out the direct roles. In these roles the school librarian serves as program administrator or manager of the school library program, including developer and evaluator of the collection. These direct roles and indirect roles are interdependent. As a teacher, an instructional partner, and an information specialist, the school librarian gains knowledge used to make decisions about the collection

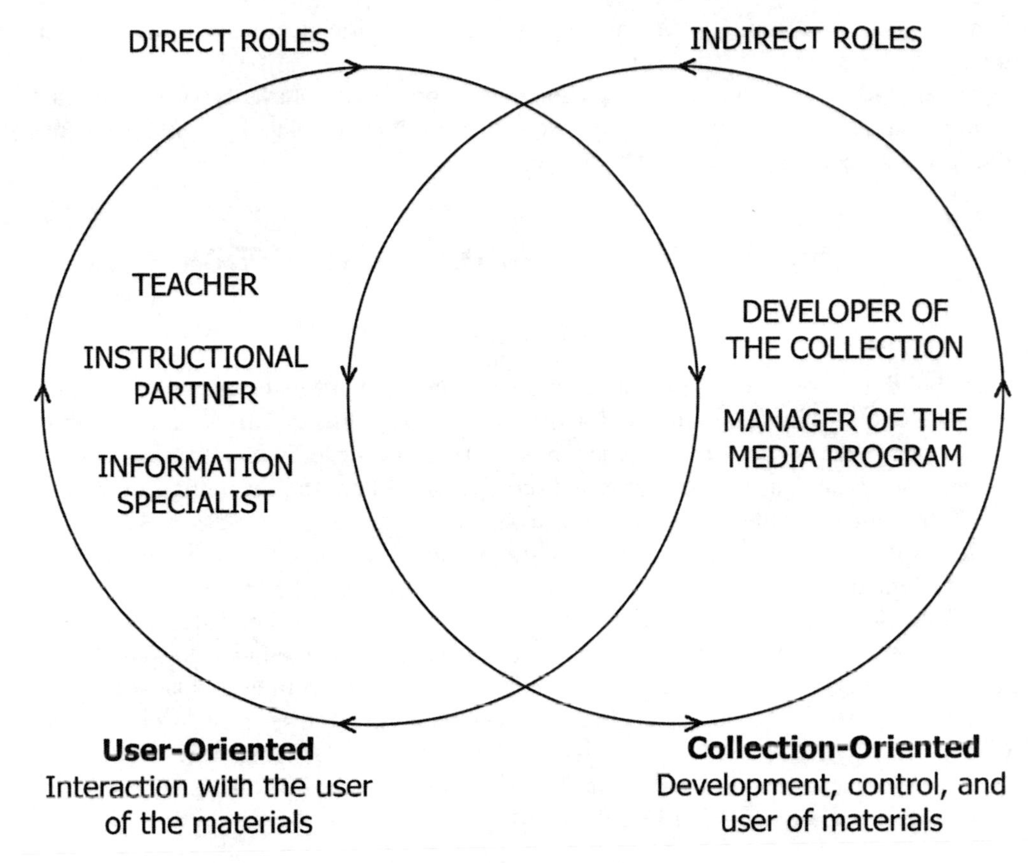

Figure 1.1. Roles of the school librarians as they contribute to the collection

As teachers, school librarians help students develop skills in accessing, evaluating, and using information from multiple sources. They work with classroom teachers and administrators to help them develop skills in information literacy, including the uses of information technology.

As instructional partners, school librarians join teachers in linking student information needs, curriculum content, learning outcomes, and a wide range of information resources. Librarians work with individual teachers to design and assess student learning tasks and to integrate these with the information and communication skills required in subject matter standards.

As information specialists, school librarians acquire and evaluate information resources, while working collaboratively with teachers, administrators, and students to make them aware of information issues. Librarians demonstrate a mastery of sophisticated electronic resources and maintain a focus on the quality and ethical uses of information resources.

As program administrators or managers of the school library program, school librarians are responsible for the management of staff, budgets, equipment, facilities, and evaluation of the program and collection. They must interpret and communicate all these tasks to school personnel and the public. In carrying out these responsibilities, librarians work to ensure that programs meet goals directly related to the collection. These goals include (a) providing *intellectual access* to information and (b) providing *physical access* to information by selecting and organizing the local collection and by acquiring information and materials from outside sources.

In any particular setting, the collection must support the librarian's roles as teacher, instructional partner, information specialist, and as a leader advocate for the effective use of information and information technology.

RELATIONSHIPS THAT INFLUENCE THE COLLECTION

District Level

Many building-level library programs (those designed to meet the needs of a single school) are units of a school district library program. The district's goals and objectives apply to the building-level library program, and the district-level library program personnel provide a wide range of resources and services to the building-level library program. The district may provide centralized purchasing and processing of materials. The online catalog or union catalog may include bibliographic and location information about items owned by the district and housed in school libraries throughout the system.

Collections housed in the district school library often include items that supplement materials owned by individual schools. District collections may contain materials that are expensive or heavily used at limited intervals, museum items with curricular value, and backup equipments. They also may include video or DVD libraries, professional collections, and materials examination collections. District-level collections are available to all school personnel within the district. Some districts also provide the transportation of items in their collections to individual schools.

Regional Level

The school library program and the school librarian have formal and informal relationships with groups and agencies within the county and regions of the state. County-level and regional-level professional associations provide programs and contacts useful to the school librarian. Some states, such as New York, have several separate Boards of Cooperative Education Services (BOCES), which provide shared educational programs and services to school districts. School library systems function within a BOCES, providing access to information and library resources and conducting professional development activities.

State Level

In the United States, education is the responsibility of each state. Each has its own philosophy, goals, and objectives for its educational programs. These responsibilities are assigned to the state education agency. The agency staff may serve as consultants and information disseminators, and their products and services may include printed publications, sponsorship of listservs or other electronic services, statewide online catalogs for the holdings of all the schools in the state, and the maintenance of materials examination centers. For school librarians working without the benefit of a district-level library program, the state school library consultant is a key contact. In addition to consultants, state educational agencies may offer recommendations and standards for the library program and collection, as well as other useful guidelines for school librarians.

Other state agencies are information resources. They provide information about all aspects of the state, sponsor websites, or offer lists of resources available from the state.

National Level

In the United States, school library programs, just like other areas of schools, are influenced greatly by national issues and legislation. For instance, society's concerns about people with physical disabilities spawned several pieces of federal legislation that affect library programs and collections. In 1990 the Americans with Disabilities Act (ADA) mandated that public services and facilities be accessible to people with disabilities. This act has had additional amendments during the past few years. It is important for school librarians to be knowledgeable about ADA and to assess whether their libraries fulfill the mandates of ADA.

Other pieces of legislation that directly affect the operation of a school library are the Copyright Act of 1976 and the amendments to the act made by the Copyright, Clarification, and Correction Act of 2010; the Digital Millennium Copyright Act passed by the U.S. Congress in 1998; and the Teach Act passed in 2002. Designed to balance the interests of authors and artists with the user's ability to access information, these laws guide librarians in carrying out their responsibilities.

The U.S. Congress also passes legislation that affects K-12 education and consequently impacts school library programs and collections. The No Child Left Behind (NCLB) Legislation signed by President George W. Bush in 2002 focuses on accountability for schools, including a high-stakes testing program for students in K-12 schools. This legislation has strongly impacted curriculum and instruction in schools in the United States and has caused much controversy. In February 2012, President Barack Obama announced that he was freeing 10 states from the central requirements of NCLB in exchange for the states developing more creative ways to evaluate student learning. Obama said he awarded the waivers because Congress had failed to revise the law even though legislators agreed that it needed revamping (*Washington Post*, 2012). Other states are expected to apply for such waivers.

Some grant programs are also part of the NCLB Legislation. NCLB programs that especially affect school libraries include Improving Literacy Through School Libraries, which helps schools improve reading achievement by providing increased access to library materials, technologically advanced school libraries, and professional certified school librarians; Early Reading First Initiative, which supports the development of excellent early childhood centers primarily intended for children from low income families; and Reading First Title I, which focuses on putting into classrooms proven methods of early reading instruction. Although federally funded, most of these programs are administered through state or local agencies (U.S. Department of Education, 2010).

The Libraries and Services Technology Act (LSTA) was signed into law by the U.S. Congress in 1996. Originally known as the Library Services Act (LSA), the program has been in existence in various forms since 1956. Funds are available to school libraries, public libraries, academic libraries, qualified private/research libraries, special libraries, library consortia, and libraries in correctional institutions to improve patron services. LSTA emphasizes improving library services to the underserved, especially to children living in poverty (American Library Association, 2011). The Institute of Museum and Library Services (IMLS) administers LSTA.

Some national professional associations provide guidance and information to school librarians. Two professional associations directly involved with school library programs are the American Association of School Librarians (AASL), a division of the American Library Association, and the Association for Educational Communications and Technology (AECT). The joint efforts of these two associations led to the publication of two past national standards for school librarians: *Information Power: Guidelines for School Libraries* (American Association of School Librarians, & Association for Educational Communications and Technology, 1988) and *Information Power: Building Partnerships for Learning* (1998).

Global Level

With the increasing availability of the Internet, the opportunity to tap into resources on a global basis is growing. Teachers and students can search the Internet for sites throughout the world. LM_NET, a listserv (discussion group), is dedicated to school librarians worldwide and to people involved with the school library field. School librarians can join this listserv and discuss various topics that focus on topics of interest to the school library community; many of the discussions are archived online (LM_NET, n.d.).

The International Association of School Librarianship (IASL) shares information about school library programs and materials for children and youth throughout the international community. Their website includes information and documents that are helpful to school librarians (International Association of School Librarianship, 2011).

CONCLUSIONS

The concept of the school library collection has changed dramatically in recent years. Accessibility, rather than just ownership, now constitutes the school library collection. Not only is there a physical collection owned by the school library, but the school library collection also includes materials that are available on databases, resources that are accessible through resource sharing, and items found online that are selected by school librarians for student use. By being a leader and serving in the roles of teacher, instructional partner, information specialist, and program administrator, the school librarian can align the school library collection with the needs of its users and with the school's mission and curriculum.

REFERENCES

American Association of School Librarians. (2007). *Standards for the 21st-century learner*. Chicago: American Library Association.

American Association of School Librarians. (2009). *Empowering learners: Guidelines for school library media programs*. Chicago: American Library Association.

American Association of School Librarians & Association for Educational Communications and Technology. (1988). *Information power: Guidelines for school library media programs*. Chicago: American Library Association.

American Association of School Librarians & Association for Educational Communications and Technology. (1998). *Information power: Building partnerships for learning*. Chicago: American Library Association.

American Library Association. (2011). *Library Services and Technology Act (LSTA)*. Retrieved from http://www.ala.org/ala/issuesadvocacy/advocacy/federallegislation/lsta/index.cfm

International Association of School Librarianship. (2011). *School libraries online*. Retrieved from http://www.iasl-online.org/*LM_NET Home* (n.d.). Retrieved from http://lmnet.wordpress.com/

U.S. Department of Education. (2010). *NCLB*. Retrieved from http://www2.ed.gov/policy/elsec/leg/esea02/index.html

Washington Post. (2012). Obama: 10 states to receive No Child Left Behind waivers. Retrieved from http://www.washingtonpost.com/local/education/10-states-to-receive-no-child-left-behind-waivers/2012/02/09/gIQAZCdY1Q_story.html

ADDITIONAL READINGS

Bush, G. (2006). The changing role of the school librarian. *Principal, 85*(4), 56–58.

Hamilton, B.J. (2011). The school librarian as teacher: What kind of teacher are you? *Knowledge Quest, 39*(5), 34–40.

Hand, D. (2011). The school librarian as instructional partner: Up with teachers to guide student learning. *Knowledge Quest, 39*(5), 22–26.

Harris, H.J. (2011). The school librarian as information specialist: A vibrant species. *Knowledge Quest, 39*(5), 28–32.

Purcell, M. (2010). All librarians do is check out books, right? A look at the roles of a school library media specialist. *Library Media Connection, 29*(3), 30–33.

Shankles, R. (2002). Not limited by space any more. *Arkansas Libraries, 59*(6), 16–17.

Steadman, W.S. (2011). The school librarian as leader: Out of the middle, into the foreground. *Knowledge Quest, 39*(5), 18–21.

Yates, S.D. (2011). The school librarian as program administrator: Just-in-time librarianship. *Knowledge Quest, 39*(5), 42–44.

HELPFUL WEBSITES

Oberg, Diane. (n.d.). *Changing school culture: The role of the 21st century teacher-librarian*. Retrieved from http://tmcanada.pbworks.com/f/TM+Canadasz+org+culture+and+chg+Apr+2010.pdf

The Unquiet Librarian. (2010). *It's broken; let's fix it: The traditional model of school librarianship*. Retrieved from http://theunquietlibrarian.wordpress.com/2010/04/27/its-broken-lets-fix-it-the-traditional-model-of-school-librarianship/

Chapter

Collection Development

Collection development is comprised of numerous activities that are dependent upon one another. The following are collection activities that are necessary to maintain and develop an effective library collection:

- Becoming knowledgeable about an existing collection
- Becoming familiar with the school and community
- Assessing the needs of the school's curriculum and other programs
- Assessing the specific needs of the users
- Establishing collection development policies and procedures
- Identifying criteria for selection of materials
- Planning for and implementing the selection process
- Acquiring and processing materials
- Participating in resource sharing
- Maintaining and preserving the collection
- Providing physical and intellectual access to materials
- Evaluating the collection

This chapter provides a general explanation of these activities. Many of these activities will be addressed in more depth in subsequent chapters.

LEARNING ABOUT THE EXISTING COLLECTION

If a collection is to serve as a communication and information base, the school librarian must know both the users' needs and the collection's available resources. Browsing is a quick way to learn about a collection. Walk through a collection and note whether you recognize titles and equipment. Ask yourself the following types of questions:

- Are you familiar with all the formats you find?
- Are signs clear and accurate?

- Are materials housed in unusual areas?
- Will students overlook any materials?
- How does the online catalog help students locate items?
- Are encyclopedias available in print, on CD-ROM, and/or online?
- How do users access electronically delivered information?
- Is there a filter on the software used to access information online? If so, can the school librarian override the filter to access sites?
- Does the school librarian collect and mark websites for student use?
- Is the collection accessible only in the school library or can students and teachers remotely access it from classrooms and from homes?

While browsing, try out the online public access catalog (OPAC) and make notes about materials or formats that are new to you. The OPAC is the online database that lists all the materials held by a library. Create a list of areas that need signs to make materials easier to find. Note whether equipment is housed in an area convenient to the materials that require it. Look to see if there is a ready reference area and note whether any of the reference materials are duplicated in the circulating collection.

Remember that some collections extend to materials housed outside the school library but that are still on the school campus. Professional journals or other materials may be located in the teachers' lounge or department offices. Check other resources in the school. Does the counseling center collect vocational materials or materials about colleges? Are there other departmental collections? Does the OPAC indicate the storage locations of these materials throughout the school?

As you gather these first impressions, examine the library's procedures manual for explanations of unusual situations. For example, 10 copies of one book title may seem unusual, but perhaps the books are used in classrooms that conduct literature-based reading programs.

Although these procedures will help you gain information about the collection, remember that it is impossible to become familiar with all items in a collection in your first semester or even in your first year as a school librarian. However, as you participate in the day-to-day operations of the school library (circulating materials, shelving books, and other frequent activities) and become involved with teachers and students, you will gain valuable knowledge about the collection.

KNOWING THE COMMUNITY

A basic consideration of all collection development activities is the interaction of the library program with the school, other educational or informational institutions and agencies, and the external environment. The community (its geographical, political, economic, cultural, and social characteristics) influences the collection. Changes in a school's mission or goals, in access to other collections, or in citizens' attitudes about education will influence decisions about the collection.

Today, the global community is a key resource. Students have computers in their homes and access to computers at school and in their public libraries. Teachers electronically communicate with colleagues around the world. Internet access can speed the delivery of an article for a student's report. All these factors affect a school library's collection development activities. See Chapter 3, "Community Analysis and Needs Assessment," for more discussion of community analysis.

ASSESSING NEEDS

To ensure that the collection fulfills the informational and instructional needs of its users, the school librarian must identify those needs. Whom does the collection serve? What are the users' informational needs? What are the subjects taught in the school? What are the teachers' instructional needs? Are there groups of students with special needs?

You can begin to find the answers to these questions by accessing the school's website for pertinent information, examining curriculum guides, asking the administrative staff for student demographic statistics, and attending departmental meetings. Analyzing past school library reports, such as circulation statistics or interlibrary loan requests, will also help provide information about the needs of the users. Conducting a survey of the students and the teachers to determine how a collection can assist in meeting specific needs is also a valuable means of assessing user needs.

More information on assessing needs is included in Chapter 3, "Community Analysis and Needs Assessment."

DESCRIBING THE PROGRAM

Students and teachers need to know when they will be able to physically access the materials in the collection. Both outside the library and on the library's website clearly post the school library's hours of operation for your users. Also, let users know how the school library is scheduled. Do you have flexible scheduling, fixed scheduling, or a combination of flexible and fixed scheduling? Is the school library open before or after school hours? Can students access the collection from classrooms and from home? Is that access restricted by hours or the number of students who can access the collection simultaneously?

You should also note whether there are special reading programs that the collection supports, such as Battle of the Books, Scholastic's *Reading Counts*, or Renaissance Learning's *Accelerated Reader*. You can answer numerous other program questions in a policies and procedures manual:

- Does the school library sponsor special programs, such as author visits or National Library Week?
- Do the library personnel conduct book fairs?
- Are there orientations for students and new faculty members?
- Are there opportunities for students to serve as volunteers or aides?
- How does the library assist with student or faculty research?
- Are copy and printing services available?
- Are there provisions or materials for students with special needs?
- Do school library personnel conduct professional development workshops for teachers?
- How are the library program and services evaluated?

All of these areas of the program may not relate directly to the collection (although many do), but it is important to have this type of information included in a school library manual or in a publication that is available to students and teachers. Chapter 4, "The School Library Program," includes more information about areas of the library program that impact the collection.

SELECTING MATERIALS

Selection policies articulate the library program's commitment to the right of intellectual freedom, and they reflect professional ethics, rights of users, and concern for intellectual property. These policies are carried out using specific selection procedures.

Criteria, or the standards used to evaluate items, are a major component of selecting print, nonprint, and electronic resources. One must establish criteria for assessing each item and its relationship to the collection as a whole. Generally, criteria used to evaluate materials include literary quality, currency, accuracy of information, appeal and value to students, application within the curriculum, quality of presentation, and format. You will also need to establish selection criteria and policies relating to specific formats, including electronic formats that are accessed online through the Internet.

Selection is the process of deciding whether an item will be a valuable addition to the collection. During this process, keep the set criteria in mind and make decisions within established policies. Personal examination and favorable reviews can provide the basis for selection decisions. Sources that provide reviews of a variety of formats include selection tools and reviewing journals. Some of the most useful selection tools for school librarians are listed and described in the "Appendix: Resources."

Use the same criteria for accepting donated materials that you use for purchasing collection items. Some materials that you select, such as DVDs, CDs, and e-books, require equipment. Therefore it is necessary for you to also establish criteria and procedures for the purchase of equipment. Many school districts provide guidelines for such purchases.

Established criteria, policies, and procedures are not the only factors that can influence a school librarian's choices. It is possible that one's values, interests, and even prejudices may influence selection decisions. To make sound decisions, you must set aside personal biases and make objective choices. Soliciting and gathering input from teachers, administrators, and students can also assist in the selection process.

The selection of materials is a major portion of collection development and includes establishing criteria for selection of many types of formats. Thus, three chapters of this book (Chapters 6, 7, and 8) address this topic.

ACQUIRING AND PROCESSING MATERIALS

After selecting materials and equipment to add to the collection, you must then make decisions relating to the process of acquiring and processing these items. In schools where clerical assistance is available in the library, an aide or clerk can be very helpful in these activities. Frequently, a school bookkeeper or financial officer is also involved in the acquisitions process.

For items such as books or magazines you may want to acquire your materials through a jobber. A *jobber* is a company that handles titles from several publishers. Using jobbers has many advantages including saving money and time spent by school library personnel. You may also decide to order some items directly from publishers or local bookstores. Some audiovisual vendors handle and distribute materials from several companies. For some selections, such as reference databases, you may need to make decisions about whether to purchase the item through an online subscription or in a CD-ROM format. Purchases that involve online access are generally more complex than acquiring a physical item and often involve price negotiation and licensing issues.

Many items can be purchased already processed, including catalog records, spine labels, barcodes, security strips, plastic book jackets, and school library stamp identification. Purchasing *shelf-ready items* (those that are processed by the jobber or publisher) can save you and your staff an enormous amount of time. The cost is affordable and varies due to the number of items purchased and the extent to which the items are processed. If you choose to do some of the processing on your own, you will need some written procedures detailing the process for this activity. More detailed discussions of acquisition and processing activities can be found in Chapter 9, "Acquisitions and Processing."

RESOURCE SHARING

Participation in resource sharing will influence your selection and acquisition decisions. Networks involving more than one library provide access to information materials and services housed outside the school's facility. A school that participates in a cooperative network has access to a plethora of resources and services; however, participation carries with it certain responsibilities and perhaps financial obligations. Some networks offer cooperative purchasing programs, cataloging and processing, computerized databases, delivery systems, production services, examination centers, serials cooperatives, and other forms of resource sharing. Generally, there are policies and procedures that are written cooperatively by representatives from the libraries involved in this type of resource sharing. These should be included in your library's policies and procedures manual. You can also participate in informal resource sharing, such as inquiring by phone or e-mail as to the availability of a particular item in another school in your district or perhaps scanning and sending a journal article from one school library to another or hand delivering an item that is needed in a nearby school.

Fitting resource sharing into a continuum of collection development activities is somewhat difficult since resource sharing can impact multiple collection development activities, including selection, acquisitions, and circulation. More information relating to resource sharing can be found in Chapter 9, "Acquisitions and Processing," and in Chapter 16, "Fiscal Issues Relating to the Collection."

MAINTAINING AND PRESERVING MATERIALS

Collection maintenance is an important and often neglected function of collection development. The school librarian must make decisions about removing (deselecting or weeding), mending, rebinding, and replacing materials. Equipment must also be kept in working condition.

You can do many things to help preserve and maintain your collection and equipment. These include teaching students the proper handling of materials, providing copy machine access, using a security system, and maintaining appropriate temperature and humidity in the school library, to name just a few. Conducting systematic inventories of materials also helps maintain a usable collection. It is important to establish policies and procedures for these maintenance and preservation activities. Chapter 10, "Maintenance and Preservation," provides additional information about how to effectively maintain a collection.

ACCESSING AND CIRCULATING MATERIALS

While some librarians may not consider accessing and circulating materials as collection development activities, they are the reasons that the other activities take place. The ultimate purpose of collection development is to make materials accessible to users. As mentioned in Chapter 1, school librarians need to provide physical and intellectual access to materials. Physical access includes having times (during school, before school, or after school) when students and teachers are able to use the collection.

You will also need to develop circulation policies and procedures to provide some guidelines for the use of the collection. Some questions to consider are as follows:

- Which types of formats circulate and to whom?
- How long can students check out materials?
- Is there a limit on the number of items that can be checked out?
- Does the limit on items vary depending on a student's grade level?
- How do the checkout policies differ for teachers?
- Are fines charged for overdue items?
- Do students need to pay for materials that are damaged during the time the materials are checked out?

Students and teachers also need electronic access to materials. It is the librarian's responsibility to provide and manage this access. This may involve working closely with the person responsible for setting up the school's network and with the school's technology committee. It is also important that acceptable use policies be written for the use of electronic materials. If there is not such a policy in place, then you should take the initiative to develop a policy. Teachers and administrators should be involved in developing an acceptable use policy since it is a policy that needs to be adopted and utilized throughout the school.

Your policies and procedures manual should contain a statement endorsing intellectual freedom. Some official documents, such as the *Library Bill of Rights* written and amended by the American Library Association Council, are valuable additions to your manual, either in the text of the manual itself or in an appendix. Such documents will be beneficial if you receive complaints about materials in your collection and you need to defend intellectual freedom. Your manual should also include a list of specific procedures to follow if an item is formally challenged. This list should be a part of your policies and procedures manual before a challenge occurs.

Copyright issues also affect access. Your manual should include a statement noting that school library personnel uphold the U.S. copyright laws and fair use guidelines. In most schools, the librarian is responsible for enforcing those laws and guidelines within the school library and is responsible for providing information to the faculty and students regarding copyright. School librarians should not serve as *copyright cops* outside the school library (a responsibility of school administrators); however, the school library manual should include how copyright information is provided to users. It is imperative to have a list of some of the guidelines that affect teachers and students.

In some instances intellectual freedom and copyright issues are addressed in the selection portion of a policies and procedures manual. Exact placement of them within the manual does not matter, but it is essential that they be included.

Circulation of materials is covered in more detail in Chapter 11, "Circulation and Promotion of the Collection." Certain intellectual freedom and copyright issues, are also discussed in Chapter 13, "Ethical Issues and the Collection."

EVALUATING THE COLLECTION

Gathering information on how students and teachers use the materials will assist you in evaluating the collection. Some evaluation techniques that involve users include examining circulation statistics, determining the in-house use of materials, and conducting surveys. Collection-centered techniques, such as directly examining the collection and comparing the materials to lists or bibliographies, can also be used to evaluate a collection. Your manual should include a plan for systematically evaluating the collection, including who conducts the evaluation, what types of measures are used, and how often the collection is evaluated. More information related to how to carry out evaluation of a collection is found in Chapter 12, "Evaluation of the Collection."

INTERACTION OF COLLECTION DEVELOPMENT ACTIVITIES

You can view collection development activities as a continuum in which one activity leads to and influences the others (see Figure 2.1). Activities are not isolated; rather,

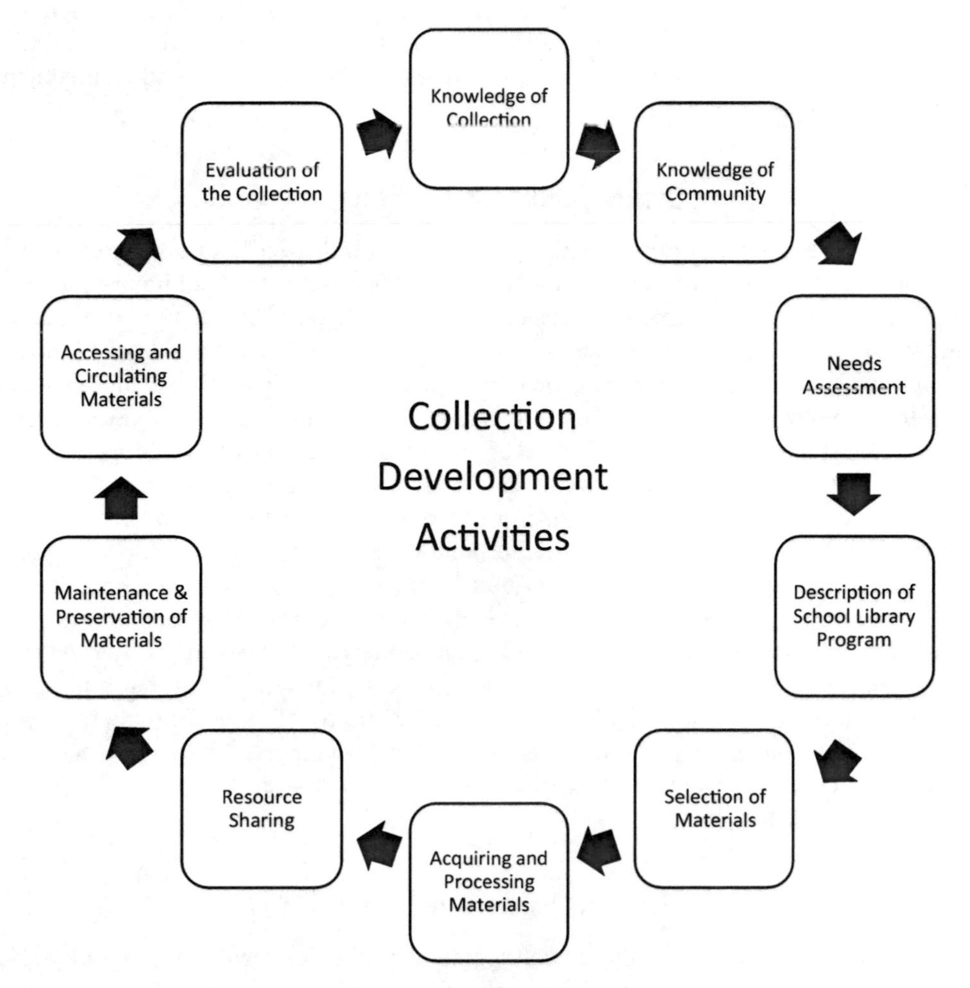

Figure 2.1. Interaction of collection development activities

their interactions are cyclical. Thus, a change in one activity affects others. For instance, if there is a change in the curriculum (part of the community analysis) and several science courses are added, this will affect selection. You should establish policies that provide guidance, but also remember that policies may need to be altered to meet changes. With the rapid developments in technology, librarians can expect to add new formats to the collection; selection criteria for these formats will then need to be incorporated into the policy.

OTHER FACTORS THAT AFFECT COLLECTION DEVELOPMENT

The school librarian is responsible for developing and implementing collection development activities. However, the librarian cannot control all the factors that influence collection development activities. The library program must operate within policies that the local board of education adopts and must also meet the goals of the district and the school. The attendance districts established by the school board may change yearly and impact the composition of the student body or potential users of the collection. State or federal legislation may dictate requirements about the student population, the curriculum, and other school programs. Shifts in the student population will impose new demands on the collection that collection development activities must accommodate. The changing availability of electronic access creates continual shifts in the equipment needed and requires librarians to update their skills.

District School Library Program

A building-level school library program that is part of a district library program offers many advantages to the entry-level school librarian. The system's school library program coordinator or director is someone you can turn to for guidance. The district-level guidelines for school library programs and the selection policy also aid the school librarian. District-level school library programs may offer services to help establish and maintain the collection program. For example, there may be opportunities to examine new materials or view exhibits and demonstrations at district-level library program meetings.

Regional centers also provide personnel and services, including consultants or technicians, cooperative collections, examination centers, staff development workshops, and clearinghouses for information about new technology. Providing distance-learning opportunities is another way these centers can extend the resources of the building school library.

Although district and regional programs offer many benefits, they may also impose constraints on a school library program. An approved buying list generated by a district-wide committee or state purchase agreements may limit the equipment that a librarian can purchase or the librarian may be allowed to order from only specific jobbers. If you encounter these situations, you should ask district-level personnel if there are procedures for ordering other items. In some districts, you must also order resources at specified times of the academic year.

Financial Support and Control

The school's and district's funding policies, including policies regulating use of outside funding sources, impose constraints on collection development. Accrediting agencies may also make budget demands. School librarians operate within the limits set by budget allocations. In addition to the size of the budget, the accounting system can affect collection activities. For example, funds designated for equipment cannot be used for books. Collection development is more successful when budgeting allows program objectives and needs to determine priorities.

The school board's or administrator's position regarding the use of outside funding also affects the collection. Some school districts opt not to use outside funds; others encourage school librarians to seek grants or endowments. Such grants or endowments may specify materials to be purchased or may limit the type of use or user for whom materials may be purchased. For example, some funding may be used only for materials for student use.

At some point in your career as a school librarian, a school official may inform you that you must spend a large sum of money earmarked for materials for special uses within 7 to 10 days. This situation does not encourage thoughtful planning or selection, but it sometimes occurs with outside funding opportunities. Try to be knowledgeable regarding what materials can be funded by outside sources and be aware when the funding will occur. You should maintain a *consideration file,* a listing of materials (with ordering information included) that you are currently considering for purchase; such a file will be a great asset in these situations.

School Facilities

Limitations of the physical plant or the physical facilities of the library can affect the collection. For instance, the lack of an adequate number of safe electrical outlets limits the use of some media. School library usage by after-school programs or programs for preschoolers may influence collection development activities. Many formats in the collection (such as picture books, art prints, and maps) require specialized storage units. As school libraries change from predominately print collections to ones with electronic collections, less shelving space is needed, but more computer workstations are required. In some instances, such as a lack of an adequate number of electrical outlets, you may need to advocate for additional wiring to be put into the library or ask for wireless access. You may need to find funding to provide the additional computer workstations or laptops that are required for electronic resources.

CONCLUSIONS

Collection development is comprised of many activities that interact with one another. Changes in one activity often affect other collection development activities. Policies and procedures should be written to address each of the activities, but school librarians should be prepared to make alterations in order to meet changing needs. Other factors, such as district-wide policies and services, financial support, and school facilities can also impact collection development.

ADDITIONAL READINGS

Collins, M.D.D., & Carr, P.L. (2009). *Managing the transition from print to electronic journals and resources: A guide for library and information professionals.* New York: Routledge.

Downs, E. (2010). *The school library media specialist's policy and procedures writer.* New York: Neil Schuman.

Gregory, V.L. (2011). *Collection development and management for 21st century library collections: An introduction.* New York: Neal Schuman.

Hoffmann, F., & Wood, R.J. (2007). *Library collection development policies: School libraries and learning resource centers.* Lanham, MD: Scarecrow Press.

Hughes-Hassell, S., & Mancall, J.C. (2006). Designing a learner-center collection: An introduction to the process. *Learning & Media, 34*(3), 6–8.

Johnson, P. (2009). *Fundamentals of collection development and management* (2nd ed.). Chicago: American Library Association.

Kerby, M. (2006). *Collection development for the school library media program: A beginner's guide.* Chicago: American Association of School Librarians.

Nebraska Educational Media Association. (2010). *Guide for developing and evaluating school library media programs* (7th ed.). Santa Barbara, CA: Libraries Unlimited.

HELPFUL WEBSITES

Library Media Service. West Hartford Public Schools. (n.d.). *Library media specialist's tool box.* Retrieved from http://www.whps.org/library/CollectionManagement.htm

Warrior Librarian. (2006). *Collection management policy.* Retrieved from http://warriorlibrarian.com/LIBRARY/policy

Chapter

3 Community Analysis and Needs Assessment

Effective collection development must be based on reliable knowledge about the collection's users (in the case of a school library: the students, teachers, administrators, and perhaps parents being served). The gathering of information about a population that a library serves is generally called *community analysis*. The demographics that should be collected about users of a school library include community information and school information.

LEARNING ABOUT THE COMMUNITY

If the students in your school live in a large city, you should include in your community analysis information about the city itself (e.g., the location of the city and its population), but additional demographics should relate to primarily the neighborhood area in which most of the students live. For smaller towns, where neighborhoods may not be especially unique, the data for the entire town may be reported.

How do you learn about the community? Some good sources of information are the school district, the local chamber of commerce, the news media, government agencies, service and civic clubs, government census data, and the public library. These sources can provide maps, surveys, brochures, community profiles, lists of local activities, and projections for future population shifts. They can also lead you to other information sources, such as planning commissions or historical societies. Almost all communities have official websites that can provide some of the information you will need to collect, and many of the groups and institutions often have their own websites. If the public library has recently surveyed the community's information needs, their findings can be helpful. United States census data, which are available online (http://www.census.gov/), provide much information for a community analysis.

The following information is helpful to include in a community analysis:

- Geographic setting
- Topographic features (near mountains, oceans, or rivers)
- Population
- Age distribution of the population
- Ethnic and racial groups
- Educational levels of the population
- Economic levels of the population
- Employment opportunities
- Businesses
- Political activities
- Modes of transportation
- Educational institutions
- Availability of libraries and museums
- Information agencies (newspapers, radio stations, or TV stations)
- Technological resources (availability of Internet via cable TV, fiber-optic cable to the home, high-tech industries)
- Recreational facilities
- Religious institutions
- Housing
- Governmental units
- Medical care facilities and organizations

In addition to the topics listed above, a community analysis might also include information that is unique to the community, such as historical development, cultural data, or future trends and plans.

The demographics can provide guidance for collection development and programming. Census data about racial, ethnic, and language backgrounds indicate some types of materials the collection needs. Ethnic organizations, such as a Hispanic council, might be willing to help meet the needs of young Hispanic students. In communities with large populations of refugees and immigrants, you will also need materials that help students and teachers understand the new members of their community.

Stability of the population also affects the collection. A community without an influx of young families may face a decline in student population, leading to closing or consolidating schools. If you are in a school with low-income work forces, there is likely to be a certain amount of transience. Children of inner-city factory workers or migrant farm workers may spend only a few weeks in your school. When working with children from such families, you may need materials in less permanent formats. In these situations, consider selecting less costly paperback books, and try not to fret about the loss of materials.

The location of the community, its climate, and its recreational patterns also make demands on the collection. Schools in areas where skiing, snowmobiling, water sports, or other outdoor activities are common need appropriate related materials in the school library collection.

Many communities support recreational and educational programs. Young people may regularly participate in functions at museums, zoological gardens, and concert venues. These interests result in demands on the collection. For instance, if a community has a planetarium that is open to students, the collection will need stronger astronomy resources than one in a community without such a facility. Active scout or 4-H programs may also indicate a need for specialized materials in the collection.

A community of young families may be more likely to support educational programs than a community of fixed-income people. The educational level of the population may be another clue to the willingness of citizens to financially support schools. Active participants in community groups might be more receptive to the importance of a school library program. Remember that neighborhoods in large school districts differ drastically. You may find pockets of support, or opposition, in various neighborhoods.

LEARNING ABOUT THE SCHOOL

Your community analysis should also include a detailed description of the school itself. It is extremely important to have knowledge about the students, teachers, and administrators who use the school library. The best sources for such information include the school website, the guidance office, and the school secretary or administrative assistant. Some states also maintain websites on individual schools. These websites can provide you with information such as student enrollment, the number of students on free or reduced lunches, and student test scores. The following is information to be included in a school analysis:

- Enrollment
- Grade levels
- Ethnic makeup of the student body
- Number of students whose second language is English
- Socioeconomic status of the students
- Number of students on free or reduced lunches
- Dropout rate
- Number of students enrolled in advanced courses
- Percentage of students going to college
- Special education population
- Standardized test scores
- Courses or units of study emphasized in the curriculum
- Extracurricular activities available
- Number of faculty members
- Background of faculty members (Do the teachers live in local neighborhoods? Do they have advanced degrees? Do they come from diverse backgrounds?)

Other types of information, such as the number of high school students who have jobs or the number of transient students in a school, can also influence collection development. The purpose of a school has implications for the collection. If you are a librarian in a magnet school, such as a performing arts or technical school, or in a parochial school where specific religious beliefs are taught, certain titles may need to be included in the collection (or perhaps excluded).

Schools with a high percentage of students in advanced placement classes will have demands different from those schools where students are entering the military or job force, rather than going on to higher education. Students taking courses through Advanced Placement or International Baccalaureate programs are likely to need materials available through interlibrary loan or on the Internet. On the other hand, students who attend vocational programs for a part of the school day will need specialized materials, such as car repair or hair fashions, that support their vocational curriculum. If an elementary school has many students whose first language is not English, you will want to include many bilingual materials in the collection. If students in a school are enrolled in distance education courses, their information needs will also need to be considered, especially if the courses they are taking are not those offered in the on-campus facility.

As a school librarian, you also should assess the needs of the teachers in your school. A well-selected professional library will be greatly appreciated by the faculty, as will instruction in accessing online materials for their courses. It could be beneficial to determine whether there are teachers in the school who are working on advanced degrees. They may need your assistance in locating print or online materials to help them complete requirements for the courses in which they are enrolled.

OTHER LIBRARIES

Some of your most valuable allies may be the public library's children and young adult specialists. If you are a new school librarian, investigate the following: What services do libraries and other information agencies offer to students? Is there a branch library near your school, or do students use a bookmobile? Do students have access to the Internet at the public library? Can they access the public library's online catalog from their home or from the school? Do school and public libraries offer cooperative programs or services? Can you borrow public library materials for classroom use? Has the school established a procedure for alerting the public library of forthcoming assignments? Do the two libraries participate in resource sharing plans? Have the libraries jointly applied for grant funds?

Visit local community college, college, and university libraries. Their collections probably include reference materials, bibliographies, and selection tools too expensive for the school's collection. If special libraries (industry, hospital, or government) in the community are open to student use, their resources can be of particular interest to high school students completing research papers or school projects.

ASSESSING USER NEEDS

While completing a community and school analysis can provide valuable information for collection development, other means of assessing student and faculty needs should also be used. Conducting separate surveys for students and teachers can be helpful. These surveys should include questions relating to the needs of the users and to the collection. The questions on a student survey should be written so students can clearly understand them. The wording of questions will vary greatly, depending on grade levels included in a school. Sample survey questions for classroom teachers might include the following:

- What units of study are you planning for this school year?
- Does the library currently have adequate materials to support your curriculum?`
- Do students in your courses need materials from the library to complete assignments?
- Will you be bringing students to the library for research?
- How can I help your students with their research?
- What areas of professional development are of particular interest to you?
- Are you currently working on an advanced degree? If so, in what area of study?

A few sample questions for students include the following:

- Is English your first language? If not, what other languages do you speak or read?
- What are your favorite leisure activities?
- What are your reading interests?
- Do you have any hobbies?
- Do you participate in extracurricular activities? If so, what are some of those activities?
- Do you check out materials from the public library?
- Are there materials needed for reports or research papers that you have not been able to find in the school library collection? If so, name some of them.

The data from surveys should be analyzed and presented in a report that includes some graphic representations so survey results can easily be understood, not only by a librarian, but also by other interested parties. In your report include collection recommendations based on the survey results. For instance, if survey findings indicate a large percentage of students whose first language is Spanish, consider applying for a grant to add bilingual materials to your collection. If you find the eighth-grade science teachers are beginning a new unit of study on oceanography, include in your budget funds for materials to help strengthen that area of the collection. If students indicated they were not able to find enough materials about gay rights, then you may want to add related print resources or collect and mark relevant websites. Consider creating *pathfinders* (lists of materials on particular topics). The pathfinders should include print, nonprint, and online resources; they are especially helpful to students who are beginning research projects.

In addition to conducting formal surveys that can impact collection development, you should also use informal means to assess user needs. One informal way to gather this information is to attend grade level or department meetings to learn about what types of projects, assignments, or units of study are being planned by classroom teachers. In the library, at lunch in the cafeteria, or at faculty meetings, chat with teachers about the types of materials and services they would like to see in the school library. Provide a suggestion box on the circulation desk where students or teachers can comment on materials they are not able to locate in the collection.

CONCLUSIONS

In order to determine the needs of the users of a school library, a librarian should conduct a community analysis, including demographics relating to both the community and the school itself. Carefully designed and administered surveys can also provide accurate and reliable data about user needs. Librarians can assess the needs of students and teachers through informal means, such as attending department or grade level meetings. Information gathered in a community analysis and through needs assessments should be major influences for collection development and the school library program.

ADDITIONAL READINGS

Worcester, L., & Westbrook, L. (2004). Ways of knowing: Community information needs analysis. *Texas Library Journal, 80*(3), 102, 104–107.

Young, T. (2010). Aligning collection development with instructional and learning needs. *School Library Monthly, 26*(10), 20–22.

HELPFUL WEBSITES

Greer, R.C., & Hale, M.L. (2008). *The community analysis process*. Retrieved from http://www.skyways.org/pathway/article.html

Sarling, J.H., & Van Tassell, D.S. (n.d.). *Welcome to community analysis for libraries and librarians!* Retrieved from http://www.skyways.org/pathway/ca_homepage.html

The School Library Media Specialist. (n.d.). *Library media program: Community analysis*. Retrieved from http://eduscapes.com/sms/program/community.html

Upper Hudson Library System. (n.d.). *Community analysis: Community survey form*. Retrieved from http://www.uhls.org/uhls/communityanalysis/

Chapter

The School Library Program

Research studies clearly indicate that in order to succeed, students need strong school library programs (Haycock, 2011; Lance & Loertscher, 2005; Lance, Rodney & Hamilton-Pennell, 2001; Lance, Rodney, & Schwartz, 2010; Rodney, Lance & Hamilton-Pennell, 2002; Todd, Kuhlthau, & OELMA, 2004). As part of those programs, all students need access to current, quality, high interest, and extensive collections (American Association of School Librarians, 1999). The school library program provides a setting where students can develop essential information skills: being able to locate, evaluate, organize, use, and create information. Here students will not only access the traditional print and nonprint resources, but they will also access needed information via virtual learning environments.

SCHEDULING OF THE SCHOOL LIBRARY

Patrons need to be informed of the operating hours of the school library, including the times they can check out materials or use the school library computers. These hours are generally affected by the librarian's employment contract, the number of professional school librarians in a school, and the presence of clerical or paraprofessional assistants. Having more school library personnel usually makes it possible to have expanded hours of access for patrons. For instance, in a high school setting where at least two professional librarians are on staff, it may be possible to stagger work hours so the library can be open to students before classes begin and after school. The operating hours of the school library should be specified in your policies and procedures manual, in a student handbook, and on or near the entrance to the school library. Additionally, patrons need to know if online materials are accessible from classrooms or from students' homes, and whether there is around-the-clock access to the online resources.

You might be able to decide whether your school library will operate on a fixed, flexible, or mixed schedule. Each of these types of schedules has advantages and disadvantages. Fixed (or rigid) schedules are sometimes utilized in elementary schools. In this type of schedule, each class is provided a prescribed time (usually once a week) to visit the library for story hours, library instruction, or materials check out. In a school that uses fixed scheduling, the visits to the library are often part of a master schedule that provides classroom teachers with planning time. Music, art, physical education, and computer are generally in the same master schedule to provide planning time for classroom teachers. More often than not, in a fixed schedule only one class is allowed into the library at a time.

Some advantages of a fixed schedule include the following:

- All students have access to the library resources at least once a week during their scheduled library time.
- The school librarian has the opportunity to teach information literacy skills to all students in the school.
- Teachers are provided with a planning period.

Some disadvantages of a fixed schedule are as follows:

- Information literacy skills are often taught in isolation and may soon be forgotten by the students.
- The school library is treated as a subject, rather than a center for resources and learning.
- Students cannot visit the library at times when they may have specific needs for resources.
- Teachers may not be able to send individual students or small groups of students for check-out or research activities.
- In a large school, a fixed schedule can occupy 80 to 90 percent of a librarian's day, leaving little time for other management responsibilities or collaborative opportunities.

In flexible (or open) scheduling, classes are scheduled as classroom teachers and the librarian define a need. For example, in one week a classroom teacher may have the students working on research projects and schedule a 40-minute block of time every day of that week. The classroom teacher accompanies students to the library and plans cooperatively with the school librarian. The schedule for teaching information literacy skills is based on need and is integrated into research activities; thus the schedule varies each week. With a flexible schedule, individuals and small groups of students use the library as often as needed.

Many important advantages of flexible scheduling include the following:

- Students have access to resources at the time of need or interest.
- Library visits and the teaching of information literacy skills are related to classroom activities and assignments.
- The librarian has time to collaborate with classroom teachers, thus improving communication, the librarian becomes familiar with the curriculum, and the teachers learn what resources are available in the school library.
- Students become more independent users of resources and gain information literacy skills for lifelong learning.

Although the AASL strongly recommends flexible scheduling, some school librarians note disadvantages:

- It is possible that some students never or infrequently visit the school library and thus do not get opportunities to check out materials for either research or pleasure.

- Some teachers may send their problem students to the library frequently, simply to get them out of the classroom.
- The librarian may feel as if there is not time to take care of other management responsibilities, such as ordering or cataloging, when there are students and teachers constantly using the library resources and needing assistance.

Some elementary school libraries use mixed scheduling, which is a combination of fixed and flexible scheduling. For instance, the librarian could have fixed classes in the morning and flexible access during the afternoon. Another frequently used mixed schedule involves having fixed classes for the lower grades and flexible access for the upper elementary grades. If a full-time clerk is available in the library, the librarian might teach classes in a fixed schedule, while the clerk assists small groups of students or individuals who come to the library from other classes. Fixed and flexible scheduling has many possible combinations. Some elementary librarians consider the mixed scheduling to be the ideal program.

Libraries in secondary schools usually operate on a flexible schedule in which teachers sign up with the librarian for times to bring their classes to the library. Other times they are allowed to send individual students or small groups of students to the library. Some middle school librarians choose to use a mixed schedule, generally scheduling fixed classes through English or social studies teachers, with specific times for students to check out books or work on special projects and yet still remaining open for small groups of students or individuals. Regardless of which type of scheduling is used in a library, students and teachers must be made fully aware of the schedule and how it affects their access to the library.

The type of scheduling used in a school library can impact the collection. If you are in a school where flexible or mixed scheduling is present, you will most likely find there is more use of the library for both personal reading and research activities; thus, you need to develop a collection that includes the materials needed to support such activities. You need to become familiar with the curriculum, possible research assignments, and the times of the year there will likely be a demand for particular resources. Additionally, you need to work collaboratively with your classroom teachers to provide integration of the teaching of information skills into the curriculum, and at the same time develop a collection tailored to the needs of the students and teachers.

GENERAL SERVICES

What general services are included in a school library program? This may vary according to the number of school library personnel, student body enrollment, grade levels included in the school, and school library facilities. General services provided to students and teachers could include the following:

- Providing orientation sessions for students and teachers
- Providing copy machines so students and teachers can make copies of library materials
- Providing access to online databases
- Making it possible to print Internet resources
- Collaborating on research projects
- Providing reading and viewing guidance for students and teachers
- Providing book talks for classes

- Preparing bibliographies and pathfinders
- Providing style sheets for students
- Bookmarking Internet sites for classroom assignments
- Providing resources and equipment for students with special needs
- Conducting professional development workshops for teachers

How are these services related to the school library collection? The collection is inescapably intertwined with the school library program. Providing the services listed and a collection that reflects the needs of the students and teachers will help create an effective, high-quality library media program.

It is essential that school library programs effectively engage students and provide programs and services that contribute to authentic student learning, learning that uses a prior knowledge baseline and has value beyond being an indicator for success in a school assignment. This includes providing learning opportunities through technology; thus, it is important to have emerging technologies available to all students. In turn, librarians need to base their technology-related instruction on student learning, rather than the technologies themselves.

SPECIAL PROGRAMS

Many opportunities are available to provide special programs in a school library. Traditionally, a high priority of library programs has been the promotion of reading. With the current emphasis on increasing standardized reading test scores, this priority has become even more of a focus and has served to closely link classrooms and the school library. In some instances special reading programs, such as computer reading programs (Renaissance Learning's *Accelerated Reader* and Scholastic's *Reading Counts*) or the Battle of the Books (a reading competition program), are school-wide activities and are closely connected to the reading curriculum. In other schools the programs are used as reading motivational tools and are administered only through the library. These programs are discussed in more depth in Chapter 14, "The Curriculum." Many librarians continue to design their own reading motivation programs and contests.

Although librarians are not reading teachers, they can collaborate with classroom teachers and reinforce the strategies and techniques used to teach reading. Such strategies include pointing out rhyming words in a poem, defining unfamiliar words, predicting what will happen next in a story, or determining an author's message. Introducing students to various genres and imparting a love for literature will also help students enjoy reading and become lifelong readers for both pleasure and information.

Other special programs that are sometimes part of a school library program include computer clubs, book discussion groups, and student library aides. Many school librarians also plan programs for special events held in the library. These include author visits, book fairs, career days, speakers, storytelling, read-ins (famous local persons or parents are invited to the library to read a book aloud), and National Library Week or Children's Book Week celebrations.

EVALUATION OF PROGRAMS

Every school library program should frequently use varied means of evaluation. Initially, a school librarian should perform some type of self-assessment of a program. One way

SCHOOL NAME | SCHOOL DISTRICT

Dear Students:

This survey is being conducted to help us understand how you use the school library and how the library program may be Improved. Please complete the survey below and return it to your school librarian. Thank you for taking the time to provide us with this valuable information.

~The Library Staff

How often do you visit the School Library? _____ Daily _____ Weekly _____ Monthly ______ Never						
When do you generally visit the School Library? ____Before School _____ At Lunch ____ With Classes _____ After School						
Please indicate your grade level: ______K-5 ______ 6-8 ______9-12						
Indicate your level of agreement by putting a check mark in the box that most closely represents your response. If this item doesn't apply, please leave the answer blank. Thank you.	QUALITY RATING					
	Strongly Agree	Agree	Neutral	Disagree	Strongly Disagree	Don't Know
SCHOOL LIBRARY RESOURCES						
The School Library provides the resources I need to complete my assignments.						
The School Library provides the resources I need for my school interests.						
The School Library promotes reading.						
The School Library Catalog/OPAC is easy to navigate.						
The School Library Web Site is useful.						
I feel well prepared to locate resources in the School Library because of the training I received.						
The skills I learned in the School Library help me to locate electronic resources through the Internet.						
The School Library has books and other resources that are of interest to me.						
The atmosphere in the School Library is conducive to learning the skills I need.						
TECHNOLOGY RESOURCES						
Please complete the following response by writing in your response.						
Do you use any of the digital subscriptions that are part of our library collection? ______Yes ________No						
If you utilize e-readers, would you like to see more e-books as part of our library collection? ______Yes ________No						
What, if any, technologies would you like to see added to our library? Response: ______________________________						
How often do you utilize e-readers and/or e-books? __________ Daily __________ Weekly __________ Monthly __________ Never						
What other technology/applications would you like to see utilized in our school library (e.g. social network applications, Podcasts, Blogs/Wikis)? Response: ______________________________						

Figure 4.1. Student school library survey

FACULTY LIBRARY SURVEY

This survey is intended to help us meet the needs of the teachers in our school. Please answer each question as completely as you can and then return the survey to school librarian. Thank you for taking the time to provide us with your valuable input!

~ Your School Library Staff

Indicate your level of agreement by putting a check mark in the box that most closely represents your response. If this item doesn't apply, please leave the answer blank. Thank you.	QUALITY RATING					
	Strongly Agree	Agree	Neutral	Disagree	Strongly Disagree	Don't Know
LIBRARY RESOURCES						
The School Library contains the print resources I need to assist me with my daily lesson plans.						
The School Library contains books and other resources that are of interest to my students and promote information literacy skills.						
The School Library staff advises me of new additions to the library collection that would be beneficial to me.						
The School Library staff solicits my input when adding resources to the library collection.						
TECHNOLOGY RESOURCES						
The School Library has access to the electronic and other non-print resources I need to support my classroom.						
There are sufficient computers, online subscriptions, whiteboard, and other technology resources in the School Library to meet my classroom needs.						
The School Library provides sufficient technology to encourage 21st Century learning skills.						
SCHOOL LIBRARY AVAILABILITY						
The School Library's hours of operation are sufficient to meet my needs.						
The School Library's staff is available to answer questions and meet my needs.						
The School Library staff assists me in the use of the library resources.						

Please complete the following by checking off or writing in your response:

TECHNOLOGY SURVEY

What technologies or other resources would you like to see added to the School Library collection? ____________________

____

Do you utilize the library's digital subscriptions? ______ Yes ______ No

Do you utilize the library's access to e-books? ______ Yes ______ No

If you answered "no" above, why not? ____________________

____

Would you support the purchase of additional e-books for the School Library collection? ______ Yes ______ No

What e-books would you like to see added to the School Library collection? ____________________

____

Would you support the purchase of e-readers for the School Library collection? ______ Yes ______ No ______ Maybe

Do you support the use of social applications like Facebook, Twitter, etc. in the classroom curriculum? ______ Yes ______ No ______ Maybe

If you answered "no" above, why not? ____________________

____

OTHER COMMENTS? If you have additional comments or would like to clarify any responses, please feel free to do so below. Thank you!

Figure 4.2. Faculty school library survey

to evaluate a program is to put in written format the mission, goals, and objectives of the school library and then compare the current program to those items.

Using a rubric will provide a more thorough evaluation and present an overall picture of the current status of your program and the areas in which you would like the program to move forward. Several school districts and states have developed program evaluation rubrics that can be used for this purpose. Check with your school district or state department of education to see if such a rubric is available for your use. If there is not already a rubric that you can use for this purpose, you can adapt other rubrics to accommodate the objectives and needs of your library. At the end of this chapter you will find website listings of some valuable program evaluation rubrics. In your rubric be sure to include items that will evaluate how well the program is developing critical problem solvers and how the program contributes to student achievement.

You also should provide opportunities for your patrons to evaluate the school library program. You can do this by interviewing students and teachers or by creating surveys in which patrons can indicate their present usage of the library and provide useful feedback for improvement of a program. Surveys should provide anonymity, be relatively brief (very short for younger students), and be written in clear, concise language.

Figure 4.1 is an example of a student survey appropriate for a school library program. Different questions might need to be used depending on the grade levels of students. You can also choose to utilize a different format for student responses.

Classroom teachers can provide valuable information about the library program, particularly if you are using a flexible schedule and teachers are accompanying their students to the library. Figure 4.2 is a sample of a survey that could be used for classroom teachers to help evaluate the school library program.

CONCLUSIONS

Research has shown that strong library programs and access to information in a variety of formats contribute to authentic student learning and achievement. Effective school library programs are dependent on a collection that is responsive to the needs of students and teachers and are integrated into the curriculum through resource-based instruction of information literacy skills. A library program should be evaluated frequently, both through self-assessments by the school librarian and by its users. School librarians must strive to ensure that the relevancy of their school library programs and instructional impact of information literacy skills are understood by administrators, teachers, parents, and the community in general.

REFERENCES

American Association of School Librarians. (1999). *Position statement on the value of independent reading in the school library media program.* Chicago: American Association of School Librarians.

Haycock, K. (2011). Connecting British Columbia (Canada) school libraries and student achievement: A comparison of higher and lower performing schools with similar overall funding. *School Libraries Worldwide, 17*(1), 37–50.

Lance, K.C., & Loertscher, D.V. (2005). *Powering achievement: School library media programs make a difference—the evidence.* Salt Lake City, UT: Hi Willow Research and Publishing.

Lance, K.C., Rodney, M.J., & Hamilton-Pennell, C. (2001). *Good schools have school librarians; Oregon school librarians collaborate to improve academic achievement*. Terrebonne, OR: Oregon Educational Media Association.

Lance, K.C., Rodney, M.J., & Schwartz, B. (2010). The impact of school libraries on academic achievement: A research study based on responses from administrators in Idaho. *School Library Monthly, 26*(9), 14–17.

Rodney, M.J., Lance, K.C., & Hamilton-Pennell, C. (2002). *Make the connection: Quality school library media programs impact academic achievement in Iowa*. Bettendorf, IA: Mississippi Bend Area Education Agency.

Todd, R.J., Kuhlthau, C.C., & OELMA. (2004). *Student learning through Ohio school libraries: The Ohio research study*. Columbus, OH: Ohio Educational Library Media Association.

ADDITIONAL READINGS

American Association of School Librarians. (2009). *Empowering learners: Guidelines for school library media programs*. Chicago: American Library Association.

Boehm, P. (2009). The new AASL program guidelines for school library programs. *School Library Monthly, 26*(1), 50–52.

Callison, D. (2007). Data on the instructional role of the library media specialist—are schools getting their money's worth? *School Library Media Activities, 23*(10), 55–58.

Franklin, P., & Stephens, C.G. (2006). Endings and beginnings in the library media center. *School Library Media Activities Monthly, 22*(10), 44–45.

Johnson, D.A. (2006). A 13-point library media program checklist for school principals. *Teacher Librarian, 33*(3), 70–71.

Klinger, D.A., Lee, E.A., Stephenson, G., Deluca, C., & Luu, K. (2009). *Exemplary school libraries in Ontario*. Toronto, OT: Ontario Library Association.

Lee, E.A., & Klinger, D.A. (2011). Against the flow: A continuum for evaluating and revitalizing school libraries. *School Libraries Worldwide, 17*(1), 24–36.

Marcoux, E. (2009). The best of the best school library programs—2009. *Teacher Librarian, 37*(4), 32–34, 36.

Marcoux, E. (2009). NSLMPY winners and their tips: A recipe for your school library. *Teacher Librarian, 36*(4), 29–31.

Marcoux, E. (2012). The 2011 SLPY award winners' words on supportive administrators. *Teacher Librarian, 39*(3).

Moreillon, J. (2009). Reading and the library program. *Knowledge Quest, 38*(2), 24–30.

HELPFUL WEBSITES

American Association of School Librarians. (2001). *Flexible scheduling*. Retrieved from http://aasl.ala.org/essentiallinks/index.php?title=Flexible_Scheduling

California School Library Association. (2004). *Standards and guidelines for strong school libraries*. Retrieved from http://www.csla.net/pdf/CSLA_Standards.pdf

Jackson, G.G., & Scott, R. (2005). *No library media center left behind: Assessing library media programs*. Retrieved from http://www.ala.org/ala/mgrps/divs/aasl/conferencesandevents/confarchive/pittsburgh/NoLMCLeftBehind.pdf

Maryland State Department of Education. (2000). *Standards for school library media program in Maryland*. Retrieved from http://www.marylandpublicschools.org/NR/rdonlyres/092A7763–3A8E-47D6-B57D-32FBDC668D0A/13091/SLMStandards1.pdf

Ohio Department of Education. (2010). *Ohio guidelines for effective school media programs*. Retrieved from http://www.ode.state.oh.us/GD/Templates/Pages/ODE/ODEDetail.aspx?Page=3&TopicRelationID=1703&Content=97092

Starr, L. (2010). *Strong libraries improve student achievement.* Retrieved from http://www.educationworld.com/a_admin/admin/admin178.shtml

The Utah Educational Library Media Association, The Utah Library Media Supervisors, & The Utah State Office of Education. (n.d.). *Standards: Utah school library media programs.* Retrieved from http://www.schools.utah.gov/curr/library/pdf/standards.pdf

Policies and Procedures

One of the most important responsibilities of a school librarian is to develop or maintain an updated policies and procedures manual. Written policies and procedures are critical to the efficient management of a school library program and collection. Such policies and procedures have numerous purposes:

- Ensure a degree of consistency
- Define the scope and coverage of the collection
- Assign selection responsibility
- Facilitate quality selection
- Provide guidance in the acquisition, processing, and cataloging of materials
- Provide for maintenance of materials and equipment
- Aid in weeding or deselection of the collection
- Impart information dealing with the circulation and promotion of the collection
- Guide evaluation of the collection
- Acknowledge the rights of individuals to ask for reconsideration of materials
- Guide staff in handling complaints
- Protect intellectual freedom
- Promote fair use of copyrighted materials
- Ensure equitable student access to materials, including those on the Internet
- Provide guidelines to protect the confidentiality of library users
- Serve as a training tool for new staff or volunteers
- Create a public relations document to inform the public of the purposes of the program and collection
- Provide a means of assessing overall performance of the school library program

Having written policies can save time, help avoid confusion, and provide guidance. For instance, if you are absent from your position for a long period of time due to illness or perhaps maternity leave, a policies and procedures manual will be invaluable to the person who is substituting in your position. If you leave your position to take another, your replacement will be able to have background on your program and collection, including a clear understanding of what policies and procedures have been in place. In difficult situations such as a materials complaint being made by an emotional parent, the written procedures for handling a challenge can provide guidance, consistency, and support. Written policies and procedures demonstrate to a reader that the program is run in a professional manner, decisions are not arbitrarily made, and overall planning is taking place.

POLICY VERSUS PROCEDURE STATEMENTS

Policy statements and procedure statements guide the activities of the collection program and tell why the collection exists. They state goals in general terms, allowing for flexibility and change. Policies establish the basis for all the collection activities by identifying who will use the collection and what will be in the collection. They need to be in place before procedures are developed. Policy documents are known by various terms including *collection policy*, *selection policy*, and *materials policy*.

Procedure statements direct the implementation of policies. They should be concrete and measurable. By defining *what, how*, and *when* questions, they address the tasks or processes for attaining the policy goals. Procedure statements explain how policies will be put into practice and identify the people responsible for their implementation. Procedures are specific and should be reviewed and updated on a regular basis. Examples of policies and procedures for specific school libraries can be found using the "Helpful Websites" listed at the end of this chapter.

As you examine documents, try to determine whether the policies and procedures are clearly distinguished. Questions you can ask yourself include the following: Does the statement

- address the purpose of the collection? (a policy)
- identify the types of materials that will be included? (a policy)
- explain how the collection will be created? (a procedure)
- state who is responsible for the collection? (a policy)
- describe the steps for maintaining the collection? (a procedure)
- explain the basis for adding or withdrawing materials from the collection? (a policy)
- identify who (students, teachers) will be involved in the selection process? (a policy)
- describe how teachers, administrators, and students will be involved in the selection process? (a procedure)
- identify student responsibilities for the use of resources in an ethical and educational manner? (a policy)

FORMULATING AND ADOPTING POLICIES

Policies need to reflect the goals and needs of the individual school library program and its institution. To be effective and responsive to these specific goals and needs, policy statements should be created at both the district and building levels. For example, usually the school district's stance on intellectual freedom and fair use are developed at the district level; however, questions dealing with the level of collecting materials on specific subjects would be at the building level. The diversity of building-level educational programs and the changing needs of users limits the effectiveness of adopting another school's policy statement. Nonetheless, it is helpful to examine statements from various sources. Doing so can prevent omissions, provide guidance for the outline, and offer suggestions for wording.

You should obtain input from others when writing specific policies for your school library. A library advisory board comprised of teachers, administrators, parents, and perhaps students can assist with the development, approval, and implementation of both policies and procedures. Each school will have its own process for approving policies. In some schools, the policy is approved only at building level. For instance, in a school using site-based management, a school advisory board composed of administrators, classroom teachers, and parents might be the group to whom policies are submitted for approval. In other school districts, there is a defined procedure that terminates with school board approval. Consult your school administrators to plan for the steps to obtain formal approval of your policies.

The following is a sample of the steps that might be followed by a governing body in formally formulating and adopting a policy:

- Decides to establish and adopt a policy.
- Appoints an ad hoc committee composed of representatives of the school community.
- This body may include parents, students, certified school librarians, administrators, people from other libraries and educational institutions, and community members. If the policy is to cover all instructional materials, including textbooks, then the body should also include subject specialists.
- Determines who will use the policy.
- Identifies when the statement might be used for evaluating the collection, preparing funding proposals, generating accreditation reports, or guiding cooperative resource sharing agreements.
- Charges the committee with the responsibility of developing the policy and establishes a deadline for the presentation of a draft.
- Distributes general guidelines to the committee to facilitate its work.
- Studies the draft before discussing it with the committee.
- Determines whether and how the policy can be easily updated.
- Solicits discussion and suggestions from legal counsel, personnel within the school (such as department heads or curriculum committees), and groups such as parent–teacher associations and teachers' associations.
- Conducts a closing review of the committee's recommendations and the comments expressed by others who studied the draft.
- Adopts a formal written statement as the approved policy of the issuing agency.
- Provides for implementation of the newly adopted policy. This involves disseminating the policy to all staff members involved in the evaluation, selection, and use of materials covered in the policy. A meeting or staff development program should familiarize the staff with the policy so they can respond to inquiries about it. Library personnel and teachers are likely to be the ones who receive requests that materials in the collection or used in classrooms be reconsidered.
- Disseminates the policy to the community.
- Plans and conducts school and community activities to make people aware of the importance of the freedom to read, speak, view, listen, evaluate, and learn.
- Establishes periodic evaluation and revision of the policy. Reviews should be scheduled on a regular basis with intervals of one to three years.
- Formally adopts changes. Dates of the original adoption and sequential revisions recorded on the document are helpful indicators of the document's history.

A graphical representation of this process can be found in Figure 5.1.

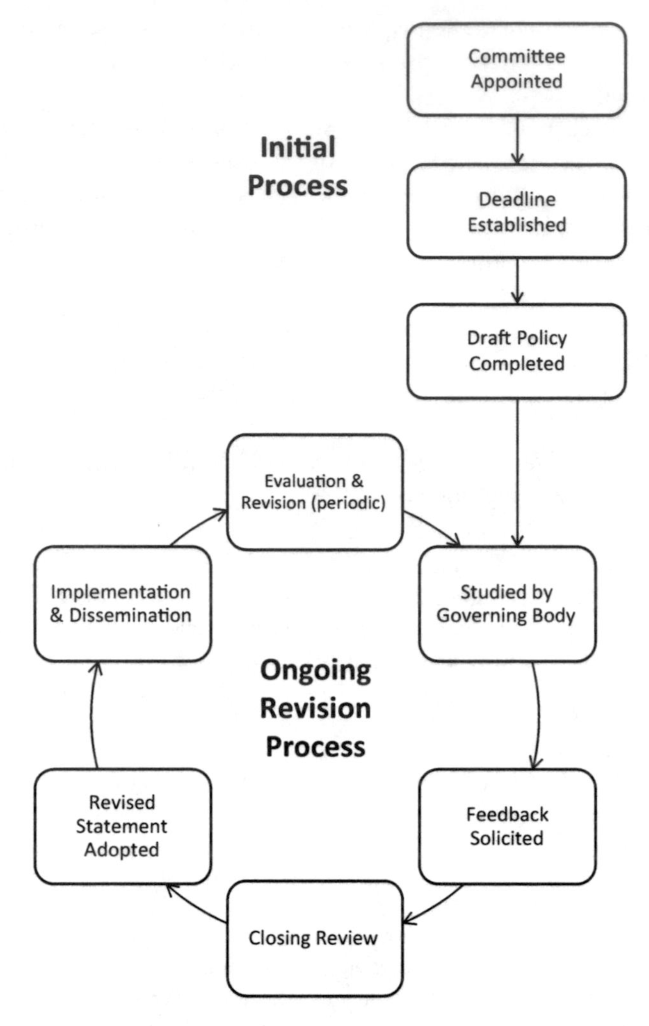

Figure 5.1. Process of policy formulation and revision

WRITING A POLICIES AND PROCEDURES MANUAL

If you take a position in a school library that does not have written policies and procedures, one of your initial responsibilities should be to begin the development of a manual that includes the policies from the district level, plus any policies and procedures specific to your school library. Policies and procedures can be integrated into one manual or you may choose to separate them into two different manuals.

Your manual should be written in third person, and proper names of persons should not be included. Instead of naming the person who performs a task or has a specific responsibility, use terms such as *the librarian* or *the library clerk* or *the principal*. These terms should not be capitalized. Using such terms will create a more professional manual and will avoid having to make frequent revisions when personnel changes are made. Other helpful hints for creating a professional manual include the following:

- Be concise; use a minimum of verbiage.
- If you use acronyms, spell them out the first time they are utilized.
- Include step-by-step instructions for describing procedures.
- Do not be too technical; make the manual simple enough to be understood by a lay person or a new employee.
- Make generous use of white space.
- Be factual; double-check for accuracy.

If desired, the manual can be created and maintained electronically; thus, it is much easier to revise the information in the manual. A table of contents should be included in the beginning of the manual to make it possible to easily find a particular policy or procedure. If you are maintaining a hard copy of the manual, then it is wise to put each policy and procedure on separate pages and place your manual in a sturdy loose-leaf binder, with various topics presented in separate sections (perhaps denoted by labeled tabs or color-coded division pages). This will make it easier for you to make revisions or additions when you want to update the manual. If at a later date you choose to add or delete a few paragraphs, printing out a couple of revised pages of a section is much more efficient than having to reprint the entire manual. When you make revisions, it is often helpful to add the date of the revision (e.g., 11/12) in a footer at the bottom of the page. If the manual is only in an electronic format, then it may be necessary in some instances to print out particular pages when needed (e.g., a printed page that lists the steps for processing a book might be needed for a volunteer who is assisting in the procedure).

You do not need to *recreate the wheel* when you are writing a manual, but if you take a substantial amount of wording from another document, you should provide a citation for the original document. This can easily be done by placing an asterisk after the original wording and putting a citation in a footer at the bottom of the page. You might want to adopt a certain style (MLA, Turabian, or APA) for your citations, but no matter what style you decide to utilize, the citations need to have enough information for the reader to access the original documents. If you are including a district-level policy or procedure in your manual, you might choose to place it in an appendix and cite the item in the text of your manual (e.g., "See Appendix A for the district policy on intellectual freedom"). You can then add into the text any other information that is specific to your school library, such as where a complainant can obtain a copy of a form for reconsideration of a challenged material. If the library in which you take a position as a librarian already has written policies and procedures, you need to carefully read and follow them until any revisions are made.

As a library school educator, the author of this book has required students to write a manual for a hypothetical school library or work collaboratively with a school librarian to develop a manual for an actual school library. This assignment can be very time consuming so often students complete the assignment in groups, making group decisions about which selection tools will be used, what steps to follow for a challenged book, whether to charge fines for overdue books, and various other topics. This creates some interesting discussions and careful consideration of all the areas that comprise collection development and management. You will be extremely busy as a new school librarian so having already carefully considered all the aspects of collection development and management and having a model to follow for written policies and procedures will be a huge timesaver in the future.

CONTENTS OF A MANUAL

Numerous topics can be included in a policies and procedures manual. The following are suggested items for all manuals:

- Table of Contents
- Community and School Analyses
- Library Philosophy or Mission Statement
- School Library Goals and Objectives
- Description of Programs and Services
- Personnel Job Descriptions
- Formats Collected
- Selection Policies and Procedures
- Acquisition, Processing, and Cataloging of Materials
- Gifts
- Maintaining Materials and Equipment
- Inventory of Materials
- Weeding Materials
- Circulation
- Confidentiality of Library Records
- Collection Evaluation
- Internet or Technology (Including an Internet Use Policy)
- Copyright and Fair Use Compliance
- Intellectual Freedom

These items do not need to be in the order listed, but they should be in a logical order. For instance, a community and school analysis should be toward the beginning of a manual since the policies and procedures are supposed to be based on the needs of the users.

Other topics or items that can be helpful to include in the text of a manual or in an appendix are: resource sharing, behavior guidelines and classroom management techniques, budget and fundraising, public relations, evaluation of the library media program, evaluation of personnel, a student handbook, a manual for volunteers, and any useful forms or surveys. As you can see, there are many policies and procedures to remember when developing a collection and managing a program. You will not want to carry all this information around in your head, and it will not serve others adequately if it is not in a written format.

CONCLUSIONS

In order to efficiently develop and manage collection activities, policies and procedures need to be developed by the school librarian, with input from others who utilize the materials. District-level policies that relate to a school library must be considered and followed.

Additionally, policies should go through an approval process. All policies and procedures should be organized in a written format so that consistency can be maintained and a clear understanding of collection activities and the library program is available. Policies and procedures should be regularly reviewed for possible revisions to make certain they are meeting the mission and goals of the library.

ADDITIONAL READINGS

Adams, H.R. (2007). Conducting a privacy audit. *School Library Media Activities, 23*(6), 35.

Brumley, R.R. (2009). *Electronic collection management forms, policies, procedures, and guidelines manual with CD-ROM.* New York: Neal-Schuman.

Downs, E. (2010). *The school library media specialist's policy and procedures writer.* New York: Neil Schuman.

Harris, C. (2010). Friend me? *School Library Journal, 56*(4), 16.

Hoffman, F.W., & Wood, R.J. (2007). *Library collection development policies: School libraries and learning resource centers.* Lanham, MD: Scarecrow Press.

Pappas, M.L. (2005). Virtual school library media center management manual. *School Library Media Activities Monthly, 21*(5). Retrieved from http://www.schoollibrarymonthly.com/columns/management/index.html

HELPFUL WEBSITES

Follett Library Resources. (n.d.) *School library collection development policies: Directory of books and websites.* Retrieved from http://www.flr.follett.com/intro/pdfs/news/grants-colldevpolicies.pdf

Resources for School Librarians. (n.d.). Retrieved from http://www.sldirectory.com/

Washington Library Media Association. (n.d.). *Policy and procedure support.* Retrieved from http://www.wlma.org/Default.aspx?pageId=951332

Chapter

6 Selection

As a school librarian you will be involved in updating a selection policy for your school. If one is not in place, you should take the lead in creating a selection policy, including guidelines and procedures that relate to requests for reconsideration of materials. As discussed in Chapter 5 "Policies and Procedures," policy statements are stronger and more effective when formulated by a group. The school librarian's professional responsibility is to ensure that appropriate policies are in place. Involving teachers, administrators, students, and members of the community is vital to the process. A major benefit to this is the participants' advocacy and support of the principles on which the policy is based. This process presents an opportunity to explain the school library's role in the educational process, to emphasize the importance of a commitment to intellectual freedom, and to discuss the concept of providing access to information.

Some states have mandates for school library selection policies that include procedures for reconsideration of challenged materials. In other states similar mandates are present at the school district level. You should contact your state department of education or department of public instruction for information about such mandates.

ELEMENTS OF A SELECTION POLICY

If you include your library's selection policy in a larger manual that deals with all policies and procedures for the library, then statements that address philosophy might be covered in an earlier section of your manual. However, if your selection policy is issued as a separate document, several elements need to be included. The following section discusses each of these elements.

Statement of Philosophy

This brief statement presents the school district's values and beliefs. It can refer to the school's mission and goals statements or language from that document. The statement of philosophy should also address how the educational resources help the school achieve its goals.

Other relevant documents can be duplicated in this section. A statement referring to the U.S. Constitution's First Amendment's protection of students' rights to access information to read, listen, view, and evaluate is important to include (U.S. Constitution). Readers can be directed to copies of documents in an appendix that support these principles. Such documents include the American Library Association's *Library Bill of Rights* and *Freedom to Read Statement*, the National Council of Teachers of English's *Students' Right to Read*, and the American Film and Video's Association's *Freedom to View Statement*.

Sample phrases in this section generally start with "The Board of [school district's name] through its professional staff 'shall provide,' 'will provide,' or 'is committed to facilitating teaching and learning by providing' . . ." One or more of the following phrases could be used to complete sentences:

- "library collections that meet both the curricular needs and personal needs of students."
- "resources in various formats and varying levels of difficulty."
- "materials that provide a global perspective and promote diversity."
- "resources that reflect the basic humanity of all people and are free of stereotypes."
- "library materials that present different points of view in an objective manner."
- "materials that will help students develop critical thinking skills and aesthetic appreciation."

Selection Objectives

This element of the policy translates the school district's philosophy and goals into collection objectives. The statements show how the collection helps the school meet its goals. Objectives identify the materials that will be in the collection, present a rationale for using a variety of resources in the school, and describe the basis for judging the educational suitability of the materials for use by students and teachers. Examples of main objective statements are:

- To make available to faculty and students a collection of materials that will support, supplement, and enrich the curriculum
- To provide a wide range of the best materials available on appropriate levels of difficulty
- To enhance the curriculum with materials representative of the points of view of the religious, cultural, ethnic, and social groupings within the community
- To select materials that present various sides of controversial issues so that students have an opportunity to develop skills in critical analysis and in making informed judgments in their daily lives
- To place principle above personal opinion or prejudice in order to assure a comprehensive collection that is appropriate to the school community
- To provide materials in a variety of formats, including both print and electronic materials, to support the students' learning needs
- To select materials that stimulate growth in factual knowledge, literary appreciation, aesthetic values, and societal standards

Responsibility for Selection

An important element of the selection policy is stating who is responsible for selection decisions. If the policy applies to all instructional materials, this statement should distinguish between those who are responsible for text materials and those responsible for library program materials.

These statements usually acknowledge that the school board is legally responsible and delegates to school librarians the authority to select. The term *school librarians* can be defined as "professional, certified personnel employed by the district."

A statement that identifies who participates in the selection process should also be included. This statement indicates the role and level of involvement of teachers, students, administrators, staff, and community members in the selection process. Some questions that might be addressed include the following: Does a committee make selection decisions? Do school librarians work independently? Is a combination of committee selections and librarian selections utilized? How is responsibility delegated? How is input for selection gathered from teachers and students?

Selection Criteria

Selection criteria generally consist of two or more parts. The first is a list of general criteria that apply to all materials and relate to the district or school goals. A statement that these criteria apply to all materials, including gifts and loans, can eliminate the need to write a separate section about such items.

General criteria commonly used include literary qualities, technical qualities, qualifications of authors or producers, and appropriateness for audience. You can obtain additional assistance for this section by consulting Chapter 7 "General Selection Criteria." Criteria that are often used for general selection indicate that the materials should do the following:

- Contribute to the instructional program's objectives.
- Be consistent with and support the general educational goals of the state and district.
- Help students gain an awareness of our pluralistic society.
- Be relevant to today's world.
- Reflect the problems, aspirations, attitudes, and ideals of society.
- Be appropriate for the age, ability level, learning style, and social and emotional development of the intended users.
- Be appropriate for the subject area.
- Meet quality standards in terms of content, format, and presentation.
- Be selected for their strengths, rather than rejected for their weaknesses.
- Reflect value commensurate with cost and/or need.
- Not represent a personal bias.
- Represent artistic, historic, and literary qualities.
- Have a high degree of potential user appeal.
- Motivate students to examine their own attitudes; to understand their rights, duties, and responsibilities as citizens; and to make informed judgments in their daily lives.

In selecting all formats for possible purchase the librarian should consider the following general criteria:

- Reputation of the author, illustrator, publisher, and producer
- Overall quality and accuracy
- Currency and appropriateness of the content
- Value in relation to cost and need
- Value to the collection

The second part of selection criteria can address criteria for specific formats of materials, including electronic formats and equipment. If you want to address the criteria for specific formats, the contents of Chapter 8, "Criteria by Format," will be especially helpful.

Some policies identify selection sources to consult and then specify that two or more favorable reviews must appear in the selection tools before an item can be considered for selection. This practice has several disadvantages that may prove to be restrictive. First, reviewing journals and selection tools often do not review the same titles. Second, a dearth of reviews exists for some formats. Third, a specific list of selection tools may not be comprehensive or may not identify sources actually used. This policy creates a problem if none of the cited sources has reviewed a particular item. The requirement of having two reviews in particular selection tools limits selections made by librarians and should not be included in policies.

While selection aids can be helpful in identifying titles to be considered for purchase, using reviews as a criterion for selection focuses on the review, rather than the professional judgment of the school librarian. However, if you choose to include procedures relating to selection of materials, you might want to list the selection tools that are recommended as consultation aids. Possible wording could be: "The following recommended lists can be consulted in the selection of materials, but selection is not limited to their listing." An annotated listing of some selection aids that could be included in such a list can be found in the "Appendix: Resources."

Gifts

If the acceptance of gifts is not included in the general criteria section of your selection policy, statements addressing criteria used for the acceptance or rejection of gifts need to be included in a separate section. Most schools apply the same criteria for acceptance of gifts as they do for purchases. However, you might want to also consider how you will handle items that are donated by businesses or commercial concerns. It is useful to note that no advertising beyond the name of the contributing company be included and that donations must relate to the curriculum. You might also wish to include a statement relating to the currency of donated materials. This may eliminate the need of having to deal with boxes of donated *National Geographic* magazines from the 1960s and 1970s. While some of the articles in those magazines might have interesting information, most of the information will be quite outdated, and your available space to put them on your shelves will most likely be limited.

Some school librarians also include a statement relating to the fact that all gifts become the property of the school district and when declared surplus can be dispensed as deemed appropriate by the librarian. This might include transferring the surplus items to another school or weeding them from the collection. A statement could read: "The library does not accept gifts with restrictions or conditions relating to their final use, disposition, or location."

Policies relating to the acceptance of monetary gifts to purchase materials should also be addressed. If accepting monetary gifts, specific procedures should be written and carefully followed.

You might also want to address some procedures relating to gifts made to the school library. The provision of letters and/or receipts to acknowledge gifts to a library should be part of such procedures. The letter or receipt should note the number and types of materials donated, but should not specify a dollar amount, unless the gift was monetary.

Other procedures might include whether notations of donated resources are included in the catalog entry and whether a bookplate or notation is added to the material itself.

Policies on Controversial Materials

You should include a section in your policy that deals with intellectual freedom and the handling of controversial materials. Most school districts have written policies that address this topic not only in regard to materials present in the library, but also for books or other formats used in classroom lessons. Thus, it is important for you to include in your selection policy any school district policies that relate to controversial materials in a school library. This can be done in the text of your selection policy, or the school district policy can be placed in an appendix and referred to from the text.

You need to include a statement that your school library supports the principle of intellectual freedom and explain why it is important to maintain. If you have not already referred to the First Amendment to the U.S. Constitution or to other documents that address intellectual freedom, you should do so in this section. Wording in this section might read as follows: "The Lincoln School Library supports the principles of intellectual freedom inherent in the First Amendment to the United States Constitution as expressed in official statements of professional associations. These include [identify statement(s)] and form a part of this policy."

Request for Reconsideration of Materials

Most selection policies also include procedures for handling complaints and for focusing the complainant's attention on the principles of intellectual freedom, rather than on the material itself. A school district may have specific procedures for dealing with challenged materials. In such a case, you will need to place these procedures in your policies and procedures document and make certain they are implemented correctly.

If the steps to follow for challenged materials are not specified by the school district, then you should meet with an advisory board at your school, develop the procedures, and put them through an approval process. Possible steps to consider in your reconsideration of materials in your school library include:

- Listen calmly and with courtesy to the complainant.
- Explain to the complainant the selection criteria used for materials that are in the library and try to resolve the issue informally by discussing the educational uses of the material in question and noting relevant sections of the American Library Association's *Access to Resources and Services in the School Library Program: An Interpretation of the Library Bill of Rights.*
- If the complainant wants to proceed with a formal request for reconsideration of a material, provide a copy of the policies and procedures related to the handling of challenged materials, as well as a copy of the school's *Request for Reconsideration of Library Resources* form.
- Instruct the complainant that the form must be completed before a formal complaint proceeds.
- Inform the principal of the challenge and the identity of the complainant. If the complaint is resolved informally, keep the identity of the complainant confidential.
- When the complainant returns the completed form, the principal will inform the superintendent of schools of a request for formal reconsideration.

- Form a reconsideration committee to include a building administrator, a classroom teacher from the appropriate grade level or subject area, the school librarian, an objective member of the community, and a student (if the challenged material is in a secondary school).
- Appoint a chairperson for the committee.
- Have the chairperson arrange a meeting of the committee to be held within 10 working days after the form is returned to the school by the complainant.
- At the first meeting, instruct all members of the committee to read the completed *Request for Reconsideration of Library Resources* form and to read, view, or listen to the material in question. The librarian may need to obtain additional copies of the challenged material (book, video, DVD, CD, or audiocassette) through interlibrary loan or through informal means before a time for the next meeting can be set.
- At a second meeting when all committee members have had ample opportunity to examine and evaluate the challenged material, discuss the item that has been questioned.
- Instruct the committee members to form opinions on the material as a whole, not on specific passages or selections.
- Have the committee reach a decision, using majority rules, to retain or remove the item.
- Have the chairperson complete a report of the committee's procedures and their decision regarding the challenged material and submit the report to the principal.
- Instruct the principal to send a copy of the report to the complainant and discuss it with the complainant if so requested. Remind the principal to also submit a copy of the report to the superintendent of schools.
- If the complainant continues to be dissatisfied with the process, inform that person that he has the right to appeal the decision of the committee to the superintendent of schools and the district school board.
- Keep challenged materials in circulation until the process is complete.

Figure 6.1 is a sample of a form for requesting the reconsideration of a library resource. You should make certain that the form that you use meets the needs of your particular school setting and has been approved. In some schools the same form is used for challenging materials in a classroom setting as for the reconsideration of materials in a library; thus, in those cases some adaptation of this sample form would be needed.

Generally speaking, procedures are written for internal use and are not necessarily available for public use; however, in the case of challenged materials, a single document for the public's use should combine both the policies and procedures for handling the challenge. This document should be readily available to the public, with a copy kept at the circulation desk. Sharing this information in a forthright manner can alleviate some of the tension that can occur in situations where materials are challenged.

Most challenges can be settled informally if one takes the time to calmly listen to the complainant's concerns and then explains the library's criteria for selection, emphasizing the principle of intellectual freedom. Assuring parents that you respect the interest that they have in their own child's reading or viewing can often satisfy the needs of parents to voice their concerns.

Challenges to materials are to be expected in most schools. The challenges may come from parents, community members, teachers, principals, or organized groups. Having a written procedure to follow and knowing how to respond to a challenge will alleviate the emotional upset that sometimes is experienced by school librarians when faced with an irate parent or an outspoken member of an organized group that challenges library materials. To ensure that all queries, whether internal or external, are treated in the same manner, each individual's complaint should be treated according to the written procedures.

REQUEST FOR RECONSIDERATION OF LIBRARY MATERIALS

The School Board of XYZ School has delegated the responsibilities of selection of books and other resources to the school librarian, and has established reconsideration procedures to address concerns about any of the selected materials. If you wish to request reconsideration of a book or other library resource, please return the completed form to the principal of XYZ School.

Title: ______________________________

Author: ______________________________

Publisher: ______________ Copyright Date: ______________

Person Initiating Request: ______________ Date of Request: ______________

Address: ______________ Phone Number: ______________

Email Address: ______________________________

Please answer the following questions completely. Use additional pages if necessary:

1. Are you representing yourself? Organization?
   Name? ______________
2. Resource Type: Book Textbook DVD Magazine
   Newspaper Electronic Resource Other
3. What brought this book/resource to your attention?
4. What concerns do you have about this book/resource?
5. Have you examined the entire book/resource? If not, what parts did you examine?
6. What other resource(s) would you suggest to provide additional information on this specific issue or topic?
7. What action would you like the library to take regarding this book/resource?
8. Would you like to make a presentation to the Reconsideration of Library Resources Committee and/or School Board regarding this material?
9. Other comments?

Figure 6.1. Request form for reconsideration of library resources

SELECTION PROCEDURES

In choosing materials, a school librarian plans and carries out certain activities that culminate in selection decisions. These activities include identifying and assessing evaluative information about materials, arranging for examining materials either through visiting exhibits or examination centers, and providing ways to involve others in the process. These steps lead to the direct acquisition of materials or obtaining materials and information through resource sharing and electronic means. For a listing of resources that can assist in the selection process, see the "Appendix: Resources."

Overview of the Selection Process

Selection is the process of deciding what materials to add to the collection. Librarians can identify potential materials through many sources. For example, administrators, teachers, and students request specific items or types of materials. The librarian learns about new materials by reading reviews, viewing the announcements of publishers and producers, and previewing materials.

You need to keep a record of suggestions and requests to purchase materials. This can be done electronically in a computer file, in a card file, or simply by keeping written notes; this record is called a *consideration file*. You should record as much bibliographic and purchasing information about the item as you can obtain, including the identifying source and the person who requested the item. The next step is to determine whether the item is already in the collection or on order. Some librarians enter the information in the online catalog so users will be aware that the item is being considered or on order.

Once an item is fully identified, the librarian must decide to include or exclude it from the collection. The librarian bases this selection decision on several considerations, including collection policy; budget; content, format, use, and immediacy of need. After the librarian has decided to purchase the item, the status of the record for the item is changed from *consideration file* to *order file*. The actions following this step compose the acquisition process.

Sources of Information about Resources

Bibliographic tools provide information about the availability of materials, their cost, and whether they are recommended. Trade bibliographies, such as *Books in Print* (R.R. Bowker), Bowker's online *New Books in Print* and *Canadian Books in Print* (University of Toronto Press), provide information about the existence of materials, but do not evaluate them. Selection tools, such as *Senior High Core Collection* (H.W. Wilson), *Middle and Junior High School Core Collection* (H.W. Wilson), and *Children's Core Collection* (H.W. Wilson), evaluate materials and may include purchasing information. They are available electronically and in print format and are especially useful if you are developing a library collection from scratch.

When considering a bibliography or selection tool for use or purchase, read the introduction and examine several entries. This will help answer the following questions about the work:

- *Purpose of the bibliography*: Does it meet your need?
- *Directions for use*: Are they clear? Does the work give sample entries with explanations?
- *Format*: Is the bibliography available in print, CD-ROM, or online?

- *Extent of coverage*: Does the resource include information about a variety of formats? Does it provide information for many items, or is coverage limited? Does it include materials for a wide range of audiences, preschool through adult? What periods of publication and production does the work include?
- *Method for collecting the information and designated responsibility*: Who wrote the entries? What are the writers' qualifications? Are reviews signed?
- *Criteria for inclusion*: On what basis are items included? Are the criteria stated? Is the selection policy provided?
- *Form and content of entry*: Does the work present information clearly? Does it use symbols and abbreviations? Symbols may indicate levels of recommendation, reviewing sources, interest level, readability, and type of media. What ordering and bibliographic information does the work give? Are the annotations descriptive, evaluative, or both? Are all items recommended equally? Are items recommended for specific situations, uses, or audiences? Are there comparisons with other titles or formats? Does the work include only materials that have received favorable reviews in other tools?
- *Organization of entries*: Are the indexes necessary to locate an item? Do cross-references direct the user to related items? Do indexes provide access by author, title, series titles, audience, reading level, and subject? Does the index include analytical entries? For example, the selection tools by H.W. Wilson Company include analytical entries for individual folktales in anthologies, biographical sketches (not limited to collective biographies), subjects, and short stories in collections. This information is helpful in locating these materials for students and teachers.
- *Date of publication*: Does the work provide the compiler's closing date? How often is the bibliography revised or cumulated? Does it provide supplements? What time lag exists between compiling the information and the issuing of the bibliography?
- *Special features*: Does the bibliography include directories for sources of materials? Does the work include appendices? If so, what is included?
- *Cost*: Does the tool provide sufficient information for a variety of users to merit the expenditure for it?

Selection Tools

Selection tools exist in a variety of formats: books, reviewing periodicals, and bibliographic essays. These tools can be in print or electronic format.

Books

Commonly used general selection tools that appear in book and electronic format are the H.W. Wilson series (*Children's Core Collection*, *Middle and Junior High School Core Collection*, and *Senior High Core Collection*). The lead time required to produce printed formats of these printed books creates a time gap between the publication of the last item reviewed and the publication date of the bibliography itself. Subscribing to the online versions of these tools can lessen this time gap. Even if published in electronic formats, the bibliographies are sometimes not as current as reviewing journals. Other print and electronic selection tools list recommended materials for specific subjects, audiences, or formats. See the "Appendix: Resources" for titles of these books.

Reviewing Journals

Reviewing journals evaluate currently published and produced materials. There is a wide range of these journals, each with unique and valuable features. Commercial firms, professional associations, education agencies, and other publishers produce reviewing journals. Generally they are written for a specific audience, such as school librarians or classroom teachers. The coverage of materials that journals review is often limited by format, potential users, subjects, or particular perspectives. The reviews are written by journal staff members or by professionals in the field. Signed reviews sometimes provide information about the reviewer's position or background.

The content of some journals such as *Booklist* are primarily reviews of materials. However, many reviewing journals, such as *Library Media Connection* and *School Library Journal*, also include articles or columns of interest to school librarians. Some professional journals, such as the American Association of School Librarians' *Knowledge Quest*, limit their reviews to materials that could be a part of a professional collection.

Journal editors have legitimate reasons for why their journals might not review a specific title. Some do not have a work reviewed unless it can be reviewed within a specific time after its publication. Some titles may be outside a journal's scope, or they might simply fail to meet other criteria set up by the journal. Such a huge number of juvenile resources are produced each year so it is impossible for a single journal to review all of them.

Locating reviews for audiovisual materials, computer software, electronic materials, websites, and online databases can be more challenging than finding book reviews. However, more review journals are including these formats than in past years. Cumulated indexes that appear in the back pages of some journals can be helpful in the search for reviews, but a more comprehensive approach to review indexing can be found in tools such as *Book Review Index* and *Book Review Digest.* These tools are available in print format and online. The cost of such tools may require that all school libraries in the district share them.

Bibliographic Essays

Bibliographic essays that describe and recommend materials about a subject, a theme, a specific use, or an audience can be found in journals such as *Teacher Librarian, Library Media Connection,* and *Book Links.* These essays can be very helpful, but they require careful analysis. Readers do not know whether the writer simply overlooked an omitted item or whether the writer deliberately omitted that item. Usually, bibliographic essays focus on a specific topic and do not provide overall assessments of the resources.

Best, Notable, and Recommended Materials

Some professional journals contain articles listing materials that have been selected as *best*, *notable*, or *recommended* for particular years. Some lists are annotated, while others simply contain the bibliographic information. Such lists can also be found online. It is important to consider authority (who has chosen the materials) when using such lists as selection aids. For instance, resources compiled by national professional library associations can generally be considered reliable since they are selections made by committees that include several librarians and library educators. On the other hand, lists found on individuals' or publishers' websites may need to be examined more closely.

Relying on Reviewing Media

School librarians use reviewing media on a regular basis. If no selection committee exists, the entire burden of selection rests with the librarian. To examine every item published or produced within a given year would be an impossible task.

What do librarians look for in reviews? Janie Schomberg (1993) writes:

> I need and expect a lot from reviews. First, book reviews should be descriptive, objective statements about plot, characters, theme, and illustrations. Second, I expect book reviews to have an evaluative statement including comparison of the title being reviewed to similar titles and literature in general. Third, the potential appeal, curricular use, and possible controversial aspects of the title need to be addressed to fully inform me as a potential selector. (p. 41)

You need to remember that reviews reflect the writer's opinion, based on the reviewers' knowledge of materials and students.

A variety of sources provide reviews. In addition to the ones noted earlier in this chapter, reviews can be found on websites of individuals, professional groups, and commercial organizations, such as Amazon.com. Like with other review sources, you should try to determine the authority and background of the reviewer and whether there are guidelines for the reviewers.

You should evaluate reviews by examining the following:

- Bibliographic information
- Purchasing information
- Cataloging information
- Description and evaluation of literary characteristics: plot, character, theme, setting, point of view, and style
- Description and evaluation of usability: authority, appropriateness, scope, accuracy, arrangement, and organization
- Description and evaluation of visual characteristics: shape, line, edge, color, proportion, detail, composition, and medium style
- Description and evaluation of comparison: author, illustrator, and other works
- Description and evaluation of sociological factors: controversial or popular
- Description and evaluation of other considerations: total artistic appearance, book design, use, and audience

Kay Bishop and Phyllis Van Orden (1998) in a comprehensive study dealing with journal reviewing of children's books noted that school media specialists need to have access to more than one reviewing journal and they should select reviewing journals that most closely suit the specific needs of their media centers. *Library Media Connection*, *School Library Journal*, and *Teacher Librarian* are three professional journals published specifically for school librarians. Each of the journals reviews a variety of formats. A summary of their reviewing coverage is as follows:

Library Media Connection: LMC

- Bibliographic information: Author, title, illustrator, year of publication, number of pages, cost, publisher or producer, ISBN, URL for web items
- Formats included: Books (fiction, nonfiction, reference, biography, poetry, graphic novels, Spanish language, and professional reading); Free Web; Subscription Web; Software-CD-ROM; Mobile Learning
- Grade level divisions: Picture Books; Fiction K-5; Fiction 6–8; Fiction 9–12; Nonfiction (listed by subjects, with grade levels at the end of the bibliographic information)
- Grade level symbols (placed in small circles at the beginning of the review text): Green K-5; Blue 6–8; Red 9–12
- Ratings: Highly Recommended (large gold star in front of the red highlighted title of the material); Recommended; Additional Selection; Not Recommended

- Reviewer information: Name of reviewer and place of employment at the end of review
- Online reviews: Some additional reviews available at the Linworth Publishing website

School Library Journal

- Bibliographic information: Author, title, illustrator, number of pages, publisher (producer and distributor for multimedia), cost, ISBN, LC (when available); URL for websites; miscellaneous information (number of hours for audio cassettes, CDs, and DVDs, teacher's guide included or available online)
- Formats included: Books (fiction, nonfiction, reference, professional); multimedia (video and DVD, audio); digital resources (covered in separate articles)
- Grade levels: Provided at the beginning of the text of the review, no grade level divisions, no grade level symbols
- Grade level symbols: None
- Ratings: Highly recommended materials in yellow highlighted boxes with a large red star placed at the beginning of the bibliographic information
- Reviewer information: Name of reviewer and place of employment at the end of the review
- Online reviews: Some reviews available at the *School Library Journal* website

Teacher Librarian

All reviews appear in various colored highlighted sidebars in different locations throughout the journal.

- Bibliographic information: Title, author, publisher, date of publication, ISBN, cost, grade levels, URL for websites
- Formats included: Books (junior fiction, young adult [YA] fiction, adult books for teens, picture books, graphic novels, junior nonfiction, YA nonfiction): websites; Software, professional resources included in separate articles
- Grade levels: Provided at the end of the bibliographic information, no grade level divisions, no grade level symbols
- Ratings: None
- Reviewer information: Name and photo of reviewer at the top of the sidebar; reviewers the same for every issue

Other journals frequently used by school librarians for reviews of materials include *Booklist, Canadian Review of Materials, The Horn Book Magazine, Kliatt, Library Journal, Resource Links* (Canadian), and *VOYA*.

Personal Examination

The ideal way to select resources for your school library is by personal examination. Depending on your school district's policies, you may be able to personally examine materials. The most practical ways include visits by sales representatives, formal previewing arrangements, visiting examination centers, and attending conferences.

Previewing is one of the most efficient ways to examine materials prior to purchasing. This is the practice of borrowing materials from an examination center, a producer, a distributor, or a jobber for a specific time for the purpose of evaluation. Previewing is an effective way to involve students and teachers in the selection process. Previewing is not a free way to supplement the collection, nor should several teachers within one building request the same item for examination at different times. The librarian is responsible for returning previewing materials in good condition within the specified time. Some companies will not allow preview of certain formats, such as videocassettes, DVDs, or computer software. Also, some school districts do not allow the request of materials for preview. However, requesting materials you are seriously considering for purchase is an excellent way to make informed selection decisions.

When attending conferences you should always set aside ample time to examine the materials in the exhibit areas. This is an excellent opportunity to not only view the materials, but to also ask company representatives questions or to provide them with suggestions. Vendors are interested in the opinions of school librarians and welcome their input into ways to improve their products. Some vendors arrange focus groups at conferences and present their new products; they then ask librarians to provide comments about the products.

Some school district staff arrange for exhibits of materials in a central location during the preopening school activities. These exhibits allow librarians and teachers to compare a wide range of materials. If your school district sponsors such exhibits, invite teachers to examine the materials with you.

Another way to personally evaluate materials is to visit an examination or preview center. These centers may serve district, regional, or state levels. They can be housed in the district school library center, at a university, or in a state agency. Often the materials in a preview center cannot be checked out, but can be examined only within the center.

Whether your evaluation involves personal examination of items or relies on reviews, some materials will, for one reason or another, remain unused or prove to be inappropriate. You should consider these situations as learning experiences. Schomberg (1993) observes, "There seems to be no way to avoid the occasional 'lemon.'... Selection of materials based upon reviews cannot be expected to be successful 100% of the time" (p. 42).

Other Sources of Information

Information about materials can also be obtained from publishers, producers, distributors, vendors, and wholesalers. The information appears in catalogs, on flyers, on television, and on the Internet. However, you should always be cautious about making selections from only these types of sources since their main objective is to sell their products.

Involving Others in Selection

The idea that teachers, students, and administrators should participate in making selection decisions is not new, but its practice is not always utilized. Common ways to involve others in the process include:

- Routing bibliographies and reviewing journals to teachers and administrators
- Attending faculty, departmental, or grade-level meetings to learn about curriculum changes and to discuss future purchases
- Conducting interest inventories with students
- Sending out forms to teachers and administrators to ask them what materials they would like purchased
- Providing a materials suggestion box at the circulation desk

School library advisory committees are another way to involve others. Teachers, community members, and students can be members of the advisory committee. In some districts, the advisory committee's responsibilities are limited to policy issues and to establishing priorities for acquisition. In other districts, the advisory committee may be involved in the selection process or in making decisions about which materials to remove or replace.

SOURCES OF ASSISTANCE

Information regarding selection of materials is available from a variety of sources, including professional colleagues and professional associations. Several school districts and individual schools have placed their selection policies online. A selected list of such policies can be found at the end of this chapter under "Helpful Websites." The American Library Association website, which includes a workbook for selection policy writing, will be particularly helpful to you if you are creating a new selection policy for a school.

A list of suggested readings dealing with selection policies, intellectual freedom, censorship, and handling challenges can be found at the end of this chapter. Additional discussion of intellectual freedom appears in Chapter 13, "Ethical Issues and the Collection."

Other organizations, besides the American Library Association, offer valuable assistance in handling censorship disputes. These include the American Association of University Women, American Booksellers Association for Freedom of Expression, American Civil Liberties Union, American Federation of Teachers, Association for Supervision and Curriculum Development, Association of American Publishers, Electronic Frontier Foundation, Freedom Forum, Freedom to Read Foundation, International Reading Association, Lamda Legal, Media Coalition, National Association of Elementary School Principals, National Coalition Against Censorship, National Council of Teachers of English, National Education Association, National School Boards Association, and People for the American Way Foundation. Contact information for these groups can be located easily by using the title of the organization in an online search on the Internet.

CONCLUSIONS

Written selection policies for materials can be a separate document or part of a larger policies and procedures manual. Many school districts have selection policies for school library materials, as well as for textbooks. It is important to include in an individual school library's policies and procedures manual any portions of the school district's policies that relate to school library materials. Selection policies should include who is responsible for selection, criteria for selecting materials, and how to handle controversial materials. Having written policies and procedures for challenged materials can ease tensions for a school librarian, as well as provide an objective process for those persons who register concerns about specific materials in a collection.

The ideal way to make selections of materials is to personally examine the resources. This can be done at conferences, special exhibits, examination centers, and by requesting materials for preview. Reading reviews of items and referring to bibliographies and special selection aids are other valuable means of selecting materials for school libraries. Teachers, administrators, and students should also be involved in the selection process.

REFERENCES

Bishop, K., & Van Orden, P. (1998). Reviewing children's books: A content analysis. *Library Quarterly, 68*, 145–182.

Schomberg, J. (1993). Tools of the trade: School library media specialists, reviews, and collection development. In B. Hearne & R. Sutton (Eds.), *Evaluating children's books: A critical look: Aesthetic, social, and political aspects of analyzing and using children's books* (pp. 37–46). Champaign-Urbana: University of Illinois, Graduate School of Library and Information Science.

U.S. Constitution, Amendment I.

ADDITIONAL READINGS

Adams, H.R. (2010). Preparing for and facing a challenge in a school library. *Catholic Library World, 81*(2), 113–117.

Barber, R. (2011). My experience with library censorship and some suggestions. *Learning Media, 39*(1), 11–13.

Friese, E.E.G. (2008). Inquiry learning: Is your selection policy ready? *Library Media Connection, 27*(3), 14–16.

Gibson, J. (2007). Championing intellectual freedom: A school administrator's guide. *Knowledge Quest, 36*(2), 46–48.

Harer, J.B. (2009). Parental involvement in selection: Mandated or our choice? *Library Media Connection, 28*(3), 18–19.

Stripling, B., Williams, C., Johnston, M., & Anderton, H. (2010). Minors & Internet interactivity: A new interpretation of the LBOR. *Knowledge Quest, 39*(1), 38–45.

Sullivan, C., & Sullivan, M. (2005). Monkey business: The intelligent design war has come to the school library. *School Library Journal, 51*(11), 42–44.

Torrisi, J., & Brimacombe, K. (2010). Free people read freely: The 14th annual report on challenged and banned books in Texas public school 2009–2010 school year. *Texas Library Journal, 86*(3), 94–101.

Wolf, S. (2008). Coping with mandated restrictions on intellectual freedom in K-12 schools. *Library Media Connection, 27*(3), 10–12.

HELPFUL WEBSITES

American Library Association. (1998). *Workbook for selection policy writing.* Retrieved from http://www.ala.org/Template.cfm?Section=dealing&Template=/ContentManagement/ContentDisplay.cfm&ContentID=11173

American Library Association. (2011). *Banned & challenged books.* Retrieved from http://www.ala.org/ala/issuesadvocacy/banned/index.cfm

Baltimore County Public Schools. (n.d.). *Selection criteria for school library media center collections.* Retrieved from http://www.bcps.org/offices/lis/office/admin/selection.html

California Department of Education. (2011). *District selection policies.* Retrieved from http://www.cde.ca.gov/ci/rl/ll/litrlppolicies.asp

Garces Memorial High School. (2010). *Selection criteria for school library media center collection.* Retrieved from http://www.garces.org/Home/Library/selectioncriteria.aspx

Hawaii Department of Education. (n.d.). *Materials selection policy for school libraries.* Retrieved from http://www.garces.org/Home/Library/selectioncriteria.aspx

Hopkins, D. M. (n.d.). *School library media centers and intellectual freedom*. Retrieved from http://www.ala.org/ala/aboutala/offices/oif/iftoolkits/ifmanual/fifthedition/schoollibrary.cfm

Lanier, G. D. (n.d.) *Conducting a challenge hearing*. Retrieved from http://www.ala.org/ala/issuesadvocacy/banned/challengeslibrarymaterials/copingwithchallenges/conductingchallenge/index.cfm

Montana State Library. (n.d.). *Collection development policy guidelines for school library media programs*. Retrieved from http://msl.mt.gov/slr/cmpolsch.html

Rainier High School. (2011). *RHS library policies and standards*. Retrieved from http://www.rainier.wednet.edu/education/components/scrapbook/default.php?sectiondetailid=987&linkid=nav-menu-container-4–13169

Chapter

7 General Selection Criteria

Selection is a complex, decision-making process and not a simple gut-level "I like this" response. Responsible collection development requires that broad considerations govern the evaluation and choice of a single item. A school librarian is responsible for the collection as an entity, as well as for individual items. You must base your choice on your evaluation of an item and its relationship to the collection. All types of materials need to be evaluated: print, nonprint, and electronic, including websites and virtual libraries that you choose to mark for use with students. You should also justify your choice of an item by assessing its contribution to the policies and goals of the collection program.

When making selection decisions, the basic criterion is quality. Two fundamental questions must be considered. Is the format appropriate for the content? Does the presentation effectively address the users' needs? When evaluating an item's presentation, consider these questions: What is the idea (intellectual content)? How is it presented? Does the medium provide the most suitable treatment for the idea? The criteria that are provided in this chapter are guides, not absolutes. The collection, the users, resource-sharing plans, and outside resources influence the applicability of each criterion to specific items.

Selection decisions require the evaluator to judge materials within the framework of given criteria. These criteria can help one evaluate the content, physical form, or potential value of materials to users or to programs. In the final selection of whether to add an item to a collection, a school librarian must consider all the criteria.

The first part of this chapter describes general criteria that one may apply to all types of materials in a school library. The second portion of the chapter discusses the purchase of equipment. For assistance in selecting specific formats of resources, see Chapter 8, "Criteria by Format."

INTELLECTUAL CONTENT AND ITS PRESENTATION

How can one evaluate the idea, or intellectual content, of a work? Criteria to help one do so include the following: (1) authority, (2) appropriateness of content to users, (3) scope,

(4) authenticity, (5) treatment, (6) arrangement and organization, (7) instructional design, (8) special features, (9) materials available on the subject, and (10) value to the collection.

Authority

The basis for the criterion of authority addresses the qualifications and credibility of the people who created the work. This includes authors, illustrators, editors, directors, publishers, producers, and anyone else involved in the creation of a work. You can judge authority by considering the qualifications of the author, illustrator, or director; the quality and acceptance of other works by the same person; and the dependability and reputation of the publisher or the producer.

Appropriateness of Content to Users

Appropriateness of content focuses on the intellectual content of a resource in relation to its intended use and audience. The concept must be appropriate to the users' developmental level. In other words, the presentation should be geared to the maturity and interest level of the intended users. Whether the content is factual or imaginative, it should not be presented in a condescending manner, nor should it supersede the users' capacity to understand. An item should be appropriate for the students who will use it and not for some arbitrary standard established by adults.

Scope

Scope refers to the content's overall purpose and depth of coverage. You can examine the introduction, teacher's guide, or other documentation for an item to learn the intended purpose and coverage. You should then evaluate whether the stated purpose meets a need of the collection and, if so, then decide whether the resource itself actually fulfills the stated purpose. When the content of the item you are considering duplicates content in other materials in a collection, you should consider whether the item presents content from a unique perspective. If it does, it may be a valuable addition that broadens the scope of the collection.

Authenticity

Information presented in materials should be valid, reliable, complete, and current. Opinions need to be distinguished from facts and, as much as possible, impartially presented. Accuracy is often linked to timeliness, or how recently an item was published or produced, especially in technological subjects where changes occur rapidly. Check with a subject area specialist, if necessary, to be sure the information is timely. Remember, however, that a recent publication date does not necessarily show that the material itself is current or accurate.

Treatment

The treatment or presentation style can affect an item's potential value. It must be appropriate for the subject and use. In the best items, the presentation catches and holds the users' attention, draws on a typical experience, and stimulates further learning or creativity. Asking the following questions can help you evaluate the presentation of an item:

- Are the material's signs (pictures, visuals) and symbols (words, abstractions) necessary to the content and helpful to the user?
- Are the graphics, color, and sound well integrated into the presentation?
- Is the presentation free of bias and stereotyping?
- Does the material reflect our multicultural society?
- Is the information accessible to those who have physical limitations?
- Does the user control the rate and sequence of the content presentation?
- With electronic information, can the user easily enter, use, and exit the program or site?

The treatment of an item must be appropriate to the situation in which it will be used. Some materials require an adult to guide the student's use of material; other materials require use of a teacher's guide to present the information fully. Treatment may present very practical limitations. For example, consider whether the length is appropriate to class periods as generally scheduled. The use of a 60-minute DVD may be problematic if the longest possible viewing period is 55 minutes.

Arrangement and Organization

Presentation of the material in terms of sequences and development of ideas influences comprehension. Content should be presented clearly and develop logically, flowing from one section to another and emphasizing important elements. The arrangement of information needs to facilitate its use. Content should be divided by headings, and information should be easy to locate. The presence of a summary or review of major points enhances effectiveness and helps users understand the work.

Instructional Design

Some materials are intended to meet certain instructional objectives. This is particularly true of textbooks, but can also apply to other books and formats. These materials need to meet the expectations of the learner or teacher. The following general questions can be asked to help evaluate such resources:

- Does the material encourage problem solving and creativity?
- Does the resource promote the understanding of ideas?
- Will users have the necessary capabilities (reading ability, vocabulary level, or computational skills) to learn from the material?
- Will the presentation arouse and motivate interest?
- With electronic materials, is direct access to specific parts of the program possible?
- Does the presentation simulate interaction?
- Are instructions clear?
- Is there effective use of color, text, sound, and graphics?
- Are there suitable instructional support resources provided?

Special Features

Some works have special or unique features that are absent from other resources on the same topic and thus they could have value to a collection. Some of these features may be peripheral to the main content of a work but still add to the collection. Visuals (maps, charts, graphs, or other illustrations) or added items, such as glossaries or listings of award-winning children's books, can serve particular reference needs in a school library. A teacher's guide to a DVD might offer suggestions for follow-up activities or contain a bibliography of related materials. These special features can be a decisive factor in selection decisions that are not clear-cut.

Materials Available on the Subject

In selecting materials to fill a need for a particular subject, program, or user, availability may outweigh other criteria. This occurs frequently with current events, such as the election of a new U.S. president. Biographical information may be needed immediately and yet little may be available for young users. By the end of a U.S. president's first four-year term, there is most likely a wide range of titles and formats from which to select, but at this time the attention to the information may be on the wane. Other examples of information that may have initially limited availability of materials for young people include new scientific discoveries, creation of new nations from former countries, and diseases that suddenly become a threat. The author of this book can remember having difficulty finding quality materials for elementary and middle school students on the subject of AIDS when it first became a frequent news item in the popular media. Availability of materials for young people on the subject was extremely limited, and yet today there is much material on AIDS that is produced with young readers or viewers in mind.

Value to the Collection

After evaluating the specific qualities of the item, the librarian needs to consider it in relation to the collection by asking some of the following questions:

- Does the item meet the needs of the school program or the users?
- Can the resource serve more than one purpose?
- Who are the likely users? How often would they use the item?
- Could a teacher in an instructional situation use the item for informational or recreational purposes?
- Is the item readily available through interlibrary loan?

Other Considerations

Series

Deciding whether to select items in a series can sometimes be problematic. It may be tempting to order an entire series produced by a company, but a school librarian should judge each item within a series independently in terms of its value and known needs. Several authors may write books in a series, but not all the authors may be equally skilled. Even if one author writes the entire series, you should consider whether that person is knowledgeable about all the subjects presented in the series. Authors of fiction may not be able to sustain the readers' interest throughout a series. Thus, you need to consider whether the works function independently of each other, or whether sequential use is required. In the case of nonfiction series, your users may not need all the topics that are covered in the series. You may have sufficient coverage in other materials for some of those topics.

Sponsored Materials

Particular organizations may produce and distribute materials often referred to as *free or inexpensive*. They include books, computer programs, games, maps, multimedia kits, posters, videocassettes, DVDs, and realia. The materials may provide more up-to-date and in-depth information than you will find in other materials. Sponsors include local, state, national, and international groups, such as government agencies, community groups, private businesses, and trade and professional associations. For example, you can obtain posters about foreign countries from airline and cruise ship companies. Embassies can provide information about their countries. The U.S. Government Printing Office and the National Audiovisual Center identifies free and inexpensive materials that are available on a wide range of subjects. Some of the materials from both of these agencies are available digitally online.

In addition to applying general selection criteria and format-related criteria when evaluating these materials, one needs to also assess whether the information presents a one-sided or biased view of the topic. Advertising and references to the company or organization should be extremely limited and not dominate the content.

PHYSICAL FORM

Although content is one basis on which to evaluate an item, you also need to evaluate the packaging of the information, or its physical form. The quality of the content can be weakened if it is not presented through the appropriate medium. Criteria to consider in this area are (1) technical quality, (2) aesthetic quality, (3) durability, and (4) safety and health considerations.

Technical Quality

In order to judge the technical qualities of items, some of the following questions may need to be considered:

- Are illustrations and photographs clear and eye catching?
- Is the balance of illustrations to text appropriate to the content and prospective user?
- Does the use of sound, visual materials, and narrative help focus attention?
- Is there a balance of music, narration, and dialogue?
- Are sound elements synchronized?
- Is the speech clear and effectively paced?
- Is the sound clearly audible?
- Is closed captioning available?
- Are the mobility of subjects, expressiveness of presenters, camera work, resolution, and clarity used effectively?

Aesthetic Quality

Aesthetics refer to a resource's appeal to the intellect, senses, and imagination. Both the external design of an item and the presentation of the content need to be aesthetically pleasing. Book jackets and CD and DVD covers should appeal to the potential user, but they also need to be appropriate. For instance, book jackets for teen romance novels should have illustrations that are vibrant and interesting, but they should not be racy or depict characters that are much older than the main characters in the story.

Durability

It is important to consider the quality of a resource in relation to its durability (how long an item will remain in usable condition with frequent use). Unfortunately many resources produced today do not compare in durability to materials that were produced many years ago. For instance, the paper and binding in many books today are far inferior to those produced in the early and mid-twentieth century. The types of bindings used to make book covers, and the quality of materials used to make videocassettes, DVDs, and CDs can all affect durability. Items that are going to be frequently used, such as those in a reference collection, should be especially durable. Print encyclopedia sets and books in elementary schools can often be ordered in special library binding, which will help them stay in good condition through heavy usage. Since most items in a school library collection circulate and leave the library itself, you want your resources to be as durable as possible.

Safety and Health Considerations

While safety and health features are particularly important when selecting tactile materials, you should consider these issues for all materials. When dealing with items in a kit, such as puppets or stuffed animals, you need to consider whether the items are constructed with nonflammable materials and whether they can be cleaned. Some real objects present a special challenge in terms of cleanliness. What can you do with a piece of salt from the Great Salt Lake that probably will be licked by most of the 1,000 students in an elementary school? Materials with movable parts can also pose problems, possibly with loss of integral parts. Models and kits may have parts that can cut fingers or be swallowed, while architectural models may collapse.

COST

Cost is an item that must be analyzed in relationship to both intellectual content and technical qualities. Once the criteria discussed previously have been sufficiently applied to an item that you are considering adding to a collection, you must then decide whether the price of the item is commensurate with the intellectual content and technical qualities of the item, the value to the collection, and the monies available in your budget. These factors, of course, are important and will greatly affect your decision on whether to purchase an item. If you determine that the contemplated item for purchase is of high quality and you are in need of the resource for your particular collection, but you do not have sufficient funds in your budget, then you should consider some other options for obtaining the item: interlibrary loan, shared collection development with another library, or fundraising projects. These options will be discussed in more detail in later chapters.

EQUIPMENT

Most school librarians also have some responsibility for selecting equipment for the library. You may be asked to help select equipment that is housed in classrooms, as well as equipment that circulates to classrooms, such as laptop computers. The author of this book remembers well when video players first became popular for use in classrooms, and she had only four video players on carts that circulated to over 30 teachers in a school. Just keeping a schedule of circulation by period and delivering the carts to the appropriate classrooms took much time and organization. Fortunately, today many classrooms have their own electronic equipment. However, there are still several types of equipment that need to be purchased for the school library, such as computers, e-readers, interactive whiteboards, copy machines, and projectors.

If you are responsible for selecting equipment, it is important to remember that many school districts put the purchase of equipment above a certain cost (sometimes $100) through a bid process in which they generally accept the lowest bid for each type of equipment. If this is the case in your school district, someone at the administrative office of the school district can provide you with a listing of the equipment and the companies from which you are allowed to purchase certain types of equipment. In your policies and procedure manual, you should include the selection criteria and procedure for obtaining equipment, noting whether certain types of equipment are put through a bid process.

Criteria that should be considered when selecting equipment include (1) quality and durability; (2) performance, compatibility, and versatility; (3) ease of operation; (4) safety; (5) maintenance and service; (6) reputation of manufacturer and dealer; and (7) cost.

Quality and Durability

Quality and durability are very important criteria to consider when selecting equipment. You should choose equipment that is constructed of strong materials and will remain intact through heavy and sometimes fairly abusive use. If a piece of equipment will circulate outside of a building, it needs to have a weatherproof carrying case. Straps and handles used to aid in moving the equipment should be strong enough to withstand the weight of the item when carried any distance.

Performance, Compatibility, and Versatility

Equipment should operate efficiently and consistently at a high level of performance. Poor quality projection or sound reproduction can negate the technical quality of materials so carefully sought during selection. The noise or light from the equipment should not interfere with its use, nor should the equipment be easily subject to overheating.

Equipment needs to be compatible with other equipment and materials in the collection. This is especially true when selecting computers. You should not purchase equipment whose use is limited to materials produced by the manufacturer.

Ease of Use

If equipment is too complex, it will discourage use; thus, it is wise to select equipment that has only the features that are needed and have clearly written directions that are easy to follow. If possible, try to examine the equipment that you are considering for purchase. The following questions will help you determine how easy it is to operate the equipment:

- What level of manual dexterity must one have to operate the equipment?
- How many steps must one follow to run the equipment?

- Does the equipment have many controls?
- Does the equipment operate efficiently with minimum delay?
- Are there parts that can be easily removed and possibly misplaced?
- Are automatic operations dependable?
- Are there options for manual and remote control?
- Are shutoff or cooling-down features automatic?
- Does the size, weight, or design of the equipment require that you use and store it in one location?
- Can one easily move the equipment to a cart?
- How much time will be needed to teach students and faculty to use the equipment?

Safety

Safety features demand consideration, especially when young children will use equipment. The school librarian should choose equipment that has no rough or protruding edges that could injure the user. Equipment should be balanced so that it will not topple easily. Also, it should not be easy for users to come into contact with potentially dangerous components, such as a fan or a heated element.

Equipment needs to meet established safety regulations. You can look for seals from the Underwriters Laboratory (UL) or the Canadian Standards Association (CSA) to help determine whether equipment meets safety standards.

Maintenance and Service

Although you want the equipment you select to be built to withstand hard use, you also need to plan for regular maintenance and service. You may be able to perform some of the easy maintenance, such as cleaning the equipment on a regular basis.

You should examine warranties and guarantees to see what conditions are covered. Also, try to determine how easy it will be for minor repairs to be made or for parts to be replaced quickly and efficiently. You might want to inquire as to whether the distributor or manufacturer offers in-service training on operating or repairing the equipment. Some distributors and manufacturers provide on-the-spot repairs, whereas others require that the purchasers send the item to a factory. Thus, it might be important to ask whether the manufacturer, vendor, or repair center provides replacement or rental equipment while they are servicing the equipment that needs repair. Finally, if the district or school has a staff person assigned to do repairs, you should consult the person regarding whether they will service the equipment that you are considering for purchase.

Reputation of Manufacturer and Dealer

If you are a new librarian and are not familiar with the manufacturers or distributors of equipment for schools, you should consider asking other librarians who they regard as the most reputable manufacturers and distributors with whom to deal. The following are some questions you could ask:

- Does the manufacturer have a reputation for honoring warranties?
- Is delivery prompt?
- Does the manufacturer handle requests for assistance pleasantly and efficiently?
- Does the dealer have outlets near the school?

- Does the manufacturer provide support service through e-mail, telephone hotlines, toll-free numbers, backups, preview opportunities, updates, refunds, and replacements?
- Is the support assistance readily available?
- Are the service hours convenient?

Cost

When selecting equipment, a school librarian should weigh quality over cost, but also consider budget constraints. You should try to determine whether a competitor offers a similar item at less cost. You can also ask if trade-ins are allowed. When purchasing a very expensive item, such as a large copy machine for the library, you will need to decide whether to purchase or lease the equipment. The answer to this question may depend on how much use the copy machine will have, whether monies are being taken in for copies, and from where the financial support for items such as paper and ink cartridges will come.

CONCLUSIONS

Several general criteria can be addressed when selecting items for a school library. For print and electronic resources, the intellectual content and its presentation, as well as the physical form of an item, should be considered. When selecting equipment for the school library or classrooms, specific criteria need to be addressed, but one needs also to be aware of any school district policies that deal with equipment selection and maintenance. For all purchases that are being considered, a librarian should strive to get the best quality within the constraints of the library budget.

ADDITIONAL READINGS

Hill, R.A. (2011). Mobile digital devices: Dipping your toes in technological waters. *Teacher Librarian, 39*(1), 22–26.

Johnson, T. (2011). S.P.I.D.E.R. A strategy for evaluating websites. *Library Media Connection, 29*(6), 58–59.

Lamb, A., & Johnson, L. (2011). Nurturing a new breed of reader: Five real-world issues. *Teacher Librarian, 39*(1), 56–63.

Simmons, M., & O'Briant, B. (2011). Product profile: Recorded books: One-click audio academic collection. *Library Media Collection, 29*(6), 60.

HELPFUL WEBSITES

Baltimore County Public Schools. (n.d.). *Selection criteria for school library media center collections.* Retrieved from http://www.bcps.org/offices/lis/office/admin/selection.html

Butler Area Senior High School Library. (2005). *Web page evaluation criteria.* Retrieved from http://www.angelfire.com/pa5/butlershslibrary/webcriteria.pdf

PCWorld. (2011). E-readers: Reviews of the Kindle, Nook, and other e-readers. Retrieved from http://www.pcworld.com/products/tablets/ereaders.html

Chapter

Criteria by Format

It is widely accepted knowledge that people gather information through their senses (seeing, hearing, touching, tasting, and smelling) and have different learning styles depending on how they utilize those senses. Excluding persons with particular physical disabilities, such as deafness or blindness, most students learn through a combination of all their senses. However, they usually have a predominant learning style: visual, auditory, or kinetic. Students learn better from media formats that incorporate their predominant learning style. Thus, a variety of media need to be included in a school library collection in order to meet the learning styles of all students.

In your library's policies and procedures manual, there should be a listing of all the media formats that are in your collection. This can be a separate listing or it can be included in your circulation section with a possible indication of which formats can be checked out by students and/or by faculty.

This chapter focuses on the characteristics of different formats and how school librarians should consider them in selection decisions. The formats are arranged in alphabetical order. Each description includes physical characteristics, advantages, disadvantages, selection criteria, implications for collection development, and copyright considerations. Even though some of the formats are being phased out of most school libraries, if they are still available for purchase, they are included to accommodate all types of school libraries, regardless of their technology capabilities or budgets. In addition to the selection criteria listed for each format, you should consider whether the item has received awards or favorable reviews. The general selection criteria from Chapter 7 should also be applied.

You can refer to the "Appendix: Resources" of this book to locate materials that will provide reviews or other guidance for selection of particular formats. The additional readings and websites listed at the end of this chapter are primarily those that relate to the newer formats that are being collected in school libraries.

ART PRINTS *SEE* GRAPHIC MATERIALS

AUDIOCASSETTES

Although not a new technology, audiocassettes remain popular in school libraries today. Combination kits of books and audiocassettes are frequently found in elementary school libraries, whereas middle school and high school students enjoy books on tape or more often today books on CDs (audiobooks). They are also extremely appealing to students who are visually impaired. Audiocassettes require tape recorders; thus, if teachers check out audiocassettes for classroom use, you should also provide quality tape recorders that make it possible for large groups of students to easily listen to the audiocassettes.

Advantages

- Tapes are portable and easy to use.
- A wide range of content is available.
- Equipment is easy to use and inexpensive.
- Information is locked into a fixed sequence, and specific sections can be easily located through use of counters on tape recorders.
- Most students are familiar with the equipment.

Disadvantages

- Listening for an extended period of time may induce boredom with some students.
- Use with large groups requires high-quality tape recorders, with adequate amplification.
- As technology becomes more outdated, cassette players become more expensive to buy or fix and require more maintenance.
- Cassettes must be rewound before circulating if a previous user did not rewind them.
- Cassettes are small and can easily be stolen.
- Cassette cases break easily; thus a supply of empty cases may need to be purchased.

Selection Criteria

- Is the sound free of distortion?
- Are the length and quality of the performance appropriate to the intended audience?
- Do labels provide enough information to distinguish one item from another (cassette #1, cassette #2, etc.)?
- Do labels provide the time required to listen to the tape?
- If the recording is based on a book, is the recording true to the original?
- Does the recording engage the listener's attention?
- Does narration begin with attention-getting words to capture the listener's interest? Are keywords or key statements emphasized to help the listener?
- Are accompanying materials, such as a teacher's guide, appropriate and useful?

Implications for Collection Development

The items should provide for individual and group use of narrative presentations, as well as for music and documentaries. For music, other formats, such as compact discs (CDs), are better choices and more appealing to most users. Most vendors now produce their audiobooks on CDs, rather than cassette tapes. Cassette tapes can be fairly easily damaged in circulation, particularly with young children.

Copyright Considerations

Although it is easy to do, it is not legal to make copies of audiocassette tapes. Converting cassette tapes to another format requires written permission from the copyright holder.

BOOKS

Most school libraries contain more books than any other format, although they are not always the most popular format among students, particularly in high school settings. Hardback and paperback books share similar characteristics, but often fulfill different needs. Hardback books with special library bindings are frequently purchased for very young patrons, while paperback books are especially appealing to teenagers. E-books, which are becoming more popular, are discussed in a separate section.

Advantages

- Books are usually designed for individual users.
- Users can set their own pace and stop in the process to recheck information or reread a section.
- The table of contents and index can provide ready access to information.
- Books are portable.
- A wide range of subjects and genres are available in books.
- Books do not require equipment.
- They are relatively inexpensive.

Disadvantages

- Use of colored artwork or photography, although adding to appeal or clarity of text, increases the cost.
- Compared to electronic formats, movement is more difficult to illustrate on the printed page.
- Large group viewing of the same material is difficult, except with *big books* (oversized paperback books).
- Interaction and feedback for students is difficult to achieve except in programmed texts.
- Students must have the appropriate reading and comprehension level skills.
- It usually takes several months to get a book published; thus, the information may not be as current as that in electronic formats.

Selection Criteria

- Are the shape and weight of the book appropriate for the intended audience?
- How opaque is the paper? Print that shows through the page may be confusing to a young or disadvantaged reader.
- Is the typeface suitable for the intended audience?

- Is the spacing between words and between lines adequate for the young or reluctant reader?
- Is the book jacket attractive? Does it reflect the content of the book?
- Are the illustrations placed throughout the text where readers can view them easily, or are they placed all together in an inconvenient location?
- Is the medium used for illustrations (e.g., pen-and-ink drawings, block prints, or oil paints) appropriate to the setting and mood of the story?
- Do the page layouts and color add appeal and clarity to the book?
- When a readability formula, such as Fry or Spache, is applied, is the text appropriate for the intended audience?
- Is the content accurate and current?

Additional Criteria for Hardbacks

- Are the bindings durable and the covers attractive and easy to clean?
- Are reinforced bindings available for titles that very young children will use or titles that will circulate frequently?
- Will the hardcover books lie flat when open?

Implications for Collection Development

Even though selections should cover a wide range of subjects and genres, one should also consider the reading and maturity levels of students. You should order additional copies of popular books; paperbacks are an inexpensive way to meet these demands. A paperback book may appeal to some users more than would the same title in hardback. Policies should address questions such as what foreign languages to purchase and whether there is a need for large-print books.

Copyright Considerations

Copyright law defines print materials as books, periodicals, pamphlets, newspapers, and similar items. A teacher may make a single copy of a chapter in a book, a short story, short essay, short poem, chart, graph, diagram, cartoon, or picture to use in teaching. Multiple copies are limited by specific guidelines:

- If a poem is less than 250 words and is not on more than two pages, the entire poem can be copied. For poems longer than 250 words, only 250 words can be copied.
- An article, story, or essay can be copied in its entirety if it is less than 2,500 words. Other types of prose are limited to 1,000 words or 10 percent of the whole, whichever is less.
- Creation of anthologies, compilations, and collective works is prohibited.

CARTOONS *SEE* GRAPHIC MATERIALS

CASSETTE TAPES *SEE* AUDIOCASSETTES

CDS

A CD is an optical disc used to store digital data. The disc is covered with a transparent coating and is read by a laser beam. CDs reached library markets in the mid-1980s.

Originally they were developed as music formats, but they grew to encompass other applications, such as audiobooks. CDs are available in different sizes, but the most common size is 120 mm in diameter.

Advantages

- CDs take up little storage space.
- CDs are small, lightweight, and portable.
- Equipment used to play CDs is inexpensive.
- CD players are easy to use, and many students are familiar with them.
- Sound on CDs is generally superior to that on audiocassettes.
- Because a track system is used on CDs, it is possible to access certain parts of a CD.
- Since nothing touches the encoding on the disc, CDs are not worn out in the playing process.
- CDs retain superb sound for hundreds of hours.

Disadvantages

- It is relatively easy to scratch a CD, thus ruining parts of the CD. The top side (label side) is particularly vulnerable and is difficult to repair.
- If using a CD with a large group, the CD player must have adequate amplification.
- Capacity is fairly limited compared to some other formats, such as digital or online space.
- CDs are small and therefore easy to steal.
- As with audiocassettes, cases are easily broken; thus, it is wise to have extra cases on hand.

Selection Criteria

- Is the sound of high quality?
- Is the content appropriate for the intended audience?
- Will the content be appealing for more than just a few months?
- Are there accompanying materials, such as the words to the songs or the time to play each track?
- Does the label provide information on the time required for playback?

Implications for Collection Development

You need to consider whether you wish to collect and circulate CDs that contain music. Although they are popular items with teenagers, they can be easily damaged and copied (thus violating copyright). Some lyrics of songs, especially in the rap music category, may not be appropriate for a school setting. Musical CDs for preschool and elementary level students are also becoming increasingly popular. If you have a generous library budget, CDs will undoubtedly be a popular format. So many selections are available that it may be difficult to decide which items to purchase. Also, some of the musical CDs (particularly pop music) may be popular for only short periods of time.

Copyright Considerations

It is illegal to make copies of any sound recordings; even archival copies may not be made. Converting CDs to another format requires written permission from the copyright owner. It is a good idea to place appropriate copyright warning stickers on CDs that circulate.

CD-ROMS

Soon after the introduction of audio CDs, CD-ROMs (compact discs read only memory) were developed. A CD-ROM is a form of a compact disc that is read by using a CD-ROM drive on a computer. CD-ROMs can provide access to very large quantities of digitally encoded information at relatively low cost. Graphics, sound, and other non-text items can mix with text. This format is used for encyclopedias, reference sources, databases, multimedia products, interactive books, games, music, OPACs, computer software, clip art, and graphics. Although CD-ROMs were very popular in the 1980s and 1990s, much of the information on them can currently be purchased online. Accessing the information online makes it easier for several users to access the information simultaneously.

Advantages

- A single CD-ROM can store the equivalent of 1,000 short books.
- A single disc can hold more than 650 megabytes of text, graphics, and sound.
- With a good index, information retrieval is flexible.
- Use of CD-ROMs helps students learn search strategies before going online.
- The quality of images is high, and they do not fade as photographic images do. The images take less storage space than if they were individual slides or photographs.
- CD-ROM discs are small, lightweight, and portable.
- The discs are durable and resistant to fingerprints.
- The laser beam reader does not come into direct contact with the disc so the disc does not wear out with play.
- Graphics may be better and faster than on websites.
- The format is appealing to students.

Disadvantages

- A CD-ROM drive on a computer is required.
- Some CD-ROM discs require specific methods of retrieval.
- Scratching on the label side makes the disk unusable.
- Capacity is limited compared to online databases.
- Information cannot be updated or changed.
- Use of a single CD-ROM is limited to one student or a small group, creating scheduling and teacher planning difficulties. Networking CD-ROMs can alleviate these problems.

Selection Criteria

Criteria for CD-ROMs and software are similar (see the discussion in the Computer Software section). Additional questions to consider are the following:

- How frequently is the CD-ROM updated?
- Does the cost of a subscription include the update?
- Is there an annual fee?

- Are on-screen tutorials provided? Are they simple and easy to understand?
- Is the menu system easy to use?
- How fast is access to the information?
- What is the quality of the video and audio production?
- What is the technical quality of the underlying program, the manual, and the support personnel?
- Does the CD-ROM contain a large amount of high-quality information?
- Are the advertisement and promotional materials accurate about the number of minutes or hours of full-motion video, high-fidelity audio, number of photographic images, and amount of text?
- Is the CD-ROM truly interactive in the sense that users can explore options?
- Would online access to the information, rather than an individual CD-ROM, better serve your needs?

Implications for Collection Development

You should plan procedures to establish (1) time limits for individual student use of a CD-ROM workstation, (2) number of printouts allowed, (3) fee if applicable, (4) security for discs, and (5) whether to have a dedicated machine for each disc. Plans should also include how to obtain appropriate licenses and how to ensure adherence to copyright issues. These plans must be flexible and are best designed in conjunction with teachers. Administrators may be involved in setting fees, if students are to be charged for printouts.

When you find recommended titles you want to consider, find out whether you can obtain a copy of the CD-ROM for a trial period on your equipment. During the trial, evaluate the technical support found in the documentation, user manuals, and telephone or online help lines. It is important to remember that free demos can supply you with a look at the content of the CD-ROM, but the demos may be technically different from the CD-ROM itself. Use of previews (often with slide shows making a marketing pitch) can give you a sense of the possible interest to your users.

Copyright Considerations

Unlike books, audiocassettes, maps, and some other formats, the physical medium (CD-ROM) is purchased, but the content is often licensed for use. For multiple users or multiple copies of the disc at multiple workstations, you will need to obtain a site or network license.

CHARTS *SEE* GRAPHIC MATERIALS

COMICS

Comic books, or the shortened form *comics*, tell a narrative by depicting sequential art. Although sometimes humorous, the subject matter varies. Popular genres include superheroes, fantasy, horror or supernatural, action or adventure, science fiction, and manga (Japanese comics). The majority of comic books are marketed to teenagers, with the two largest U.S. publishers being Marvel and DC (Diamond Comics).

Advantages

- Comic books are particularly appealing to teens and will attract students to the school library.
- Reluctant readers of books will often read comic books.
- Visual learners like the graphic format, which can assist them in understanding a narrative.
- Comic books can lead readers to explore other literature.
- Comic books can help students develop an appreciation for art and different artistic styles.
- Many comic books address themes that are important to teens and preteens, including acceptance, prejudice, social issues, and triumph over adversity.
- Comic books are inexpensive.

Disadvantages

- Comic books are not very durable.
- School librarians may not be very familiar with comic books and might need assistance in selecting the best ones for a collection.
- Some teachers, administrators, and parents may think that comic books do not have educational value and thus should not be included in a school library collection.

Selection Criteria

- Can you obtain sample copies to help you in selection?
- Is the content appropriate for the intended audience?
- What is the reputation of the publisher?
- Is the writing and art of good quality?
- Have the comic books won any awards?
- Will the selected titles be popular with students?
- Are the comic books available as trade paperback collections?

Implications for Collection Development

Comic books are particularly appealing to preteens and teenagers and will attract them to the school library. Since they are not very durable, it is wise to treat comic books similarly to magazine subscriptions where use is generally limited to the library and the materials are often placed in magazine protective covers. If you wish to circulate comic books, you can purchase trade comics (stories collected in paperback format). Specialized comic book subscription agents and mail order services offer subscription plans for comic books. Subscriptions can also sometimes be arranged through local comic book stores, or are sometimes available from the major magazine subscription agencies like EBSCO. You should preview materials before placing them on the shelves and be prepared to address possible censorship issues.

Copyright Considerations

Although not specifically addressed in fair use guidelines, comic books would most likely be similar to picture books. Two pages of picture books may be copied as long as the two pages do not make up more than 10 percent of the book.

COMPUTER SOFTWARE

Computer software is available through educational institutes and consortia, commercial vendors, software companies, and textbook publishers. Shareware (courseware available at no cost or more often on a trial basis) is available from the educational agency or other body that produced it. After the software has been evaluated and retained, the user is expected to register the program and pay a voluntary fee. Public domain software is a computer program that the author has released and can be copied by anyone. Such software is often on Internet websites dedicated to public domain use. The title screen of the program indicates that the program is in public domain.

Most computer software is currently produced on CD-ROM discs. See the selection criteria under CD-ROMs in addition to the following section, which emphasizes instructional software.

Advantages

- Software can be used for creative problem solving, drill and practice, testing, recreation, and guidance.
- Individual and self-paced interactions are special instructional features of computer software.
- Programs can provide the reinforcement and stimulation needed by students who have learning disabilities.
- Programs with branching allow the student with correct answers to move into more difficult questions, while allowing those who need to review and repeat responses opportunities to do so.
- Rapid information retrieval is possible.
- Use of computer software can be highly motivating for many students.
- Desktop publishing allows students to design and enhance their presentations.
- Teachers can use recordkeeping programs to monitor students' progress.

Disadvantages

- Incompatibility of software and equipment can limit use.
- Some software can contain poor computer programming.
- More software programs are designed to appeal to boys than to girls.
- Students and teachers may have unreasonably high expectations of how quickly learning will happen.
- Some programs will not accept creative or original student responses.
- A high level of student use can limit the amount of interaction between teachers and students.

Selection Criteria

- Are the software and equipment compatible?
- Is content more appropriate for presentation on a computer than on other instructional media?
- Is the program designed to run on the user's computer? The computer's brand, model, memory size, operating system, storage format, display technology (monitor and graphics system), and accessories (mouse, game paddles, etc.) must be compatible.

- Is the computer's disk operating system compatible with the software program?
- Does the user control the rate and sequences of the content presentation (unless timing is an integral part of the program)?
- Is the student able to enter, use, and exit the program with relative ease and independence?
- Are the responses or feedback to answers (both correct and incorrect) appropriate?
- Will the software design lead students to correct answers or to remedial instruction when they need assistance?
- Are on-screen instructions clear and easy to understand?
- Are the student guides and worksheets, the teacher guide, and the technical information adequate and comprehensive?
- Does the program require students to be familiar with special terms or symbols related to computers?

Implications for Collection Development

As mentioned previously, many computer software programs are now available on CD-ROM format or online. You will need to consider the scope of the software collection and whether it will circulate, and to whom it will circulate (only teachers or to both teachers and students). Some software has limited licensing; in such cases, it may only be used in the library or installed on a limited number of computers. It is wise to obtain teachers' opinions in deciding purchases.

Copyright Considerations

One archival or backup copy of each program is permitted. It may not be used at the same time as the original. For use at more than one computer, such as on a LAN (local area network) or WAN (wide area network), a site license agreement must be obtained. Any computer software programs that circulate should have copyright warning stickers placed on them.

DVDS

DVDs (digital versatile discs) are compact optical discs read by laser beams. DVD discs are the same diameter and thickness as compact discs, but are capable of storing up to 13 times the data contained on one side of a CD. Both sides of a DVD can be utilized for storage data; thus it offers 26 times the power of a compact disc. Movies, documentaries, and music are all available in DVD format. DVDs are rapidly replacing videos, laser discs, CDs, and CD-ROMs.

Advantages

- DVDs can deliver video that is near studio quality and audio that is better than CD quality. The pictures are characterized by more color detail and color resolution than videos.
- Content can be easily searched and specific sections can be quickly accessed.
- Interactive menus are available.
- Many DVDs have extra features, such as additional footage, interviews, commentaries, links to online resources, and biographical materials.

- Some DVDs have additional materials, such as accompanying booklets or viewers' guides.
- The compact size is easy to store, and portable players are available.
- Discs are durable.
- Wear does not occur from playing, only from physical damage.
- DVDs do not deteriorate in quality over time.
- Unlike videos, DVDs are not affected by magnetic fields.
- DVDs can be played on a computer that has a DVD drive.
- DVDs are inexpensive.

Disadvantages

- Careless production can create visible artifacts (anything that was not originally present in the picture), such as banding, blurriness, fuzzy dots, and missing details.
- The production of materials has centered mostly on the home entertainment center; however, the production of DVDs designed for educational and instructional purposes is growing.
- Most DVD players must be connected to a television set.
- Some television sets need to have the controls adjusted to take advantage of the DVD's capabilities.

Selection Criteria

Criteria applied to video, audiocassettes, and computer software should be applied to materials on DVDs. As with other technology, there are additional questions to consider:

- Is the content connected to the curriculum?
- Is the standard used to judge the content the same as for other materials in the collection?
- Do users have convenient access to a player?
- Would purchase of the item duplicate something easily available in public libraries?
- Is a DVD the best format for the message?

Implications for Collection Development

Development and availability of DVDs should be monitored for its replacement of audiocassettes, CDs, videotapes, laser discs, and CD-ROMs. When you add DVD drives to your systems, look for those that are designed to play CD-ROM titles, as well as DVDs.

Copyright Considerations

A number of copy protection schemes are used with DVDs. One is the SCMS (serial copy generation management system), which is designed to prevent copying. The copy generation management system (CGMS) is embedded in the outgoing video signal, and one must use equipment that recognizes the CGMS. The U.S. Digital Millennium Copyright Act (DMCA), in which *don't copy flags* are incorporated by the producers, became law in October 1998. Although perfect reproductions can be made of a DVD, copyright restrictions do not allow archival copies to be made of DVDs. DVDs bought in stores are protected by the copyright law and are not intended for use outside the home. However, fair use guidelines permit the use of the DVDs in face-to-face instruction if they are part of the curriculum. Any movies that are to be shown in a school for entertainment purposes require a Movie Copyright Compliance Site License.

E-BOOKS

Many different types of electronic books (e-books) are available. Some can be accessed electronically and are meant to be printed out for reading; others are distributed electronically but are intended to be read on a computer or on e-book readers. Most e-books use EPUB, a free and open standard created by the International Digital Publishing Forum (IDPF). Some school librarians have been fairly reluctant to purchase e-books, but this has been changing as younger library users are comfortable accessing all types of information through electronic formats.

Advantages

- Books are available 24 hours of the day.
- If allowed by the licensing agreement, several students can access an electronic book at the same time.
- Since some e-books also include sound files and moving images, they are particularly interesting to reluctant readers.
- E-books save shelf space in a library and do not have to be transported.
- The books cannot be lost or damaged by users.
- Search functions can be used to locate specific parts of the book.
- In some e-book formats, notes can be inserted right into the text, thus providing instructional features for a classroom teacher.
- E-readers allow adjustments to size and contrast and thus aid students with visual impairments.

Disadvantages

- Special software and hardware are required to access and read e-books.
- E-book reading devices are more expensive than books.
- Some users prefer a physical book, rather than an electronic version.
- Some book titles are not available in the e-book format.
- E-books can cause eye strain in some users.
- E-books do not have a defined life span. Paper has a longer life span than most digital forms of storage.

Selection Criteria

When evaluating e-books, school librarians should apply traditional criteria and also consider both the licensing arrangement and the equipment necessary for using them. As with other developing technology, basic questions are whether the library will circulate the materials and whether the library will provide the equipment needed to use the materials. Some additional questions that should be asked are as follows:

- What titles are available in e-book format?
- Will students and teachers use the e-books?
- How much will the books cost in comparison to purchasing print versions of the titles?

Implications for Collection Development

Many book titles are already in public domain and available for free. The Project Gutenberg website has a large collection of public domain e-books as does the University of

Virginia website and the Internet Public Library. The International Children's Digital Library, which was developed by a team at the University of Maryland, provides free access to children's books from around the world. Before purchasing e-books, a school librarian should promote the use of these sites and then determine whether teachers and students want or need access to additional titles.

Copyright Considerations

Copyright restrictions introduced by the DMCA in 1998 apply to e-books, as well as to other digital technologies. It may be necessary to sign a licensing agreement for e-books that are purchased and abide by the copyright restrictions of the agreement. Some agreements limit the number of users who can access the e-book simultaneously, the number of pages that can be printed within a certain time limit, the amount of cut-and-paste that a user can perform, and the amount of time an item can be checked out.

E-JOURNALS

E-journals or electronic journals are serial publications that are in digital format. Some e-journals are free of charge and are published only on the Internet. Such journals are generally referred to as open access journals. Other journals appear only in electronic format and are available by subscription, while still others appear in both electronic format (on Internet or on a CD-ROM) and also have print versions. Some electronic journals are peer-reviewed scholarly journals, while others are not quality controlled. Thus, the term *e-journal* is not always specific. There are even more e-journals (many thousands) than e-zines. Some academic libraries attempt to maintain lists of e-journals, but it requires too much time for school librarians to provide this collection service.

Advantages

- E-journals can be read around the clock from any location that has Internet access.
- They can be delivered to one's computer desktop.
- More than one person can read an e-journal at a time.
- They can be published much more quickly than print versions of journals.
- E-journals can be searched.
- They can be retrieved directly through links when accessed through an indexing database.
- Hyperlinks to information can be inserted into articles.
- E-journals do not take up space on the library shelves.

Disadvantages

- The main disadvantage is that one must have a computer to access e-journals.
- Unless the e-journal also has a print version, one must sit at a computer to read it.
- Some journals do not include illustrations, and if they do, the illustrations may not be in color or as clear as the print version.

Selection Criteria

The selection criteria for e-journals are similar to those of print periodicals. See Periodicals. Additional selection questions include the following:

- How does the cost compare to the print version of the periodical?
- Can you negotiate the cost of the e-journal according to the number of students in your school or the number of users who will access the e-journal?
- Is the journal title included in vendor databases, such as ProQuest or EBSCO?
- Is the journal easily available to students in informational databases provided by the state or by a public library?
- Will enough students use the journal to make the cost of its electronic access feasible?
- Are back issues of the journals available?

Implications for Collection Development

One must carefully consider whether to purchase periodicals in print version or electronically. Few school libraries purchase the same title in both formats. Students in secondary schools enjoy reading print versions of popular periodicals such as *Sports Illustrated* or *Seventeen* so you should consider having these types of periodicals available on shelves in the library. Electronic access to periodicals can be provided for those journals that are used primarily for research purposes. This will save enormous amounts of shelf space in a middle or high school library. Generally elementary schools provide their periodicals in print format.

Copyright Considerations

Students can make one copy of an article for research purposes. Teachers should not make multiple copies of an article for classroom use unless they obtain copyright permission from the publisher of the journal or the need meets the spontaneity guideline (not enough time to get a timely reply to a request for permission to copy).

E-ZINES

E-zines are publications (magazines or newsletters) that are distributed by e-mail or posted on a website. They usually focus on a particular subject and are free. Often one person or a small group of people who have special interest in a topic publish e-zines on the web. Some e-zines are updated constantly so do not have regular distribution, while others are periodically updated. Far too many e-zines are available (thousands) to try to include them in OPACs, but if you want to help students locate e-zines, the following sites are helpful: <http://e-zinedirectory.com/> and <http://www.ezine-dir.com/>. The University of Oregon Libraries maintains an e-zine entitled *New Breed Librarian*, which is intended to foster a sense of community for those new to librarianship. As a new librarian, you may want to check out their website. Access to their e-zine can be found at <http://scholarsbank.uoregon.edu/dspace/handle/1794/1071>.

GAMES

Games are recreational or educational activities involving one or more persons. They involve either reaching some type of goal or following a set of rules. Games can be categorized by those that involve skill, those that require strategy, and those that rely on chance. Many games involve a combination of skill, strategy, and chance. Some games require using a computer or other special equipment. Educational games in classrooms have become quite popular in many schools.

Advantages

- Participants become involved in solving problems.
- Some games simulate realistic environments.
- Participation usually generates a high degree of interest.
- Students receive immediate feedback.
- Some games contribute to effective learning by motivating and supporting learning and attitudinal changes.

Disadvantages

- Games can be very time consuming.
- The limited number of players can create problems if others want to participate.
- Some games have parts that can be easily lost or damaged.
- Some teachers may not be aware of the learning value of games, and thus may not understand why they are included in a collection.

Selection Criteria

- Is the packaging designed to store and quickly identify missing parts?
- Can lost pieces be easily replaced?
- Are the items durable?
- Are the directions clear?
- Are the content, reading level, time requirements, and required dexterity appropriate for the intended audience?
- Does the game require a computer? Will it run on the school library's equipment?
- Is the game too costly or elaborate for its intended use?

Implications for Collection Development

Games can serve many purposes, but it is wise to get input from teachers and administrators on the inclusion of games in the collection and whether to make them available for use in a library. You should also carefully consider whether to circulate games to students, particularly if the games have many parts that can be easily lost. More elementary libraries than secondary school libraries tend to have games available for student use. However, some secondary libraries have chess or checker sets, board games, or computer games available.

Copyright Considerations

Generally copyright considerations are not involved with games, unless the games are in a different format, such as on computer software. In those cases, the same copyright considerations apply as to computer software. See Computer Software and CD-ROMs.

GRAPHIC MATERIALS

Graphics are nonmoving, opaque, visual materials that provide information. In a school library these materials include posters, graphs, charts, tables, diagrams, cartoons, art prints, study prints, drawings, and photographs.

Advantages

- Graphic materials are widely available and generally inexpensive.
- Carefully selected graphics can help prevent or correct students' misconceptions.
- Graphic materials are easy to use.

Disadvantages

- Sizes and distances are sometimes distorted.
- Lack of color or poor quality may limit proper interpretation.
- The size of the material must be large enough for all members of a group to see the same detail.
- Motion cannot be simulated, only suggested.

Selection Criteria

- Is the information presented in a precise manner?
- Are less important elements de-emphasized or omitted?
- Is the presentation unified? Are the basic artistic principles of balance and harmony observed?
- Is lettering clear and legible?
- Is the size appropriate for the intended audience?
- Does an art print give an accurate reproduction of the original work's color and detail?
- Is the item durable?

Implications for Collection Development

Many graphics are now available electronically on the Internet. Some search engines make it easy to locate specific graphics. Many school librarians and teachers are projecting these images onto large screens. Thus, there are fewer needs for purchasing graphic materials. If, however, you anticipate purchasing prints for group lessons, look for ones that provide information on the back of story or study prints. If you circulate graphics, consider either laminating them or protecting them in some manner. Special storage units may be needed.

Copyright Considerations

Graphics such as study or art prints are usually copyrighted and cannot be duplicated. Graphic materials in periodicals can be copied provided they meet the copyright test for illustrations: one chart, graph, diagram, drawing, cartoon, or picture per periodical. If you have questions about whether a graphic is copyrighted, you should check with the publisher.

GRAPHIC NOVELS

Although some librarians have considered graphic novels as a fad, their popularity with young people has certainly earned them a place in school libraries. It is important to remember that graphic novels are not a genre, but rather a separate format. They are stories in a comic form that are published as books. Storylines in graphic novels are longer than those found in comic books and are often more complex and serious. The modern types of graphic novels began in the 1970s, but in recent years they have become extremely popular and many librarians include them in their collections. The majority of the titles come in trade paperback versions.

Advantages

- Visual learners are able to connect with graphic novels.
- Graphic novels can lead students to explore other types of literature.
- Boys who are reluctant readers are often attracted to graphic novels.
- They are useful for ESL students or students who read below grade level.
- Having graphic novels in a collection will attract young people to a library.

Disadvantages

- Some teachers and parents may think that graphic novels do not belong in a school library collection.
- Some titles are not available through jobbers.
- The contents of some graphic novels are not appropriate for young people.
- Some school librarians are not familiar with the format and may need assistance in selecting titles for the collection.

Selection Criteria

- Is the content appropriate for the intended audience?
- Are students able to follow the art format?
- Is the title one that will be popular with students?
- What are the reputations of the author, illustrator, and publisher?
- How relevant is the content to existing coverage in the collection?
- Are you able to locate a review of the title?

Copyright Considerations

Graphic novels were not invented when the fair use guidelines were written; however, they most likely would be considered as picture books. Two pages of picture books can be copied as long as the two pages do not comprise more than 10 percent of the book.

KITS

A kit contains a variety of formats in one package. In some kits the materials are preselected to present information in a fixed sequence. Other kits and packages are less structured, such as a collection of related materials that can be used singly or in any combination by an individual or a group.

Advantages

- Various formats relating to a specific subject are combined in one package.
- The various formats can meet different student learning styles.
- One kit may include material designed for several grade levels.
- Kits that include sound recordings of accompanying text materials can help learners who have difficulty reading.

Disadvantages

- Some kits may include materials that duplicate items in the collection.
- Kits can be expensive.
- Lost non-replaceable parts may render a kit unusable.

Selection Criteria

- Does the kit create a unified whole? Is there a relationship among its parts?
- Is special equipment needed to use the materials in the kit?
- Does each item in the kit meet the criteria for that particular format?
- Is the kit easy to use?
- Are the directions clear?
- Is adult guidance needed?
- Does the kit fulfill a unique purpose that other materials in the collection do not meet?
- Is there sufficient space to store the kit?

Implications for Collection Development

Select kits on the basis of their potential use and appeal. Students and teachers may prefer to create kits using materials from the collection.

MAGAZINES *SEE* PERIODICALS

MAPS AND GLOBES

Materials included are flat maps, wall maps, and globes. When a map is published in a book, evaluate it in light of the criteria listed under that format.

Advantages

- Maps can provide a wide range of information: place locations and spellings; significant surface features; distances between places; and scientific, social, cultural, political, historical, literary, and economic data.
- Several people can simultaneously study wall maps.
- Unlabeled outline maps or globes encourage children to learn the names, shapes, and locations of political and topographical features.
- Maps are readily available at a wide range of prices.

Disadvantages

- If a group of students need to examine the same detail in a map, multiple copies or a transparency may be needed.

- Cartographic details, especially those on geographic, scientific, or political topics, quickly become outdated.
- Wall maps take up wall space that might be needed for book shelves or displays.

Selection Criteria

- Does the color code help the user interpret the information?
- Is the depth of detail suitable for the intended audience?
- Are symbols representational and clearly designed?
- Is the item durable?
- Is a laminated surface that allows erasable writing for instruction available on large wall maps?
- Is the map aesthetically pleasing?

Implications for Collection Development

The collection should include maps of various sizes to meet the different needs of individuals and groups. Maps and globes should be easily accessible. Because geographic names of countries tend to change fairly frequently, you should set aside monies in your budget to replace maps and globes on a regular basis.

Copyright Considerations

Wall maps, globes, and flat maps are usually copyrighted by the company that produces them. Simple flat outline maps are not eligible for copyright and may be copied. More complex maps require the same criteria as graphics.

MODELS

Models and dioramas are representations of real things. A model is a three-dimensional representation of an object and may be smaller or larger than the real object. Cutaway models show the inside of an object. Dioramas provide an impression of depth, with three-dimensional foreground against a flat background.

Advantages

- These formats offer a sense of depth, thickness, height, and width.
- They can reduce or enlarge objects to an observable size.
- They can simplify complex objects.
- The model can be disassembled and reassembled to show relationships among parts.

Disadvantages

- The size of models may limit their use with a group.
- Some models are difficult to reassemble.
- Loose parts are easy to misplace or lose.
- Specially designed shelving and storage units may be needed.

Selection Criteria

- Are size relationships of the part to the whole accurately portrayed?
- Are parts clearly labeled?
- Are color and composition used to stress important features?
- Will the construction withstand handling?

Implications for Collection Development

The size of many of these materials creates storage and distribution problems. Packaging models for circulation may also be difficult. Materials produced by staff and students may lack the durability needed for permanent inclusion in the collection.

NEWSPAPERS

Newspapers are commonly found in library collections in secondary schools. You may also want to subscribe to a local newspaper if you are in an elementary school setting. Today many newspapers are available online and can be used for current events, as well as for research purposes.

Advantages

- Newspapers are a familiar format as a source of information to students.
- Having print copies of newspapers in a school library frequently draws students and teachers into the library.
- The information in newspapers is current.
- Some newspapers, such as *USA Today,* pictorially display data, making them accessible to those comfortable with figures and graphs.
- More than one user can simultaneously access online formats of newspapers.

Disadvantages

- Storage of print newspapers can be difficult.
- Only one person at a time can read a print newspaper, unless the newspaper is separated into sections.
- Many users tend to not leave the print newspaper in its original order and condition.
- Online subscriptions to some newspapers may be costly.

Selection Criteria

- Is the content of interest to students and teachers?
- Are subjects treated clearly in a well-organized manner?
- Are illustrations pertinent and adequately reproduced?
- Do the strengths of the newspaper fulfill a need within the school?
- Is the paper directed to a local, regional, national, or an international audience?
- Does the newspaper feature visual materials with attention-getting pictorial information and clear graphics?
- In which formats (print, CD-ROM, or online) are the newspapers available?
- Is the content the same in all formats?
- How frequently is information updated?
- How easily can one retrieve back issues?

Implications for Collection Development

Local, state, and national newspapers should be represented in secondary school library collections through print subscriptions or through access on the Internet. Elementary schools should have at least a local newspaper available in the library. If classes subscribe to instructional newspapers, the school librarian may find it useful to have a copy of the teacher's edition in the library.

Copyright Considerations

A teacher can copy a chart, graph, diagram, cartoon, picture, or an article from a newspaper for instructional use. Word limits for multiple copies for classroom use are 250 words for poetry and 2,500 words for articles. A copyright warning notice should appear on each copy. Online newspapers that require subscriptions may be subject to licensing agreements.

ONLINE DATABASES

Online databases provide electronic access to organized collections of data through the use of a computer that is connected to the Internet. Numerous databases are available to libraries. Some contain data of special formats, such as indexes to periodicals, and others provide information from more than one format. Some vendors provide *bundled databases* or *aggregator databases*. Aggregator databases are databases selected by a vendor and put together as a package to which you can subscribe. Thomson Gale, ProQuest, and EBSCO are examples of vendors who provide bundled databases to libraries. Types of databases are the following:

1. Full text: includes all the information available for a certain record. Examples are encyclopedias, journal articles, and entire newspapers.
2. Bibliographic: provides citations and may include abstracts. An example is a magazine index or *Books in Print*.
3. Directory: provides a list of information. An example is a faculty and staff directory.
4. Numeric: contains numbers. Examples are population and census figures provided by the government.
5. Mixed: includes a mixture of the other types of databases.

Advantages

- Information is current.
- Users can easily and quickly locate information.
- Users can modify searches during the process.
- Immediate feedback lets users know whether information is available and whether their search strategy was too narrow or too broad.
- The information provides complete citations.
- Bibliographies are easy to generate.
- Users can save search strategies.
- Many students prefer to access information electronically, rather than use print formats.

Disadvantages

- Not all the subjects in the curriculum may be included.
- Users may need training in developing search strategies.

- Users may need training in evaluating and selecting information.
- Users may need training in interpreting bibliographic information.
- Teachers and librarians may be unable to quickly determine whether students are downloading information without analyzing it, evaluating it, or synthesizing information from several sources.
- Teachers may need assistance in designing assignments that call for evaluation of information, rather than merely locating a predetermined number of sources on a topic.
- Materials cited may not be available locally, and interlibrary loan requests may increase.
- Information generated before 1970 might not be included, limiting historical searches.
- Full-text information might not include graphics from the original work.
- Monographs are not covered as adequately as periodical articles and newspapers.
- Downtime and malfunctions that occur on a network may frustrate users.

Selection Criteria

- Are the intellectual level and the reading level appropriate for the intended users?
- Will students use the disciplines covered in the database?
- How is the database indexed?
- Can students conduct searches using title, author, and keywords?
- Can searchers use Boolean logic, connecting search terms with *and, or,* and *not*?
- Are cross-references provided?
- How frequently is the database updated? Is this appropriate for the curriculum needs?
- How accurate is the information?
- What years does the database cover?
- What services does the vendor offer?
- How clear is the written documentation? Does it include sample screens and other aids?
- If there is a print version, is the online search time less than that required for searching the print version?
- Is the screen easy to read and are directions clear?
- What criteria or standards were used in creating the database?
- Can the users access the database from home after school hours?
- Is the vendor willing to negotiate cost and having the database available during after school hours?
- If the databases are bundled, can you search simultaneously through more than one database?

Implications for Collection Development

Important questions arise when making a decision on whether to subscribe to online databases. Costs for subscriptions can usually be negotiated with a vendor. The costs may vary depending on a school's enrollment, number of persons able to simultaneously access the database, and whether the students have around-the-clock access to the databases. These are all parts of the licensing agreement that you will sign when subscribing to a database or to bundled databases. Agreements with such vendors can affect use. The number of interlibrary loan requests may increase as searchers identify resources not available in the library and not available in full text in the databases. Future funding concerns may necessitate the formation of resource-sharing plans to accommodate the increase in requests for resources the school library does not own.

Copyright Considerations

License agreements usually define what the publisher considers to be fair use of the product. Limitations may include the amount of information that users can download or the number of users who may access the service at the same time.

PAMPHLETS

Pamphlets are multiple-page, printed materials that are frequently housed in the vertical file, rather than shelved as books. Local, state, and national governments, as well as associations or businesses, publish them. Pamphlets and other vertical file materials can provide a wealth of current information and special treatment of timely subjects. Government documents frequently provide concise and up-to-date information about a topic, although the vocabulary may be beyond the elementary school pupils' comprehension.

Advantages

- Pamphlets are inexpensive or free; librarians can readily obtain duplicate copies for topics of high interest.
- Often information found in pamphlets is more current than that in other print media, except magazines and newspapers.
- Pamphlets can provide a variety of viewpoints on a subject.
- Pamphlets often discuss subjects unavailable elsewhere in the collection. Their treatment is usually brief, focusing on a specific subject.

Disadvantages

- Because of their size and format, pamphlets are easily misfiled.
- The flimsy construction of pamphlets limits repeated use.
- Free pamphlets issued by organizations or corporations may take a specific position on issues or contain a great deal of advertising.
- It takes much time to set up and maintain a vertical file containing pamphlets.

Selection Criteria

- Because groups or businesses sponsor many pamphlets, school librarians must consider the extent of advertising. Does advertising dominate the presentation and distract from or distort the information?
- Regardless of whether the item contains advertising, is the message presented without bias and propaganda?
- Is the information provided elsewhere in the collection?

Implications for Collection Development

Since much of the information that is contained in pamphlets is now available through Internet access, many school librarians have eliminated collecting pamphlets and setting up vertical files. However, if you decide to collect pamphlets, they are an inexpensive way to provide balanced information on controversial issues. Materials should be readily accessible, and librarians should review them periodically for timeliness. Because many pamphlets are undated, librarians find it helpful to date them as they file them. This simplifies the reevaluation process. As new versions of pamphlets arrive, the old ones should be removed.

Copyright Considerations

Some pamphlets have copyright limitations. Others, particularly those that government agencies produce, frequently have no copyright restrictions. The user needs to examine each pamphlet for copyright information.

PERIODICALS *SEE ALSO* E-JOURNALS AND NEWSPAPERS

A periodical is a magazine or other publication that is issued on a regular basis. The following section deals only with magazines. Hundreds of magazines are available that can be included in a school library collection. Some popular magazines that are read primarily for entertainment are *Ranger Rick, Rolling Stone,* and *People*. Others, such as *Scientific American, U.S. News and World Report*, and *American Heritage*, are used heavily for research. Many of the professional magazines are referred to as journals. Examples of ones that you might have in your professional library are *Reading Teacher, School Library Journal*, and *Journal of Science Education and Technology*.

Advantages

- Periodicals offer short stories, participatory activities for young users, and extensive illustrations.
- Some magazines solicit contributions of writing or illustrations from students.
- Many periodicals suggest activities that adults can use with students.
- Reluctant book readers often enjoy reading magazines.
- Having a collection of popular magazines will attract teen users to the school library.

Disadvantages

- Circulation controls are difficult to establish.
- Periodicals lend themselves to theft and mutilation.
- When a large number of children are involved, reader participation activities (such as fill in the blanks, connect the dots, or puzzles) need to be copied or laminated so they can be used more than once. Copying is subject to copyright restrictions.
- Storage space that provides easy access to several volumes of a journal may be difficult or expensive to provide.
- If foldouts and cutouts are removed from periodicals, portions of the text may be eliminated.
- The number of advertisements in journals may detract from their usefulness.

Selection Criteria

- Is the content of interest to students and teachers?
- Are subjects treated clearly in a well-organized manner?
- Are the illustrations pertinent and adequately reproduced?

- Is the format appropriate for the purpose of the magazine and the intended audience?
- Do any users need large print items?
- Is the journal indexed?
- Does the electronic version have the same coverage as the print version?
- How easy is it to access back issues?
- How is the electronic version updated?
- Does the electronic version provide links to other electronic sources?
- How easy is it to download articles?

Implications for Collection Development

The length of time one keeps print versions of periodicals depends on their use and the availability of storage facilities. Anticipated use plus cost are key factors in deciding whether to obtain periodicals in print, online, or in CD-ROM formats.

Copyright Considerations

A teacher can copy a chart, graph, diagram, cartoon, picture, or article from a periodical or newspaper for instructional use. Word limits for multiple copies for classroom use are 250 words for poetry and 2,500 words for articles. A copyright warning notice should appear on each copy. Creation of anthologies, compilations, and collective works are prohibited.

POSTERS *SEE* GRAPHIC MATERIALS

REALIA *SEE ALSO* GAMES, MODELS, AND TOYS

Realia are three-dimensional objects from real life that can be used for classroom instruction. Coins, tools, stamps, postcards, and fossils are examples of realia. They bring the real world into the hands of inquisitive users.

Advantages

- Students can handle and closely examine real objects.
- One can inexpensively acquire some objects, such as stamps and postcards, from a wide range of sources, including the students themselves.
- Teachers can check out realia and use them in classroom lessons.

Disadvantages

- Students can easily drop and break some realia.
- Some items may be too fragile or too small for more than one person to use at a time.
- Other items are hard to keep clean or to retain the original shape.

Selection Criteria

- Does the item serve an instructional purpose?
- Is the item durable?

- Is there a display area where several students can observe one item at the same time?
- Are items safe to handle?

Implications for Collection Development

You should avoid duplicating specimens found in other departments of the school, such as the science laboratory. Items should not be put in the collection unless they can potentially serve an instructional purpose. Realia may require special storage facilities.

SLIDES

Two types of slides are (1) two-by-two-inch slides used with projectors with trays, carousels, or cartridges, on slide sorters, or in individual viewers and (2) microslides of biological specimens used with a microprojector.

Advantages

- Color slides are economical to produce.
- The size of slides permits compact packaging and storage, with ease of distribution and circulation.
- Instructors can adapt sequencing and can edit according to their needs.
- With proper equipment, sound can be added.
- Microslides permit an entire class to view microscopic materials, rather than requiring each student to have a microscope.
- Slides can be projected for an indefinite time to accommodate discussion.

Disadvantages

- Single slides are difficult to access rapidly.
- Although slides are inexpensive to process or duplicate, this takes time and depends on the quality and speed of local laboratory services. Copyright restrictions apply to duplication.
- Older technologies, such as overhead projectors, must be kept in order to use slides.

Selection Criteria

- Are art slides faithful to the original?
- Are mountings durable?
- Is there continuity to the set of slides?

Implications for Collection Development

Effective group use of slides requires projectors with remote-control features and lenses of appropriate focal length. Student-produced and teacher-produced slides should meet the same criteria as purchased items. Newer technologies, such as digital photos, have replaced most of the use of slides in schools. Students and teachers are now able to access photographs of art and science specimens via the Internet. They can also develop their own slide presentations through the use of digital photos and presentation software.

Copyright Considerations

Copying slide sets in their entirety, altering a program, or transferring a program to another format requires written permission.

SOFTWARE *SEE* COMPUTER SOFTWARE

STUDY PRINTS *SEE* GRAPHIC MATERIALS

TEXTBOOKS AND RELATED MATERIALS

Materials include textbooks (basic and supplementary), workbooks, and multimedia items. Commercial companies and educational agencies develop these materials. Textbooks may be used as chief sources of information or as supplementary information sources. Some school districts are moving to the use of online textbooks, which eliminates some of the disadvantages of print textbooks such as the need for storage space on shelves. Articles relating to the use of online textbooks can be found in "Additional Readings" at the end of this chapter.

Advantages

- Instruction is in a fixed sequence but is usually flexible enough for the instructor to reorganize.
- The table of contents and index facilitate rapid access to information.
- Each student can have a copy.
- The teacher's editions offer suggestions for related materials and activities.
- Textbooks are field tested, and one may request and evaluate the results of those tests.
- Users can move at their individual pace.

Disadvantages

- Textbooks can limit a teacher's creativity.
- Textbooks can encourage rote learning rather than stimulate exploration.
- A textbook's bibliographies may cite out-of-print materials or fail to reflect appropriate resources in the collection.
- Textbooks take up much shelf space if they have to be housed in the library.
- Adoption of textbooks often implies they will be used over a number of years.

Selection Criteria

Teachers, in consultation with librarians, usually select the textbooks or other instructional systems. In some situations, the librarian may not participate, but the criteria presented here provide basic information necessary to consider in making selection decisions. A librarian may want to buy a single copy of a particular text for its informational content, even though it is not used in a classroom.

- Is the content accurate and objective?
- Does the content represent a broad spectrum of viewpoints on a given topic?

- Are the visual materials keyed to the text?
- Are bibliographies up to date? Do they include a wide range of formats?
- Is the treatment appropriate for the intended purpose and audience?
- Is the arrangement chronological or systematic?
- Is the presentation free of racial or sexual stereotyping?
- Is the type clear and are the pages uncrowded?

Implications for Collection Development

In some schools, librarians are responsible for the organization, storage, distribution, and inventory of textbooks. Regardless of whether you have this responsibility, you need to be aware of the content, the materials recommended in the bibliographies, and the potential use of textbooks as information sources. Individual titles may be useful as information works or for anthologies of short stories or poetry. You may want to include textbooks in the professional collection.

Copyright Considerations

Users may not copy workbooks, exercises, test booklets, and other consumable works.

TOYS

Toys (dolls, stuffed animals, puppets, cars, etc.) allow students opportunities to develop coordination and to learn through touch, manipulation, and sight.

Advantages

- Play is a way of exploring natural laws and relationships.
- Toys can help develop perceptual motor skills.
- Dolls and stuffed animals can help develop affective skills.
- Toys are inexpensive.

Disadvantages

- Parts can be lost.
- The various shapes of toys can create storage problems.
- Germs and lice can be spread through the use of toys. Toys need to be cleaned and sanitized.
- Safety requirements must be observed.
- Toys can be used by a limited number of people.

Selection Criteria

- Can a student play with the toy independently or is adult guidance needed?
- Has the user's developmental stage been considered in the selection of the toy?
- Is the toy durable?
- Will the toy withstand use by children?
- Can one buy replacement parts or make them in-house?
- Is the material nonflammable?

- Can one wash or clean the toy?
- Are the parts of the toy safe for children to use without injuring themselves?

Implications for Collection Development

Selection should be based on knowledge of children's developmental needs. You may need to provide duplicate items so more than one student can use the same toy or so that the toy can be used in the library and can also be circulated. You will need to consider carefully whether you want to collect and circulate toys.

VIDEOCASSETTES

Videocassettes contain magnetic tapes on which both audio and video can be recorded simultaneously. They were first developed in the 1970s so movement in addition to sound could be recorded. The two major standards for videocassettes were Sony's Betamax (Beta) and JVC's VHS format. The VHS format eventually squeezed Betamax out of the consumer market. Although videocassettes can sometimes still be purchased today, the DVD format has overcome VHS as the most popular for playback of recorded video.

Advantages

- The videocassette can be stopped or replayed.
- Videocassettes are easy to store, maintain, and use without damage.
- The format is familiar to users.
- Several people can view a video at the same time.
- Showing videos over closed-circuit televisions can make a presentation accessible to a large number of viewers in different locations.

Disadvantages

- Small monitors limit the size of the audience, unless one can provide multiple monitors or video projector systems.
- One cannot jump to specific sections as easily as in DVDs.
- Compatible equipment is necessary.
- DVDs produce a clearer image than videocassettes, and many producers have moved to DVDs, rather than videos.

Selection Criteria

- Is the content of the video appropriate for the intended audience?
- Are there reviews available for the video?
- Is it possible to preview the video before purchase?
- Is the case protective?

Implications for Collection Development

This format became popular because of its ease of use and range of selections. If possible, you should preview video media before making a purchase. If they meet the selection criteria, videos produced by students, teachers, and staff can be placed in the collection. Video recordings of teleconferences and educational television programs can also be added to the collection.

Copyright Considerations

Copying or altering an entire video requires written permission. Off-air recordings may be retained for no more than 45 calendar days; then they must be erased. They may be shown to a class twice within 10 teaching days. If further use of the video is sought, then one needs to obtain a license. Although there are devices available for transferring videos to DVDs, it is illegal to transfer any copyrighted materials to another format. Thus, school librarians need to retain video playing equipment for any videos that they have in their collections.

WEBSITES

Website refers to a collection of pages of documents accessible on the World Wide Web (WWW or the web). This environment on the global computer network allows access to documents that can include text, data, sound, and video. The user can move from one location to another within the website or use *links* to move to related websites. Access is by the website's address or by the *uniform resource locator* (URL). The URL identifies the name of the host computer, the server, the name of the directory, the domain, the directory or server, and the web page or the actual filename. The domain is identified by three letters describing the sponsoring organization: .com for commercial site, .edu for educational, .k12 for a school, .org for a nonprofit organization, .gov for a government agency, and .net for an Internet Service Provider, among others. The tilde symbol (~) designates a personal web page. These letters and symbols give a clue as to the author (and authority) of the information.

Advantages

- The web provides access to information on a global basis.
- The information is generally current.
- The process is quick, cheap, and efficient.
- The links connect related sources of information.
- The information may be presented through text, sound, graphics, animation, video, and downloadable software.
- Users can interact with the website at their own pace.

Disadvantages

- Sometimes searching for information takes place without the guidance of an index or a classification scheme.
- The content of some websites, including the identified links, are not updated on a regular basis.
- The advertising on some websites can be distracting.
- Content may not be age appropriate.
- Students can easily get lost or lose focus when accessing numerous links.

- Students can download a file, alter it, and (illegally) claim it is their own work.
- Internet safety and literacy must be taught to ensure proper and effective use.

Selection Criteria

- Is the following information provided: name of sponsoring organization or individual, their qualifications, the full mailing address, the e-mail address, the date the page was created, the date the information was updated, and copyright information?
- Is the content and vocabulary appropriate for the intended audience?
- Is the purpose clearly stated?
- Does the website fulfill its purpose?
- How long does it take to access the website?
- Is it easy to navigate through the various pages of the website?
- Are the links updated so that one does not get an error message indicating that the link no longer exists?
- Does the design add to the appeal for the intended audience?
- Does the type and background make the pages readable?
- Is there a link back to the home page on each page?
- Is a table of contents or outline provided for longer documents?
- Does the website have its own search engine for searching all the pages?
- Has the site been reviewed? If so, what did the reviewer say?
- If the website offers a fee-based service, is it a justified and reasonable price?

Implications for Collection Development

Selection of websites for assignments should be the librarian's responsibility, rather than having users rely solely on search tools. The school library's website can be one way that users learn of links to selected sites related to their needs and interests. The library's own website should be updated on a regular basis. If you are subscribing to a fee-based website, you may be able to negotiate the cost.

Copyright Considerations

All web pages are copyrighted. The design of the page, the HTML code, the graphics, and the collections of links are copyrightable. A notice will inform users if they may copy the materials. If you do not find a notice that you can reproduce the material, you must obtain permission to make more than one copy for personal use. If you are subscribing to a website, you will need to adhere to the licensing agreement.

CONCLUSIONS

It is important to include a variety of formats in a school library in order to meet the needs of all users. When selecting materials, librarians should consider who will use the materials, what formats they prefer, how they will use the materials, and whether appropriate equipment is available. Few collections will include every format described. Some materials may be outside the scope of a school's collection policy; others may not be suitable for a particular group of users. Each format has advantages, disadvantages, and selection criteria that may be specific to that particular media format. School librarians should also be familiar with copyright laws and fair use guidelines and how they relate to each format. Advances in technology will continue to bring new formats to the market. As new materials and formats appear, librarians need to consider their relevance to the collection.

ADDITIONAL READINGS

Brenner, R.E. (2008). *Understanding manga and anime*. Westport, CT: Libraries Unlimited.

Everhart, N. (2011). Digital textbooks in Florida: Extending the teacher-librarian's reach. *Teacher Librarian, 38*(3), 8–11.

Foote, C. (2011). E-books: Just jump in! *Library Media Connection, 29*(4), 58–59.

Ford, D.B. (2011). Redefining reading: Comics in the classroom. *Library Media Connection, 30*(3), 36–37.

Gorman, M. (2008). *Getting graphic*. Columbus, OH: Linworth.

Gorman, M. (2011). Getting graphic: Best of the best: 2010. *Library Media Connection, 29*(4), 46.

Grover, S., & Hannegan, L. Hear and now: Connecting outstanding audiobooks to library and classroom instruction, *Teacher Librarian, 35*(3), 17–21.

Harris, C. (2009). Meet the new school board: Board games are back—and they're exactly what your curriculum needs. *School Library Journal, 55*(5), 24–26.

Haynes, E. (2009). Getting started with graphic novels in school libraries. *Library Media Connection, 27*(4), 10–12.

Hutchinson, D. (2007). *Playing to learn*. Westport, CT: Teachers Idea Press.

Johnson, D. (2010). The e-book non-plan. *Library Media Connection, 29*(2), 106.

Lamb, A., & Johnson, L. (2009). Graphic novels, digital comics, and technology-enhanced learning: Part 2. *Teacher Librarian, 37*(1), 70–75.

Lincoln, M. (2010). Information evaluation & online coursework. *Knowledge Quest, 38*(3), 28–31.

Mayer, B. (2009). Got game? *School Librarian's Workshop, 29*(4), 3–4.

Mayer, B., & Harris, C. (2009). *Libraries got game: Aligned learning through modern board games*. Chicago: American Library Association.

Medeiros, N. (2010). Books, books everywhere, but nary a one in print: Cushing Academy eliminates print books from its library. *OCLC Systems & Services, 26*(1), 5–7.

Moorefield-Lang, H., & Gavigan, K. (2012). These aren't your father's funny papers: The world of digital graphic novels. *Knowledge Quest, 40*(3), 30–34.

Pappas, M. (2009). ebooks—ready for school libraries? *School Library Monthly, 26*(2), 48–52.

Porter, M., & King, D.L. (2010). E-books, e-book readers, and next steps. *Public Libraries, 49*(6), 20–23.

Rudiger, H., & Schliesman, M. (2007). Graphic novels and school libraries. *Knowledge Quest, 36*(2), 57–59.

Samet, R. (2010). Get graphic novels into your elementary collection. *School Library Monthly, 26*(5), 12–13.

Sanborn, L.D. (2011). eBook collections for high schools. *School Library Monthly, 28*(1), 37–38.

Sheehan, K. (2011). Learning brick by brick: How Lego can expand the minds of your students. *The School Librarian, 59*(2), 70–72.

Stephens, W. (2012). Deploying e-readers without buying e-books: One school's emphasis on the public domain. *Knowledge Quest, 40*(3), 40–43.

Troutner, J. (2009). Online textbooks. *Teacher Librarian, 37*(2), 60–61.

HELPFUL WEBSITES

Buffalo & Erie County Public Library. (n.d.). *Get graphic*. Retrieved from http://www.getgraphic.org/

Copyright Website. (2011). Retrieved from http://www.benedict.com

International Digital Publishing Forum. (2011). *The global trade and standards association for electronic publishing*. Retrieved from http://idpf.org/

Kannenberg, G. (2010). *ComicsResearch.org*. Retrieved from http://www.comicsresearch.org

Lavin, M. (2008). *Graphic novels: Resources for teachers & librarians*. Retrieved from http://library.buffalo.edu/libraries/asl/guides/graphicnovels/

Samet, R. (n.d.). *Raya Samet's e-portfolio*. Retrieved from http://rayasamet.weebly.com/graphic-novels-resources.html

Schrock, K. (2011). *Teacher helpers: Critical evaluation information*. Retrieved from http://school.discovery.com/schrockguide/eval.html

TOON Books. (2010). *TOON in the classroom*. Retrieved from http://toon-books.com/classroom.php

Slides

Realia See also Games, Models, and Toys

Chapter 9

Acquisitions and Processing

Acquisition is the process of obtaining materials. This involves confirming that materials are available, verifying order information, identifying and selecting sources of materials, arranging for orders to be sent, allocating funds, keeping records, and producing reports on expenditures of funds. Obtaining electronic products, reviewing license agreements, and negotiating for leases are also included in the acquisition procedures. Speed, accuracy, and thrift are common goals of the acquisition process.

The school librarian can acquire materials through purchase, lease, or solicitation of free materials, gifts, or exchanges. Schools participating in resource-sharing programs also borrow and lend materials that are available through interlibrary loan.

This chapter focuses on the components of the acquisition process that are most likely to involve the building-level person directly. It also reviews the relationship of acquisition procedures to acquisition policy, identifies the distribution systems for materials, describes procedures for acquiring materials (including electronic materials), discusses the relationship between library professionals and vendors, and describes possible processing and cataloging procedures. Obtaining materials through resource sharing is also discussed.

POLICIES AND PROCEDURES

Policies establish procedures to follow and the rationale for such procedures. Procedures describe how a process will take place and who will be responsible for implementing the steps in the process. An acquisition policy might state that materials will be purchased from the least expensive and most efficient source, for instance, a jobber. The policy might also indicate that a school librarian may buy an item locally if the need is immediate. In a high school, a policy could state that a paperback format is preferable to buying fiction books in hardback format.

In many school districts acquisition policies are uniform throughout the schools. The school district might also dictate the acquisition procedures. For example, the district's

Materials Acquisition Request

Requestor:

Name:

E-mail: Phone:

Status (please check one):

___ Teacher ___ Administrator ___ Student

Source of Citation (where you found information about the material):

____

Book (complete as much information as possible):

Author or Editor:

Title:

Publisher: Year of Publication:

ISBN#: Price:

Magazine or Journal (complete as much information as possible):

Title:

Publisher:

ISSN#: Price:

Audio-Visual Material (complete as much information as possible):

Type of Material (audiocassette, video, CD, DVD, etc.):

Producer:

Distributor: Price:

Figure 9.1. Materials acquisition request form

purchasing agent may specify the order forms that one should use. Some school districts may have agreements to use a particular jobber or to order their materials from an online catalog. Procedures for accounting and record keeping are frequently established at the district level. As a new school librarian you should ask the director of the district school library program or a school administrator for a copy of district policies and procedures that affect the school library. In some school districts you can find this information online.

In order to obtain input from teachers, administrators, and students, you may want to create a materials acquisition request form. An example of such a form can be found in Figure 9.1. This form can be printed out and made available to library users, perhaps at the circulation desk or at faculty meetings. Ideally, the form should be available electronically through the school library website so users can access the form from classrooms or homes.

DISTRIBUTION SYSTEMS

Choosing the best source for ordering materials or equipment is an important decision in the acquisition process. Chief distributors of materials include jobbers, distributors, publishers, producers, subscription agencies, dealers, and local sources such as bookstores and video stores. Any for-profit organization that markets a product or service to libraries can be considered a *vendor*. Other possible sources for materials include museums, online businesses, and garage sales. *Remainders* (publishers' overstocks) and out-of-print materials can sometimes be obtained from online vendors and from both new and used book stores. Websites that can help you identify some of these sources are found at the end of the chapter under the heading "Helpful Websites."

Using Jobbers

Jobbers, wholesalers, and distributors are intermediaries between publishers or producers and the buyer, the school librarian. The term *jobber* is used interchangeably with the word *wholesaler*. Jobbers buy materials from publishers and producers and sell them to bookstores and libraries. For example, one can buy books and videocassettes directly from the publisher or producer, but the same items are often available at a lower price from a jobber or a distributor. The word *distributor* is often used for audiovisual materials. Distributors may serve a region of the country or the entire country. Some jobbers and distributors provide newsletters, product hotlines, and websites.

The many advantages for dealing with jobbers are:

- You avoid the cost and paperwork of ordering through many publishers or producers.
- You have only one source to contact for follow-up on orders.
- Libraries receive better discounts from jobbers than from publishers or producers.
- You obtain indirect access to publishers who refuse to deal directly with libraries or give poor service to small orders.
- Most jobbers provide full processing, cataloging services, security devices, and plastic jackets for materials.
- Preselection plans (approval plans in which the librarian examines new titles at the usual discount rate, with full return privileges) are sometimes available.
- Many jobbers offer online ordering services.

Utilizing the services of jobbers also has disadvantages:

- It sometimes takes a month for jobbers to fill orders, whereas publishers can deliver in one to two weeks.
- The availability of older titles depends on the wholesaler's inventory.
- No wholesaler can supply every available title. Some titles, such as materials that professional organizations produce, can be purchased only through direct order.
- Policies on the return of defective or damaged copies may say that credit or replacement is not granted until the wholesaler has received the returns.

Librarians can expect jobbers or wholesalers to have a large inventory of titles, to fill orders promptly and accurately at a reasonable cost, and to report on items not in stock. If you receive an order and do not obtain satisfactory information about whether a book is out of print (OP), out of stock indefinitely (OSI), or temporarily out of stock (TOS), you should contact the publisher or producer to inquire about why an item was not received.

If a librarian has a standing order with a publisher, it is not necessary to initiate orders for titles that the publisher delivers under the conditions of the standing order. A *standing order* is an agreement that is made to purchase all items that match certain terms, such as Caldecott Medal Award-winning books or materials on a particular subject. Many school librarians have standing orders to renew their magazine subscriptions with vendors, such as EBSCO or WT Cox. In such a case, the vendor sends the librarian a list of all the subscriptions (either by mail or online) that are to be renewed, and the librarian can delete items or add items to the list. As a new school librarian, you need to check to see if your library has any standing order agreements in effect.

Selecting Jobbers

Selecting jobbers who meet the needs of your library can be critical. Thus, you should do some research about the various jobbers before making a selection. You can ask a jobber to provide you a list of schools in your state that use their services and then inquire with other school librarians about their satisfaction with the use of that jobber. This can also be done on school library listservs. The following are some questions that you might want to ask:

- What types of discounts does the jobber offer?
- Does the jobber change prices of items without prior notice?
- On the average what percent of an order gets filled?
- How long does it take to get an order filled?
- Does the jobber provide information about items that are not received?
- If the jobber is a magazine vendor, is there a claim procedure in place and how long does it take to obtain missed issues?
- Does the jobber follow your specifications for processing and cataloging?
- Is the cataloging information accurate?
- Are the items packaged well and in good condition when you receive them?
- Are you able to return items?

Some websites that will help you identify possible jobbers, distributors, and publishers who deal with library materials, supplies, and equipment are listed under "Helpful Websites" at the end of this chapter. These companies can also be found by looking for advertisements in professional school library and other library journals. Some jobbers that are frequently used by school librarians include Baker & Taylor, Brodart, Follett, Mackin, Ingram, Bound To Stay Bound, and Perma-Bound. When you obtain your first school library position, you will also find that you automatically begin to receive catalogs and advertising brochures from companies that deal with library items. It is wise to keep these catalogs in an organized file and replace old catalogs as you receive newer versions.

Establishing and maintaining good working relationships with jobbers and distributors is partially your responsibility. You need to make certain that your requests are reasonable, that you keep jobbers informed about your collection needs, and that invoices are processed promptly. To stay in business and provide quality services to libraries, vendors need to have large volumes of sales and have good cash flow. Thus, any way that you can contribute to these goals will be appreciated by the vendors with whom you do business.

ACQUISITION ACTIVITIES

An initial goal of acquisitions is to avoid duplication, both of effort and of the item itself. Thus, the first step that should be performed when receiving a material request from a teacher or student is to check to see if the library already owns the item or whether it is on order. The school library's online public access computer (OPAC) can provide information about current holdings, as well as materials that are on order (as long as this information has been entered into the OPAC). If on-order materials are not entered into the OPAC, then you will need to refer to all orders that you have made to check for duplicates.

Bibliographic Verification

When teachers or students request that you purchase an item for the library, they often do not include the full information needed for ordering or they may even provide some inaccurate information (the title might not be exactly correct or they do not remember the publisher correctly). Thus, it is necessary to verify the bibliographic information needed to order the item. The verification procedure consists of two steps. The first is to establish the existence of a particular item. The second is to identify the correct author, title, publisher or producer, and other necessary ordering data, such as ISBN (International Standard Book Number) or ISSN (International Standard Serial Number).

To learn whether an item is available, one can start with a special type of bibliography called a *trade bibliography*. These tools provide ordering information for materials that are currently in print or otherwise available. Bibliographic tools that indicate availability may also state additional information such as whether the item is available through purchase, rent, or loan and the purchase or rental price, whether one must order the item directly from a publisher or producer or whether it is available through a jobber, distributor, or vender, and if there are postage or delivery charges.

The information included for each item may vary from one tool to another. For print formats, the bibliographic entry usually includes the author, title, editor, publisher, date of publication, series title and number, available bindings, price, and ISBN or ISSN. For audiovisual items, the bibliographic entry usually includes the title; production and release dates; producer or distributor; physical characteristics (e.g., color or black and white, captioned or sound, audiocassette or videocassette, length or running time, and special equipment needed); number of pieces included (e.g., four study prints and one teacher's guide); languages; price; and special conditions of availability.

Many bibliographies can be used for the verification process. *Books in Print* (Bowker), *Books in Print Supplement* (Bowker), and *Children's Books in Print* (Bowker) are frequently used to verify information for books. These resources are available in book format. *Books in Print* and *Children's Books in Print* are also available online. Other Bowker products that can be used to verify information include *The Complete Directory of Large Print Books and Serials, Bowker's Complete Video Directory, Books Out Loud*, and Ulrich's *Periodicals Directory*. You should use the latest edition of these tools for the most current information on price and availability.

If you do not have access to these tools that need to be purchased or subscribed to online, other options are available. One place to find out whether titles are correct and whether a work is in print is through commercial online bookstores. A word of caution, however, is that the bibliographic information in these online bookstores is not always completely accurate. Another option is to look on the publisher's or producer's websites. The bibliographic information for ordering will be available, as well as frequent listings of forthcoming titles.

Publishers' and jobbers' catalogs can also assist in bibliographic verification. Catalogs provide price and availability information, but they should not be used for reviews. Remember that catalogs exist to sell materials, not to offer evaluative reviews. When catalogs do quote reviews, full citations to the reviews are usually not given, so the librarian needs to consider the limitations of incomplete reviews, words taken out of context, and the absence of more critical comments that reviews offer.

Ordering

After a jobber or other vendor is selected, materials then need to be ordered. Each school or school district has a procedure that must be followed in order to purchase items. This consists of filling out standardized purchase orders (POs). Some jobbers and publishers provide online access to ordering. Follett's *Titlewave* is an example of an ordering tool that can save you much time. You can find the website information for *Titlewave* under "Helpful Websites" at the end of this chapter. You should contact financial personnel at your school to determine whether you are able to use online ordering opportunities and how that should be coordinated with the school's purchasing process.

Common information that vendors need to provide materials include shipping address, author or editor, title, publisher, date of publication, price, number of copies, order number, instructions regarding processing and shipping, invoicing, and method of payment. Vendors may also request ISBN or ISSN numbers.

Receiving

Care must be taken when unpacking shipments of materials. Special training might be necessary for clerical personnel and student assistants. The first item to locate is the packing slip or invoice (itemized list). This may be attached to the outside of the package or buried underneath the materials. If you do not find the packing slip, you should keep all the items in that shipment separate from those in other shipments.

As each item is received, check it against the packing slip or invoice for title match. In the case of audiovisual or computer materials, this step must take place before you remove the shrink wrap because many jobbers and distributors will not accept returns of unwrapped electronic materials. Check the item for damage or missing parts. Know the jobber's or vendor's policy on returns and whether they will give credit for damage that occurred in shipping.

Common problems include wrong editions, items added to or deleted from the list, wrong number of copies, and damaged or incomplete items. After all items have been checked, stamp the school library name on them. Then enter the barcode into the database. Finally, approve the invoice for payment.

Record Keeping

Acquisition activities involve large amounts of detail work. You can handle the tracing of orders either manually or electronically. Manual systems often consist of keeping binders or files for POs by categories such as *outstanding*, *completed*, or *to be paid*. Another possible organizational category is using budget account numbers.

Computer software can simplify accessing information and generating records. *Consideration files* (the record of desired items) can be organized with a database management program, enabling one to print, in priority order, a list of items to be ordered from a single vendor. As materials are ordered and received, you can update these records. Some systems allow you to transfer the information to a different file, such as outstanding orders or new arrivals. Some systems also allow the administrator to create categories, such as a subject area, a specific format, back orders, or specified jobbers. You can use word processing programs to create a template to print specific information on preprinted continuous forms, including POs. You can also use a spreadsheet program to keep track of budget reports and projections.

If your school district is not using computer programs for management activities, consider the following questions: What jobs can best be handled through the use of computer programs? What equipment resources are available? What are the implications for staffing? What is the capability of existing software programs? Does your automated program permit online ordering, electronic invoicing, and credit-card payments?

Online Subscriptions

Most school libraries are purchasing databases through online subscriptions, rather than purchasing many materials in print or CD-ROM formats. Thus, while ownership through purchase used to be the traditional method, that is now being replaced by access to materials through license. It then becomes necessary to negotiate licenses with vendors. Such a license is a legal agreement of acceptable understandings and commitments that is often negotiated between the vendor and the school librarian.

Both the cost and the terms of a license can usually be negotiated with a vendor. The cost often depends on the enrollment of your school, the number of users who can simultaneously access the materials, and whether you want remote access to the materials from classrooms and users' homes. It is important that you read through any license agreement and understand the terms. If you do not understand the terminology used in an agreement, you should ask the vendor to define the terms in vocabulary that is appropriate to school library use.

If the quoted cost for access is more than your budget allows, you should not automatically give up on the idea of subscribing to online materials. Rather, you should explain your situation to the vendor representative and ask how the cost can be reduced. The online subscriptions are well worth obtaining since it makes access to materials much easier and also saves valuable space in the library.

Equipment

In most school districts or schools, equipment that costs over a certain amount (sometimes $100) must be put out for bid. In such instances, specifications for the bids must be drawn up. It is important to include every characteristic that you wish to have for the piece of equipment, for instance, the amount of memory needed in a computer, the size of the monitor, the size of the processor, and any other specifications you require. You should instruct bidders not to include taxes in their bids since schools are usually tax-exempt institutions. The business office of the school district or a regional center will handle the bidding process and the awarding of bids. You will be provided with the name or names of vendors from whom you must order the equipment. If for any reason you know that a vendor does not provide quality products or service, you should share this information with the business office so the vendor is not included in the bids that are considered.

For equipment that costs less than those requiring bids you should check with your business office to see if there are any requirements regarding vendors. For instance, in some schools you may not be able to purchase from local dealers but must order from catalogs. In other instances you may not be able to order from online vendors. Regardless of the way you order equipment, you will need to keep records of your purchases.

In most instances materials in a school library are either purchased outright or obtained through licensing agreements. Although equipment is usually purchased, large, costly equipment, such as a copy machine, are sometimes leased from a commercial vendor. In these cases the school librarian must read the leasing agreement carefully and keep track of the cost effectiveness of leasing the equipment in comparison to purchasing the item.

PROCESSING ACTIVITIES

The final stage in the acquisition process is preparing the materials for use. This involves cataloging and classifying each item, identifying the library as owner, adding security strips and circulation barcodes, putting needed labels on the materials, and providing protective cases or other packaging for circulation of the materials. You should place copyright warnings on audiovisual and computer materials.

Some school districts have their own central processing of materials, particularly of books. In these cases, the books are sent directly to the central processing office where they are cataloged, have barcodes placed on them, and have the name of the school stamped on the items. If there are no such central processing services, then you should definitely have the vendor provide as much processing as you want, particularly the cataloging, which is a very time-consuming process. All major vendors of library books and many who deal with audiovisual materials offer commercial processing for reasonable costs (often from $1.00 to $2.00 per item). This is a bargain when you consider the amount of time that it takes to fully process a book (generally between 30 minutes to an hour, depending on the difficulty of cataloging and classifying the item).You will need to fill out a specification form that indicates your processing requests so that the items match your current cataloging and you receive all the processing services that you need.

Some school librarians order their materials processed, but ask that the school library stamp not be added to the item. This makes it much easier to return materials that are not wanted after examining the items.

Interlibrary Loan Request Form

Please fill in details below and return to librarian

Name:__________________ Grade:_________Homeroom Teacher:________________

Course:_________________ E-mail:____
(for arrival notification)

Please indicate your status:
Faculty/Staff_____ Student_____

BOOK LOAN:

Book Title:____

Author:__________________________

Publisher:_______________ Publication Date:___________________

Edition or Volume Number:__________

Notes/Comments for Library Staff:____

OR:

PHOTOCOPY OF ARTICLE:

Title of Journal/Periodical:____

Title of Article:____

Author:____

Volume:_____________ Issue No.:_____________

Date:______________

Notes/Comments for Library Staff:____

If article is available as a pdf, I would like it sent directly to my e-mail
address: Yes: ☐ No: ☐

Figure 9.2. Interlibrary loan request form

If you are employed in a school that is required to do its own processing of materials, it is possible for you to purchase software to help with the cataloging. Many of the vendors of library automation systems provide software for this purpose.

Almost all school libraries use the Dewey Decimal Classification System (DDC) for classifying materials. The *Abridged Dewey Decimal System Classification* (OCLC) will usually fill the needs of a school librarian who needs to do original cataloging. Other tools that will assist in original cataloging are: *Anglo-American Cataloging Rules* (American Library Association, Canadian Library Association, and Chartered Institute of Library and Information Specialists) and *Sears List of Subject Headings* (H.W. Wilson). These tools are all available in print or online. Since some of these materials are expensive, they can sometimes be shared by more than one school or the school district can negotiate for licenses to access the resources online.

RESOURCE SHARING

Another way in which materials can be acquired (temporarily) is by borrowing them from another library. This is generally referred to as *interlibrary loan*. Some types of interlibrary loan are formalized with networks to which libraries belong. A school that belongs to such a network has access to a plethora of resources and possibly to some additional services. However, participation carries responsibilities and perhaps financial obligations. Some school librarians also use informal methods of interlibrary loan by e-mailing or phoning librarians in local schools to see if particular items can be borrowed. This is very helpful when multiple copies of an item are needed or when an item is requested very infrequently. Figure 9.2 is a sample of an interlibrary loan request form that could be used in a school library. It is important to remember, however, that interlibrary loan should not be used in place of purchasing books or other materials that are frequently requested.

CONCLUSIONS

Acquisition activities consume time and energy. Much of the work involved is detailed and should not be performed in haste. Although clerical assistants can perform some of the acquisition activities, they need to receive training in which accuracy is emphasized. A librarian's organizational abilities, mathematical skills, and business sense frequently come into play during acquisition activities. Errors or misjudgments can be costly. Using computer management systems can simplify procedures, while controlling the information in a timely manner.

ADDITIONAL READINGS

Bussey, H. (2007). More bang for your buck. *Information Outlook, 11*(6), 35–36, 38–40, 43.

Chapman, L. (2008). *Managing acquisitions in library and informations services, revised edition.* New York: Neal-Schuman.

Farkas, M. (2011). Let's not borrow trouble. *American Libraries, 42*(3/4), 24.

Koehn, S.L., & Hawamdeh, S. (2010). The acquisition and management of electronic resources: Can use justify cost? *Library Quarterly, 80*(2), 161–174.

Rosen, J. (2007). Getting teachers to pay attention. *Publishers Weekly, 254*(19), 26.

Shirley, B. (2006). Building the partnership: TexShare and K-12 databases. *Texas Library Journal, 82*(2), 72–74.

Weare, W. H., Jr., Toms, S., & Breeding, M. (2011). Moving forward: The next gen catalog and the new discovery tools. *Library Media Connection, 30*(3), 54–57.

Williams, L. A. (2011). The Fenn fallout. *Publishers Weekly, 258*(7), 4–5.

Williams, V. K. (2010). Assessing your vendors' viability. *The Serials Librarian, 59*(3/4), 313–324.

HELPFUL WEBSITES

AcqWeb. (2010). *Welcome to the new AcqWeb!* Retrieved from http://www.acqweb.org

Block, M. (2008). *Book bytes: How to find out-of-print books.* Retrieved from http://marylaine.com/bookbyte/getbooks.html

Follett Library Resources. (2011). Retrieved from http://www.titlewave.com

Lamb, A., & Johnson, L. (2010). *The school library media specialist: Overview: Collection development resources.* Retrieved from http://eduscapes.com/sms/overview/selectiontools.html#8

Lamb, A., & Johnson, L. (2010). *The school library media specialist: Program administration: acquisitions.* Retrieved from http://eduscapes.com/sms/administration/acquisition.html

PMA, the Independent Book Publishers Association. (n.d.). *Remainders book expo.* Retrieved from http://www.pma-online.org/remaindr/remain.cfm

Yahoo. (2011). *Small business: Library services>supplies and equipment.* Retrieved from http://dir.yahoo.com/Business_and_Economy/Business_to_Business/Information/Library_Services/Supplies_and_Equipment?o=a

Maintenance and Preservation

An effective collection maintenance program serves two purposes. First, materials and equipment should be readily available for use. Second, policies and procedures for preventive maintenance help ensure economical and efficient management of the collection. Maintenance activities include keeping accurate records of what is in the collection (an inventory); inspecting materials; and repairing, replacing, or removing items.

Policies and procedures of the maintenance program are the focus of this chapter. The "Additional Readings" and "Helpful Websites" listings at the end of this chapter identify works with more specific information about the preservation and maintenance of items in the collection.

MAINTENANCE POLICIES

Maintenance policies, particularly those relating to equipment, sometimes exist at the district level, rather than at the building level. However, if such policies are not present, you need to create them at the school level.

The overall policy should specify who repairs materials and equipment, whether the school library personnel do any troubleshooting with equipment, who replaces equipment bulbs and conducts preventative computer maintenance, what preventative measures are taken to maintain equipment, who is responsible for weeding the collection, the criteria used to weed the collection, what is done with discarded materials, whether an inventory is taken of the collection, and who is responsible for the inventory.

In preparing the budget, developmental items (those increasing the size of the collection) can be distinguished from replacement items (those maintaining the current level of service). The librarian can base the replacement of materials and equipment on the rates at which the items become unusable because of wear or dated content.

Another factor to consider is loss. A loss rate greater than two percent suggests that a replacement or loss factor must be a budget item. *Information Power: Guidelines for*

School Library Media Programs (American Association of School Librarians [AASL] & Association for Educational Communications and Technology [AECT], 1988) offers two budget formulas for materials and equipment. For example, to replace lost, damaged, and out-of-date books, one formula multiplies by five percent the number of books in the collection times the average price of a book. The example uses the following illustration: for a collection with 6,000 volumes, five percent of the volumes (300 books) should be replaced. If the average cost of a book is $15, then 300 times $15 means $4,500 is needed to cover the replacement costs (p. 128). Although this formula can be helpful, it is important to remember that the average cost of a hardback book has risen significantly from the figure used in the example from *Information Power: Guidelines for School Library Programs*. Curriculum Materials Information Services (CMIS) listed the 2010 average cost for children's (elementary) nonfiction hardback books at $35.63 and hardback fiction at $23.36, while paperback nonfiction was $23.47 and paperback fiction was $15.46. The 2010 average cost of nonbook items (videos, audiocassettes, compact discs, charts, games, and realia) was $37.85 for nonfiction items and $32.47 for fiction items (Curriculum Materials Information Services, 2011).

Information Power: Guidelines for School Library Media Programs (AASL & AECT, 1988) also provides a formula for replacing equipment. These formulas, along with other valuable information in the appendices, are in themselves good reasons to purchase or locate a copy of this book, despite its copyright date. Later national school library standards unfortunately do not include these valuable appendices.

Equipment

Policies related to equipment maintenance address the following issues:

- When and why equipment will be traded in or discarded.
- The type of repairs and maintenance that will be handled at the building level, at the district level, and through repair contracts.
- The records to be kept on equipment usage, repair, and maintenance.
- The quantity and type of usable pieces of equipment to be provided, including a replacement schedule.
- How school librarians should handle the transfer or disposal of equipment.

Materials

With tight budgets in most school libraries, it is essential to make efforts to preserve materials that are in the collection. Maintenance policies for materials should include who is responsible for the maintenance of materials, as well as addressing the weeding and inventory of materials. *Weeding* of materials refers to the removal of the resources from the collection. Often this is referred to as de-selection or reevaluation of the existing collection.

The process of carefully weeding a school library to remove outdated and unused materials is as important as the process of selection. A weeding policy should include who is responsible for weeding the collection, the criteria for weeding materials, and what is done with weeded materials.

The school librarian is responsible for weeding a collection, but the expertise of faculty from various fields or grade levels should be enlisted. Classroom teachers can provide information relating to the curriculum that can assist the librarian in making professional judgments about which materials can be discarded without affecting curriculum needs.

Physical qualities of a material, suitability of the content, recentness of the material, and accuracy of the information are all factors to be considered when making decisions to withdraw resources from a collection. In general, materials should be weeded from the collection for the following reasons:

- Poor physical condition
- Unattractive appearance
- Poor circulation record
- Old copyright date, with outdated or inaccurate information
- Duplicates of titles no longer in demand
- Subject matter unsuitable for users
- Topics no longer of interest
- Biased or stereotypical portrayals
- Inappropriate reading levels
- No longer needed because of a change in the curriculum

Some librarians like to use what is known as the CREW (**C**ontinuous **R**eview, **E**valuation, and **W**eeding). The CREW method uses an acronym, MUSTIE, to help librarians decide when an item should be weeded or removed from the collection.

- **M**isleading—In other words, factually inaccurate. This may include materials that fail to include substantive periods of time because of the age of the material.
- **U**gly—Tattered or worn out and beyond mending.
- **S**uperseded by a newer edition or better source. This may include use of the Internet resources that provide more up-to-date sources.
- **T**rivial—Meaning having no obvious literary or scientific merit and/or without sufficient reason or use to justify keeping it.
- **I**rrelevant to the needs and interests of the library patrons and/or not used even though it may be deemed interesting.
- **E**lsewhere—Meaning the resource may be easily borrowed from another source or found by using an electronic resource and/or the Internet.

Having guidelines for materials also assists in adhering to the weeding criteria that you establish for your library. Table 10.1 provides some suggested guidelines. You may want to alter the table to fit the needs of your school.The policy can also identify materials that are not to be discarded. Examples include local and state history materials; major publications of the school, such as yearbooks or school newspapers; classics (unless newer versions are available); and items incorrectly classified or poorly promoted that might circulate under changed circumstances.

The policy might recommend continuous, intermittent, or periodical weeding. The continuous plan, which takes place on a daily basis, may be difficult to handle without disrupting established routine. The intermittent plan calls for designating specific times of the academic calendar for reevaluating and weeding specific areas or types of media. The periodic plan makes use of days when the school library is not scheduled for use. Careful planning can and should avoid disrupting services to students and teachers.

Inventory

Some school districts have policies that require a complete, annual inventory of school library materials and equipment. You need to inquire about district policies related to this

TABLE 10.1. AGE AND CIRCULATION GUIDELINES

Class	Subject or Format	Age	Last Circulated (Years)	Comments
000	General Works	5	2	
030	Encyclopedias	5	NA	Replace one set each year; do not put old sets in classrooms
100	Philosophy/Psychology	10	3–5	Self-help books should be current
200	Religion	5–10	3–5	Retain basic titles
290	Mythology	10–15	3–5	
300	Social Science	5–10	3–5	Retain balance on controversial topics
310	Almanacs/Yearbooks	1	NA	Have latest edition; may circulate year-old editions
398	Folklore	10–15	5	Retain standard works
400	Language	10	3–5	Retain basics
500	Pure Sciences	5	3–5	Retain basics, such as Darwin; examine any item over 5 years old, except botany and natural history
600	Applied Sciences/ Technology	5	3-5	Monitor changes in health materials
700	The Arts	NA	NA	Retain all basic items, especially art history
745	Crafts	NA	5	Retain well-illustrated materials
770	Photography	5	3	Discard dated techniques and equipment
800	Literature	NA	NA	Retain all basic materials, especially criticism; discard minor writers

900	Geography and History	10–15	5	Monitor geopolitical changes; retain local history
920	Biography	NA	3–5	Keep until demand wanes
E	Easy/Everyone	NA	2–5	Keep high-demand materials
F	Fiction	NA	2–5	Keep high-demand materials; evaluate literary merit; replace classics with newer, more attractive editions
Ref	Reference			
	Indexes	3–5	NA	As newer editions appear, discard old copies
	Atlases	5	NA	
	Maps and Globes	10	NA	Check for accuracy
	Newspapers	1 week	NA	Retain 1 week; access older editions online
	College Catalogs	2	NA	
	Periodicals	5	NA	Discard non-indexed titles after circulation
A-V	Audiovisual materials			Discard worn or out-of-date items

topic. If there is not a district-level policy in place, you should create written policies to address when and by whom inventory of materials and equipment will take place. Usually the librarian, with assistance from school library staff, supervises inventory. Technologies, which include portable scanners capable of reading barcodes that have been placed on materials and equipment, makes it possible to use responsible students or adult volunteers to assist in the process.

You may also want to include in your policy a requirement that the school librarian submits a report of each inventory to the school principal. Discussing an inventory report with a principal is also a wise idea as it will help an administrator understand the process and possible problems, such as large numbers of lost items. Future budget needs for replacement of books or a security system are more apt to be met if a principal is kept aware of inventory results. A copy of each inventory report should be filed in the library.

MAINTENANCE PROCEDURES

Working within parameters of the district policies, the school librarian is responsible for establishing collection maintenance procedures for systematic inspection of all materials and equipment. While technicians and aides can repair and clean materials and equipment, the librarian identifies maintenance problems, diagnoses causes, establishes corrective measures, and monitors the quality of the work completed by staff or an outside contractor.

Routine internal maintenance procedures include the following:

Books and Print Materials: Replacing protective jackets, repairing torn pages, reinserting separated pages, eliminating minor scribbling, taping and labeling spines, and purchasing heavily used books in library bindings.

Audiovisual Materials: Splicing tapes, wiping CDs and DVDs, storing discs and videos upright (book style) in plastic cases, returning materials to storage cases immediately after use, and storing materials in cool, dry environments.

Equipment: Cleaning areas of heavy use such as playback heads and lenses, using antistatic wipes on monitors and screens, keeping warranties, manuals, and repair records in an accessible file, training library staff and students in the proper operation and care of equipment (including replacement of bulbs), covering machines when they are not in use, fastening televisions and VCRs to designated carts, not allowing students to transport equipment, maintaining an area or workspace with basic tools for minor repairs, replacing, and properly disposing items such as light bulbs and printer cartridges, preventative computer maintenance such as defragmentation, data back up, and virus scans, and keeping equipment in climate-controlled areas (Streiff, 1992).

You and your school library staff should also educate students and teachers about the proper care of library materials and equipment. You can offer professional development workshops to teachers on the proper use of equipment, especially if new equipment is purchased.

When students first begin to use the library, they should be taught to handle books carefully by turning pages only by the corners, keeping books in safe locations out of the reach of young siblings and dogs, not writing in books or placing objects in books, and refraining from reading books while eating or drinking beverages. Older students should be instructed on how to properly copy pages of materials on a copy machine, emphasizing not pressing down forcefully on the spines of books. If students are using CDs or DVDs, they should be shown how to handle these items properly, holding the discs carefully by the edges and making certain they do not get scratched.

Providing bookmarks at the circulation desk will alleviate the use of inappropriate items being used to mark places in a book or *dog earring* pages for the same purpose. Librarians have reported finding gum, chewing tobacco, pickles, and numerous other strange items in books returned to their libraries. Additionally, keeping a supply of plastic bags near the exits of the school library can reduce damage to books caused by rain or snow.

Having access to a copy machine in the library (with reasonable charges for copying pages) will cut down dramatically on damage to books when students tear out pages that they want for research. Installing security systems, particularly in secondary schools, will also help maintain the collection by reducing the loss of materials through theft.

Ensuring appropriate temperature and humidity in the school library to preserve materials and equipment is also one of your maintenance responsibilities. This is particularly important during the summer in hot, humid climates. In such environments, custodial personnel should be instructed to operate air conditioning systems for a part of every day. Not doing so can result in mold and mildew damage and possibly leave equipment inoperable.

Weeding

Psychologically, one of the most difficult tasks of beginning school librarians is weeding a collection. You, like most librarians, are probably a lover of books and other materials that are found in libraries. Librarians give many reasons and excuses for avoiding weeding. Typical attitudes are these:

- Books are sacred objects; only vandals destroy books.
- Someone may need this in the future.
- I don't have enough time to examine every item in the collection.
- There will be a scene if teacher X wants this item.
- I don't have time to remove the bibliographic and holding records for all these items.
- Our policy doesn't justify the removal of materials bought with public funds.
- I cannot decide when a fiction title is out of date.
- Kits are expensive to replace, and this one has at least half of the original items.
- This software package has gone through several revisions, adding features we could learn to use, but many of us already know how to use this version.

Weeding a collection has many benefits including the creation of more space, ensuring accurate materials, avoiding the cost of maintaining unwanted items, obtaining and keeping a reputation as a source of reliable information, and saving time in locating items. After weeding a collection of dull or drab materials, you will also find that you have created a more attractive collection and an orderly, neat environment.

In your policies and procedures manual, you should make a step-by-step listing of how to remove weeded items from the collection. This can vary somewhat from one library to another, but generally it involves removing the school identification marks from each item, writing with a permanent marker "Discard" on the items (generally in large letters on the front end pages of a book), removing the items from the OPAC, and finally discarding the items. In some cases the items can be recycled or there may be usable materials that can be transferred to another school or given to an organization. Some states do not allow you to sell the items since they were purchased with tax monies, but you might be able to donate useable items to a nonprofit organization, such as Boys Club or Girls Club. Most librarians have found that it is not a good idea to put library materials into a school library trash can since parents and teachers often do not understand why the items are being thrown away, and it may create the impression that the school library is not in need of funds for materials. It is better to box the items, tape up the boxes, and have them placed directly into a dumpster or arrange for them to be picked up for recycling. For report purposes, you will need to keep a listing of the number of items that you have discarded, and in some school districts you also need to maintain the title and barcode number of each item.

As in other aspects of collection management, school librarians should involve teachers and others in the decisions about what items to remove. Teachers and their students can provide subject area expertise. For example, high school science students can help spot inaccurate information in science materials. Teachers can be encouraged to bring to your attention materials that are no longer useful. Different techniques are used for involving users in the decision-making process about which items to remove. One technique is to display materials with tags on them on which the faculty can check off "retain," "discard," or "don't know" and then initial the item. Another technique is to use the *book slip* method. In that approach, you put a colored label on duplicate or low-use titles. The call number, the date, and a notice of the intent to remove the item from the collection should be clearly visible. Users are asked to remove the slip and turn it in at the circulation desk if they think the item should be kept. Six months or a year later, the staff checks for materials with slips and removes those materials from the collection, following the procedures written in the policies and procedures manual.

Inventory

The importance of establishing and holding to a designated time for inventory cannot be overemphasized. *Inventory* is the process of verifying holding records. During the process the school librarian assesses the physical condition of each item. In this context, inventory is more than mere matching of barcodes with records to obtain a count of the holdings. Inventory, as described here, is the process of examining each item physically and also checking the records for accuracy. A video may be in the wrong container, or a teacher's guide for a DVD may be missing. A detailed examination of materials can uncover problems overlooked during the routine checking of items at the circulation desk.

Some schools close collections for inventory, thus freeing the staff from other duties so they can review the collection in depth. However, closing the collection during the school year is in direct conflict with efforts to work collaboratively with school personnel. Some school districts recognize this conflict and hire library personnel for a period when schools are not in session. In one school district a team is appointed to inventory and weed various collections throughout the summer months. This practice can help prevent the emotional strain on school librarians that removing items sometimes entails. The disadvantage of this practice is losing the insight of the person who knows the needs of the school.

Other districts rotate sections of the collection for inventory, including reevaluation, over a three-year period. Inventory can take place when items are in circulation. Through notations on the holdings by checking circulation records in the electronic management systems, librarians can determine whether unexamined materials are on the shelves or circulating. The size of the staff, the size of the collection, available time, and user demands influence the decision whether to evaluate the entire collection at once or one section at a time.

Again, in your policies and procedures manual there should be a listing of the steps to conduct an inventory. This procedure usually includes putting the books or other materials in proper order on the shelves, passing a scanner over the barcodes on each item, running a report of the inventory to show which items are missing, attempting to locate the missing items (checking circulation records, items on display, or items in an area for repair), removing from the report any items that are successfully located, and printing out a final report. It is a good idea to share the record of missing items with teachers in case some of the materials can be located in classrooms. Also, one can check student lockers when students clean them out at the end of a school year. Providing boxes near the lockers with labels that ask students to place library materials in the boxes can also help retrieve missing items.

Today most school libraries have automated circulation and card catalogs, which makes inventory and weeding much easier. If you are in a school that is not automated, the inventory process will be much lengthier as each item must be manually matched to the shelf list of the print card catalog. The weeding process will also take more time as all catalog cards (author, title, and subject) will need to be removed when an item is discarded.

Emergency Planning and Security

Although hopefully you will never need to use them, you should have procedures in place for emergencies, such as fires, floods, hurricanes, or break-ins. It is important to find out if the school district has such plans and to make copies of those plans. It is wise to keep copies of the plans at home, as well as in a file in the library. Emergency telephone numbers of people who can give advice on how to deal with fire- or water-damaged materials should be in the plan. The plan should also include which school personnel have a copy of insurance policies, and what evidence is needed to make a claim.

Most school library automation systems can produce holding records of materials and equipment, although they will take a long time to print if your collection is large. Copies of electronic or printed holding records should be kept in a location outside the school, in a school safe, or on a secure server. These holding records need to be updated periodically to include new materials and to exclude discarded items so the holdings of the library are accurate. In an emergency, such as a fire that destroys the library, a listing of all materials and equipment can be produced for both insurance and replacement purposes.

CONCLUSIONS

Policies and procedures need to be created for the maintenance of school library equipment and materials. Educating students and teachers on the proper handling of materials and operation of equipment will help preserve these items. Weeding the collection will improve the appearance and use of the collection, as well as ensure that the information in school library materials is accurate and up-to-date. An inventory of the collection is needed to verify that the records in the OPAC are accurate and to help librarians plan for replacement and security needs. Teachers and students can assist in both the weeding and inventory of a collection, but a librarian should supervise these procedures. Emergency plans should also be available to assist school librarians in case of disasters such as fires, floods, hurricanes, or major thefts. Copies of a library's holdings should be kept in a secure place in case such emergencies occur.

REFERENCES

American Association of School Librarians (AASL) & Association for Educational Communications and Technology (AECT). (1988). *Information power: Guidelines for school library media programs*. Chicago: American Library Association.

Curriculum Materials Information Services. (2011). *Average price of resources*. Retrieved from http://www.det.wa.edu.au/education/cmis/eval/library/avprice/

Streiff, J.E. (1992). *The school librarians' book of lists*. West Nyack, NY: Center for Applied Research in Education.

ADDITIONAL READINGS

Allen, M. (2010). Weed 'em and reap: The art of weeding to avoid criticism. *Library Media Connection, 28*(6), 32–33.

Dearman, D., & Dumas, E. (2008). Weeding and collection development go hand-in-hand. *Louisiana Libraries, 7*(2), 11–14.

Fleischer, S.V., & Heppner, M.J. (2009). Disaster planning for libraries and archives: What you need to know and how to do it. *Library & Archival Security, 22*(2), 125–140.

Martin, L.J. (2011). Needing a weeding: How judging a book by its cover can help. *Library Media Connection, 30*(2), 18.

Rais, S., Arthur, M.A., & Hanson, M.J. (2010). Creating core title lists for print subscription retention and storage/weeding. *The Serials Librarian, 58*(1–4), 244–249.

Soma, A.K., & Sjoberg, L.M. (2011). More than just low-hanging fruit: A collaborative approach to weeding in academic libraries. *Collection Management, 36*(1), 17–28.

HELPFUL WEBSITES

American Library Association. (n.d.). *Disaster preparedness and recovery*. Retrieved from http://www.ala.org/ala/issuesadvocacy/advocacy/federallegislation/govinfo/disasterpreparedness/index.cfm

American Library Association. (2009). *Weeding library collections: A selected annotated library collection evaluation*. Retrieved from http://www.ala.org/ala/professionalresources/libfactsheets/alalibraryfactsheet15.cfm

Arizona State Library, Archives and Public Records. (n.d.). *Weeding*. Retrieved from http://www.lib.az.us/cdt/weeding.aspx

Dartmouth College Library. (2009). *A simple book repair manual*. Retrieved from http://www.dartmouth.edu/^library/preservation/repair/index.html

Klopfer, K. (n.d.). *Weed it! For an attractive and useful collection*. Retrieved from http://www.wmrls.org/services/colldev/weed_it.html

Library of Congress. (n.d.). *Digital preservation*. Retrieved from http://www.digitalpreservation.gov/

Library of Congress. (n.d.). *Preservation*. Retrieved from http://www.loc.gov/preservation/

Western Massachusetts Regional Library System. (n.d.) *Weeding the collection*. Retrieved from http://www.wmrls.org/services/colldev/weeding.html

Chapter 11: Circulation and Promotion of the Collection

Although perhaps not always included in the concept of collection development, the circulation and promotion of collections are primary considerations in the management of collections. Policies and procedures related to them are essential to an effective collection program. The best school library collection is of little use unless the materials in the collection are promoted and circulated to students and teachers.

CIRCULATING THE COLLECTION

Circulation Policies

Circulation policies that require consideration include which items should circulate, to whom the materials should circulate, whether there should be limitations on the number of items that circulate to an individual, and how long the materials should circulate. These questions have no right answers since circumstances in your library will affect how you respond to these questions. Such circumstances include the population makeup of your school, the number of items in the collection, curriculum needs, access to online information, and your budget (particularly funds for replacement of items).

Formats

Generally books, with the exception of reference books, circulate to students, teachers, and administrators. Most librarians do not check out reference books to patrons since the concept of reference books is that the materials be available and referred to as needed by persons using the library. However, in some school libraries, teachers are allowed to check out reference materials to classrooms for short periods of time (perhaps during the time that a class is working on a particular assignment). Some librarians, particularly in secondary schools, also have a policy that allows overnight check out of reference materials.

Audiocassettes, especially if they are books on tape or parts of book or audiocassette kits, are also usually circulated to teachers, administrators, and students. More differences may be in place regarding circulation of formats other than audiocassettes and books. For instance, some librarians allow students to check out videocassettes or DVDs, while other policies limit video and DVD check out to teachers. Sometimes teachers request that students not be allowed to check out videocassettes or DVDs since the teachers use the items in their classroom instruction. Such a request was made by the teachers in the high school in which this book's author was a librarian for eight years. Students who were absent on the day that a video was viewed in a classroom, however, were allowed an overnight checkout of the video. If a school has a large collection of videos and teachers do not object to student checkout, then students should definitely be allowed to check out videocassettes and DVDs. Students at all grade levels are especially fond of these items and will appreciate a circulation policy that allows their circulation. Undoubtedly it is an effective means of attracting reluctant readers to a school library.

Differences are found in policies related to the circulation of periodicals. Often elementary school libraries have fairly generous policies, allowing students to check out back issues of magazines. In secondary schools, the periodical titles are usually indexed, and back issues may be kept in the library for research purposes. In both elementary and secondary schools, current issues of periodicals are available for use in the library and usually do not circulate.

Policies relating to the circulation of CD-ROMs and CDs vary from one school library to another. The circumstances previously mentioned, as well as the content (whether it is instructional), will affect decisions on whether and to whom these formats circulate. Although equipment generally circulates only to teachers and administrators in most schools, there are school libraries that circulate digital cameras, video cameras, e-book readers, and even computer laptops to students.

In some schools parents are allowed to check out materials, usually books, videos, and DVDs. Often this policy exists in schools that collect materials that are aimed at parents, and the items are placed in a special, labeled section of the library. Allowing parents to check out materials, however, can complicate automated circulation by requiring parents to have patron barcodes or identification cards similar to those used by the students. In order to avoid this added task, parents can be allowed to check out materials on the students' cards, but if there are limitations on the number of items that a student can check out, this may affect a student's use of materials.

Number of Items

Unless you have a large collection in comparison to your enrollment, you will most likely need to have a limitation on the number of items that students check out. Sometimes a limitation is set to help students keep track of the materials checked out and to be responsible for them. In elementary libraries the lower grades often are allowed fewer books than the upper grades.

In secondary libraries, policies usually allow for a larger number of items to be checked out by students. Some high school libraries have no limitations on the number of items, unless there is high demand for the books that are being checked out.

Teachers at all levels are generally not limited by the number of items they can check out from a library. This is particularly true if teachers are checking out materials that are being used by students in their classrooms. In such cases, the teachers will need to be able to check out large numbers of materials.

Time Limitations

Policies related to time limitations for the circulation of materials depend on the needs of patrons. Usually students in an elementary school have a one-week checkout period for materials, with the date due being the day that the class comes to the library if the school is on a fixed library schedule. Sometimes the upper elementary grades are given a longer checkout period, perhaps two weeks. If you have a flexibly scheduled library and a large collection where there is not frequent demand for titles, it is advantageous to consider a longer circulation period. Some school librarians have experimented with having only one date each month when materials are due, regardless of when materials are checked out. It is important to remember that you want to have circulation policies that will encourage the use of materials.

Secondary schools should have a longer checkout period, especially when books are being used for research purposes. If research assignments are stretched out over a long period in a high school, it makes sense to have at least a four-week circulation period for books. Having less time will result in very long overdue lists and will frustrate students, teachers, and librarians. Options for renewing materials should be made at all school levels. The number of times an item can be renewed, however, may be limited, particularly if titles are in high demand.

Teachers appreciate not having time limitations on materials they check out from a school library. However, it is advantageous to let faculty know what materials they have checked out since it is easy for teachers to put materials into a cabinet or closet and forget that they have not returned items to the library. Most library automation systems allow individual patrons to view which items they have checked out, but many teachers neglect to use this feature.

Overdue, Lost, and Damaged Materials

For many years the collection of fines for overdue materials was controversial. Today most elementary schools do not collect such fines, partly because of the time and effort it takes to deal with the collection of small amounts of money and also because elementary librarians should be encouraging reading and the use of the library. In some cases, parents do not allow their children to check out books if they are consistently forgetting to return books and having to pay fines. Having some positive methods to encourage the return of materials is a better alternative for young children. This might be giving out stickers to all children who return books on time or maintaining a record of classes in which all children return books each week and then providing some type of treat (e.g., a pizza party or special field trip) to the class who has the best record at the end of each grading period. Some school librarians do not let children check out other books until the students return the materials that are due.

Secondary libraries sometimes collect fines from students. Some school librarians and also teachers think that older students need to learn responsibility for the return of materials on time. Other librarians like to have the monies collected in fines to use for special purposes, such as purchasing holiday gifts for student volunteers or developing a special collection (graphic novels or CDs) that would not be possible within the general library budget. It is the author's opinion that even at the secondary level it is preferable to use positive means, rather than punitive, to encourage the return of materials. The collection of fines at any grade level should be discussed with administrators and teachers before a policy is implemented or revised.

All students and sometimes teachers should be responsible for damaged or lost materials. Assessment for damaged or lost materials can be made either at replacement value (including processing charges), cost of original purchase, or percentage of replacement, depending on how long the item has been in the library collection. Some policies do not charge teachers for damaged or lost items unless there is obvious irresponsibility and unreasonable loss. In such instances it is wise to involve the principal and inform the administrator of the monetary amount of such loss.

Figure 11.1 is a sample of circulation policies for an elementary school library. Sample circulation policies for a high school library center can be found in Figure 11.2.

ANY Elementary School Library
Circulation Policies

The following items may be checked out by students: books, audiocassette kits, videos, DVDs, and back issues of magazines.

Students in kindergarten may check out one book at a time during the first semester and two during the second semester.

Students in 1st and 2nd grades may check out three items at a time.

Students in 3rd, 4th, and 5th grades may check out four items at a time.

Parents may check out four items at a time.

Library materials are checked out to students and parents for a two-week period.

Reference books and current issues of magazines are generally to be used only in the school library.

Teachers may check out as many items as needed. There is no time limit for materials checked out to teachers; however, at the end of each grading period, the librarian will send each teacher a listing of materials checked out to that teacher.

Materials can be placed on reserve by teachers if used for a student assignment. These materials can be used only in the library and will be returned to the library collection after the assignments have been completed.

No overdue fines are charged.

Students will be charged the full replacement cost for any lost materials or items damaged beyond repair.

Figure 11.1. Elementary school library circulation policies

SAMPLE High School Library
Circulation Policies and Procedures

The following policies are used to ensure fair access to information for all library patrons.

Students

- Students must present their school identification card in order to check out library materials. At the initial time that a student requests to check out an item, a patron barcode will be placed on the back of the school ID card.
- Ten items (books, videos, DVDs, CDs, and back issues of magazines) can be checked out at one time.
- All items are checked out for four weeks.
- All items may be renewed one time. Renewals can be done in person or by using the "My Account" feature of the library's online catalog.
- Reference materials are generally to be used in the school library, but with special permission can be checked out overnight and are due the following morning at 8:30 a.m.
- There is a one-week grace period for overdue materials. If items are returned after the grace period, an overdue fine of $.25 per day needs to be paid.
- Students are responsible for lost or damaged items. Any item that is overdue for more than 30 days will be considered lost. The cost will be based on the amount of damage or the price paid for the item plus a processing fee. A receipt will be issued. If the item is found and returned in good condition within the school year, a portion of the collected fee will be returned (generally one-half the fee paid by the student).
- Students withdrawing from the school need to present a withdrawal form for the librarian's signature. The librarian will note on the form any outstanding obligations.

Teachers

- Teachers are responsible for all materials borrowed, whether the items are for class use or for personal use. Teacher patron barcodes are kept in a file at the circulation desk.
- There is no limit on the number or types of items that teachers can borrow from the school library.
- Teachers may put materials on reserve for use by their students in the library. Teachers should contact the librarian or library clerk for assistance in this procedure.
- All items must be returned to the library at the end of each semester.
- Teachers are responsible for returning all library items in good condition.

Interlibrary Loan

- Teachers and students may request items that are not available in the school library by filling out the appropriate form for interlibrary loan. The forms are available in the school library.
- If the item requested is available at another school in the school district, it will be delivered to SAMPLE High School Library.
- The librarian will notify the teacher or student when the item has arrived and is ready to be checked out. The process generally takes three to five school days.
- If the item is not picked up by the patron within five school days, it will be returned to the loaning library.

Figure 11.2. High school library circulation policies

CIRCULATION PROCEDURES

The procedures for circulating materials should be included in your policies and procedures manual. If a school library is not automated, then checkout cards and pockets to hold the cards will need to be ordered from a library supply company and attached to all library materials that circulate outside the library.

Most school libraries today, however, are automated, which makes circulation procedures much more efficient. Specific procedures vary according to the library automation system that is used. Generally, each student and teacher has an identifying barcode, which is referred to as the patron barcode and serves as a library card. The barcodes that are placed on library items are material barcodes and are different from patron barcodes. Although the same laser reader is used for all the barcodes, the automated library system will be able to identify whether the barcode that is being read by the laser is a patron or material barcode.

In some libraries a Rolodex file is kept at the circulation desk with identifying patron barcodes attached to the file cards; sometimes the barcodes are covered with a special, thin plastic made specifically for that purpose. When a patron wishes to check out an item, the library staff member finds the student's name in the file and passes the laser reader over the correct barcode.

Barcodes can also be placed on sheets of paper and retained in manila files, with the classroom teacher's name on the outside of each file. This works well for school libraries that are on fixed schedules. In one school that the author of this book visited, students decorated bookmarks on which their patron barcodes were placed. Each time the class came to the library, the librarian placed the bookmarks on a small table next to the circulation desk and all the children found their own bookmarks when ready to check out books. The librarian collected all the bookmarks before the students left the library so they would be available the next time the class came to the library. Students who had been in the school for several years enjoyed seeing the bookmarks that they had made when they were in kindergarten.

Some schools require that students bring their own barcodes with them each time they check out items from the library. This is often problematic in elementary schools in which students are not carrying wallets or book bags where they can safely keep their identifying barcodes.

Large secondary schools usually require students to have their barcodes with them when they check out materials. These barcodes can be placed on the back of photo identification cards that are issued by the school administration or the library staff can create cards using an automated library management system. Having the barcodes as part of a photo identification system is particularly helpful in large schools where it is difficult to know all the students. Unfortunately some secondary students tend to borrow other students' library cards and items thus get checked out to the wrong students.

Usually the same patron barcode is used throughout the years that a student is in a school. If a school library is on a fixed schedule it is necessary for the librarian to get a list of students in each class at the beginning of the school year in order to organize barcodes into classes. If a library is on a flexible schedule it is still helpful to have class student lists so the librarian knows where to send overdue notices. In secondary schools the expected graduation date of a student is often entered into the automation system, along with the identifying barcode number. This makes it possible to retire large groups of student barcodes all at once. It is important that each barcode number is unique until students leave a school.

Material barcodes must also be unique. You can purchase barcodes from library supply companies, but you will need to keep track of the number range that you purchase to make certain you are not purchasing duplicate numbers. Some jobbers will also provide the barcodes and attach them to materials, but again you must provide the number range that is to be used.

In all schools, teachers and administrators will appreciate not having to carry their patron barcodes with them each time they come to the library. Instead their barcodes can easily be kept on a Rolodex or in a separate file at the circulation desk. School librarians can also locate teacher barcode numbers by typing names of teachers in the computer program that manages circulation.

If barcodes are not placed on all material formats and equipment, then separate circulation systems will need to be created for those items. This might consist of paper forms, checkout cards, or for equipment a checkout board, where the names of items and teachers can be written with erasable markers.

Procedures also need to be established for requests to reserve materials and equipment. Most library automation systems provide methods of reserving or holding items for patrons. Reserves for equipment that do not have barcodes attached can be handled by having a large laminated calendar on a wall, where teachers can write their names, the piece of equipment requested, and the times the equipment is needed. If equipment is checked out permanently to a room, it is best to either barcode the equipment or to keep a separate file for such items. The serial number of each piece of equipment should be indicated on the checkout record.

On many automation systems it is possible for patrons to renew barcoded items on their own, perhaps by accessing the card catalog from a classroom or from home. If you enable such a feature on an automated online catalog, then you will need to inform students and teachers that the feature is available to them.

PROMOTING THE COLLECTION

School librarians spend much time and school monies developing collections to meet the needs of students and teachers. Yet in many cases the collections are not used to their fullest. Therefore, librarians should be aware of techniques that can help promote all or certain parts of the collection.

School Library Web Page

One of the most effective ways of promoting a collection is through the use of a library web page. If the library in which you are employed does not have a web page, you should definitely create one. Today's students and many teachers spend large amounts of time accessing information online; if you create a helpful and interesting web page, they will use it. Your web page should be the default page on the computers in the library so students and teachers are well aware of its existence. You can also advertise its use in newsletters or the school newspaper. The home page should be organized to serve many purposes, including collection development and promotion of the collection.

To promote your collection on a library web page, you can feature new materials as they arrive in the library. Also, if you know that a grade level will soon be studying a particular unit, select some of the best resources that are in the library on topics in the unit. Write short, useful annotations on the resources. You can include eye-catching pictures from online sites that provide royalty-free clip art. Spend time locating quality web pages on the topics and provide links to those pages.

You can also offer to post teachers' assignments on the web page under a "Teachers' Assignments" page. You can then direct students to the print and online resources that will assist them in completing the assignments.

You can promote titles by having online book discussion groups in which you list titles of books that can be used in discussions, perhaps selecting a book of the week. Summer reading lists should be posted during the last grading periods, and students can be encouraged to begin reading the titles on the list. Try to make it possible for students and teachers to check out materials during the summer months. During certain seasons of the year, books on holidays, current sports, or special events can be featured on the web page.

If you continuously update the collection information on your web page, it will keep the interest of your patrons. Of course, maintaining a library web page can be time consuming so try to recruit the assistance of students or parents. Parents who cannot ordinarily volunteer during the day because of work or family obligations might be very willing to spend some time in the evening or on a weekend working on web page projects that will help promote the collection.

Reading

Sponsoring reading motivation programs is another excellent means of promoting a library collection. The use of electronic reading programs, such as Renaissance Learning's *Accelerated Reader* or Scholastic's *Reading Counts* will certainly impact the circulation of books in a library. However, if you have some philosophical problems with the use of these programs to motivate reading, you can easily create your own programs or projects to promote reading (and thus the library collection). The following are a few such ideas:

- Organize book discussion groups that can meet at lunch, or before or after school.
- In collaboration with classroom teachers sponsor fun reading contests where everyone has the opportunity to win a prize or the principal agrees to some outrageous activity (dyeing his hair green or kissing a pig) if a certain number of books are collectively read by the students.
- Sponsor a poetry reading event, such as a poetry slam; set up a coffee house atmosphere and provide coffee, tea, and pastries.
- Hold programs on a variety of topics such as collecting baseball cards, making films, or physical fitness; invite speakers and provide displays of materials on the featured topics.
- Have a mock Caldecott or Newbery Award election, featuring some of the notable current books.
- Show DVD clips of movies based on books; have copies of the books and DVDs, available for checkout.
- Encourage your school to have a DEAR (Drop Everything and Read) program for the entire school, including teachers and administrators.
- Sponsor an Evening of Stars and invite local celebrities (mayor, sports figures, TV weatherman, etc.) to come in and read aloud from their favorite books.
- Present exciting book talks when you meet with students in the library or in their classrooms; have multiple copies of the books available for checkout.
- Have students present book talks on the morning news announcement program.

- Make large Read Posters of teachers reading their favorite children's or young adult books and hang the posters in the library and in halls.
- Help organize a Battle of the Books contest.
- Hold a Library Center Preview Party for the faculty when new purchases arrive; provide refreshments and free bookmarks.
- Create attractive handouts or pamphlets of materials on specific topics or genres—mysteries, romances, graphic novels, and books for college-bound students.
- Enlist the Parent Teacher Student Association (PTSA) or a local bookstore to help sponsor an author visit to your school.
- Sponsor a Rock and Read corner in the library, with comfortable rocking chairs and baskets of specially selected books and magazines next to the rocking chairs.
- Practice your informal reading advisory skills by spending time at the circulation desk and making positive comments about each book that is checked out ("This dinosaur book looks interesting; tell me about it when you return it" or "I know another great book about surviving in the wilderness. Would you like to check it out, too?").
- Sponsor a Catch Them Reading program in which you give out chocolate candy kisses to students and teachers when you see them reading books outside the library.
- Create a Wall of Readers with photos of teachers and students in various poses reading their favorite books or magazines.
- Sponsor a weekly Where is the Principal Reading? contest in which a photo of the principal reading somewhere outside the school is posted, and the first person to identify the location is given a prize.

Additional ideas for promoting the use of particular collections, such as graphic novels, or digital library materials can be found in some of the articles listed under "Additional Readings" at the end of this chapter.

Displays and Bulletin Boards

One of the best ways to promote a school library collection is to display items that you would like to have circulated. This can be done in a variety of ways. The glass display cases in many schools, whether in the library or in the hallways, are ideal places to create displays on specific themes or particular authors. If you are not fortunate to have access to such cases, you can make your own displays in the library using the tops of book shelves, tables, file cabinets, or wide window ledges. Library supply companies also have furniture that can be used for displays. The revolving paperback stands are particularly effective for promoting materials in secondary school libraries.

The manner in which you display books on regular bookshelves can promote specific items. This can be done by turning books to show their covers, instead of the book spines. Moving books from very low or very high shelves to eye-level shelves can be effective if certain materials are not circulating.

Students are sometimes asked to create pictures, dioramas, or models depicting scenes or characters from books. Displaying such student artwork in the library will create interest in the books.

Eye-catching bulletin boards have always been a great way to promote a library collection. Creating attractive bulletin boards that feature the promotion of books and other library materials is definitely an art. However, if you do not have that special talent, you can easily find ideas for bulletin boards in books or online. Student aides and parent volunteers can also be of great assistance in preparing materials for bulletin boards.

One of the simplest and yet most successful promotion bulletin boards that the author of this book created in an elementary school library with flexible scheduling was to talk with students when they returned a book to the library and invite them to write the name of the book on a colorful Post-it®, along with their name, one brief sentence or phrase about the book, and a recommendation of which of their classmates they thought would enjoy the book. The students were then asked to stick the Post-its® on a bulletin board that was simply covered with white paper. As soon as word about the bulletin board spread, students came to the library to check the board and see if anyone had recommended that they read specific books. Circulation of books greatly increased during the month of the Post-its® bulletin board.

Professional Collection

Many school libraries have a special collection of professional materials for the teachers, support staff, and administrators in the school. This collection is sometimes referred to as the *professional library*. Often it is the collection that needs the most promotion.

It is important to have this collection in an area that is easily accessible for teachers and staff. If there is a teacher workroom located in a room adjacent to the library, that room is an ideal location. If you are fortunate to have an extra room in your library (even a very small room), placing the professional collection in a room with one or two comfortable chairs, a pot of hot coffee and a plate of cookies, will do wonders for the promotion of the professional collection. If you have no extra rooms, then by using low shelving around two or three sides of a large table in the library, you can create a work area for teachers. The materials can then be placed on the shelves for easy access, and materials that you want to promote can be put on display on the shelf tops or on the table.

School librarians can also promote the professional collection by e-mailing teachers and inviting them to come to the library to view new issues of professional journals or materials that might be helpful in their instructional areas. Presenting brief book talks on professional library materials at monthly faculty meetings is another possibility. An even better idea is to recruit the principal or classroom teachers who have checked out professional books or journals to share how they used the information in their work.

CONCLUSIONS

To encourage the use of library materials, school librarians should develop workable circulation policies and procedures that are positive, rather than punitive. Circulation policies generally vary according to library scheduling and the needs of the students in a particular school. Taking advantage of the many circulation features of automated library systems can save time for the library staff, as well as for patrons.

Librarians should try various techniques to promote their collections and encourage the use of all types of materials. By working collaboratively with classroom teachers to sponsor school-wide reading contests, author visits, and other special events, librarians can promote both reading and the library collection. Making creative displays and bulletin boards that feature library materials are other ways of promoting the collection. Strategically locating the professional collection and bringing teachers' attention to the items in the collection can encourage the use of professional materials.

ADDITIONAL READINGS

Adams, H.R. (2010). The "overdue" blues: A dilemma for school librarians. *School Library Monthly, 26*(9), 48–49.

Brannock, J. (2009). Creating an exhibit in special collections and using it to promote collections and educate users. *Mississippi Libraries, 73*(2), 32–34.

Dickinson, G., Gavignon, K., & Pribesh, S. (2008). Open and accessible: The relationship between closures and circulation in school library media programs. *School Library Media Research, 11.* Retrieved from http://www.ala.org/ala/mgrps/divs/aasl/aaslpubsandjournals/slmrb/slmrcontents/volume11/dickinson.cfm

Enochs, E.L. (2010). Features of elementary school library poetry collections: A collection analysis study. *School Libraries Worldwide, 16*(2), 64–79.

Gavignon, K., Pribesh, S., & Dickinson, G. (2010). Fixed or flexible schedule? Schedule impacts and school library circulation. *Library & Information Science Research, 32*(2), 131–137.

Lippincott, J.K. (2007). Beyond coexistence: Finding synergies between print content and digital information. *Journal of Library Administration, 46*(2), 17–26.

Moreillon, J. (2009). Reading & the library program: An expanded role for the 21st-century SLMS. *Knowledge Quest, 38*(2), 24–30.

Toren, B.J. (2011). Bam! pow! Graphic novels fight stereotypes in academic libraries: Supporting, collecting, promoting. *Technical Services Quarterly, 28*(1), 55–69.

Young, T.E. (2010). Marketing your school library media center: What we can learn from national bookstores. *Library Media Connection, 28*(6), 18–20.

HELPFUL WEBSITES

Lemmon, M. (n.d.). *"Model" ideas for promoting KBA in the school library.* Retrieved from http://kba.nku.edu/promote/ideas_for_promoting_kba.pdf

North Dakota State Library. (n.d.). *Promoting your library (or how to motivate the media to work for YOU)!* Retrieved from http://www.library.nd.gov/publications/marketingyourlibrary.pdf

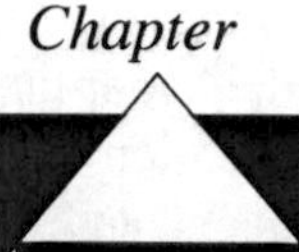

Chapter 12

Evaluation of the Collection

The evaluation of any library collection, including a school library collection, should be based upon how well the collection serves the needs of its users. It should also take into account the goals and objectives of the library program. In your policies and procedures manual, you should include who evaluates the collection, what types of evaluation measures are used, and when evaluation of the collection takes place.

School librarians should oversee evaluation of the collection. However, it is helpful to have input from faculty and students. Experts in subject areas can also assist with some evaluation methods.

Several different methods of evaluating library collections have been developed. Sometimes techniques are used independently, but more often several methods are collectively used. While there is no one correct method of collection evaluation to use in all libraries, three general types of measures can help school librarians evaluate school library collections. Collection-centered measures include checking lists, catalogs, and bibliographies; examining the collection directly; age analysis; compiling comparative statistics; applying collection standards; and collection mapping. Use-centered measures include circulation studies, in-house studies, user opinion surveys, shelf-availability studies, and analysis of interlibrary loan statistics. Simulated-use studies include citation studies and document delivery tests.

As a new librarian, you should set aside a time to develop a plan for evaluating the school library collection. The plan should include what methods of evaluation will be used, when data will be gathered, and what will be done with the results of the evaluation.

WHY EVALUATE?

Those who fund library programs need facts on which to base funding decisions, shifts in financial resources, expansion of programs, and cutbacks. As managers, school librarians need information on which to base decisions about collections and for communicating collection needs to administrators. The evaluation process can reveal answers to the following questions: Does the collection meet the users' needs? Is the collection integral to curricular and instructional needs? Does it provide access to materials from outside the school? Does it include formats that users prefer? Does it hinder or facilitate the library program? Is the collection responsive to changes in the school's program? These questions identify general areas of investigation that are broad and complex. One cannot examine all these questions simultaneously; to do so would be an overwhelming task. However, a school librarian can evaluate smaller issues, components of the larger questions. Before beginning an evaluation project, one must identify what information to collect, how to record it, how to analyze it, how to use it, and with whom to share it and why.

A project to obtain library funding through analysis of school library collections was reported by Everhart and Curtis (2001). The criteria used in this project were the currency of the collection, size of the collection, and the items per student of 15 representative schools in the Baltimore Public Schools. The team working on the project requested and received more than 10 million dollars over a three-year period of time to bring the secondary school library collections up to the state standards with resources that were current, age-appropriate, and supported the school curriculum. The strategy used by the team was to make connections between student achievement and access to quality information resources.

Further evidence of the power of objective data to gain support is reported in *Managing and Analyzing Your Collection* (Doll & Barron, 2002). They also provide directions and useful work forms for analyzing collections in terms of (1) collection percentages, (2) copyright dates of the collection, (3) average age of the collection, (4) collection use, (5) comparison of the collection to standard bibliographies, (6) comparison of the collection to textbooks or periodical indexes, (7) teacher requests, (8) evaluation of a limited area, (9) estimating update costs and benefits, and (10) comparison of information in various formats.

EVALUATION AND MEASUREMENT

Evaluation is the process of deciding worth or value; measurement, a component of the evaluation process, is the process of identifying extent or quantity. We can count the number of items that circulate in any given period, but that information is not evaluative; counting provides quantitative data, an objective measure. The count gives us information about the number of items that circulated but no information about who used the materials (or whether anyone did) and under what set of circumstances, whether additional materials were used in other places, or even what materials were used within the school library. Merely counting the number of circulated science titles does not measure how adequately the collection supports the science curriculum. One must interpret additional quantitative data and perhaps consider some qualitative assessments before beginning to evaluate. The purpose of evaluating a collection determines whether one should use quantitative or qualitative techniques, or a combination of both. Although quantitative data lack the element of judgment found in qualitative data, quantitative analysis does give us an objective basis for changing a collection policy.

Measurement can lead to meaningful evaluation. Professional judgment helps us decide what to measure, whether we can measure it, and how we interpret the results. The process can provide knowledge about alternatives, possible consequences, the effectiveness of operations, and insight into the managerial aspects of the collection program.

Evaluation produces information that can be judged by four criteria: validity, reliability, timeliness, and credibility. If the information is essential to a decision, it has validity. If we can reproduce the information when repeating the same techniques, the evaluation has reliability. If the information reaches the decision-makers when they need it, it has timeliness. If decision-makers trust the information, it has credibility. One should consider these criteria when planning how and when to evaluate.

BARRIERS TO EVALUATION

As with weeding, school librarians can fall into the trap of finding reasons for putting off or avoiding evaluation. Baker and Lancaster (1991) identify five barriers to evaluation. First, some people believe library services are intangible and library goals are impossible to measure objectively. However, librarians who use a planning process recognize evaluation as a crucial component in the process. Assessment occurs in the context of each collection's philosophy, mission statement, constraints, users, and environment. Long-range goals guide the direction of the organization. The process also involves short-term, measurable objectives to guide day-to-day activities. Strategies help us to meet the objectives and identify measures for evaluating them.

A second barrier is concern about lack of staff time. Automation answers this argument. Automated circulation systems provide means to easily obtain circulation figures and to analyze use of a collection. This information helps one see patterns in a school library. Online public access catalogs can help librarians analyze other aspects of the collection, including the number of books in specific categories and the average copyright date of materials. These analyses can lead to evaluation, which in turn can lead to more efficient and effective operations, thus saving staff time.

Third, school librarians may lack experience with or knowledge about collecting and analyzing empirical data. Some ways can be used to overcome this problem. For example, other members of the school's faculty can be asked to help with these operations. University courses and workshops on research methods provide opportunities to gain confidence in these activities.

Fourth, people who are unfamiliar with evaluation may fear the results. The results should be objective data that identify program strengths and weaknesses. The data can help one make collection decisions. An informed manager can use documented weaknesses to gain additional support of funds.

A fifth barrier is uncertainty about what to do with the results. Those responsible for the collection, including those who provide the funds for collections, must be ready to use the results to make necessary changes. The results of evaluation need to be shared and used, not filed away (Baker & Lancaster, 1991, pp. 4–7).

TECHNIQUES FOR MEASURING COLLECTIONS

The value of a collection can be measured in many ways. The following sections describe the most commonly used techniques for measuring collection value. As you read about them, think about their appropriateness for your purposes. How will the results help you present the school library program to others? What type of data will you collect? What effort must you make to collect the data? How many people will you need to assist in evaluating the collection? What will the costs be? How much time will it take? Once you have obtained the information, how should you organize it? With whom can you share the information? How can you use the information to communicate with others? Analyzing measurement techniques with these questions in mind can help you select the most appropriate technique.

Collection-Centered Measures

To determine the size, scope, or depth of a collection, one can use collection-centered techniques. These are often used to compare a collection with an external standard. They include checking lists, catalogs, and bibliographies; examining the collection directly; age analysis; compiling comparative statistics; applying collection standards; and collection mapping.

Checking Lists, Catalogs, and Bibliographies

In this procedure, the titles in the OPAC are compared to a bibliography, list, or catalog of titles recommended for a certain purpose or type of collection. During the procedure, you should record the number of titles the school library owns and does not own. From this data you can obtain the percentage of recommended titles that the collection contains.

Lists that you can use for this technique include specialized bibliographies; basic subject lists; current lists; reference works; periodicals; lists designed to meet specific objectives; citations in textbooks or curriculum guides; or catalogs from jobbers, publishers, and producers. Examples of current lists include the Association for Library Service to Children's *Notable Children's Books*, *Notable Children's Videos*, and *Notable Children's Recordings*; or the Young Adult Library Services Association's *Amazing Audiobooks for Young Adults*, *Best Books for Young Adults*, *Best Fiction for Young Adults*, *Fabulous Films for Young Adults*, *Outstanding Books for the College Bound, Great Graphic Novels for Teens, Popular Paperbacks for Young Adults*, *Quick Picks for Reluctant Young Adult Readers, Readers' Choice*, and *Teens' Top Ten*. Current lists of this nature identify highly recommended titles, but you must determine whether your collection needs those titles.

If your purpose is to measure the general coverage of titles appropriate for the audience served, standard catalogs, such as the H.W. Wilson series titles *Children's Catalog, Middle and Junior High School Core Collection*, and *Senior High Core Collection* are useful. If comparison reveals that the collection has many of the recommended titles, then, presumably, the collection is successful. The more closely the purpose of the tool matches the purpose of the collection, the more beneficial the comparison will be. The collection development policy can provide a basis for judging the appropriateness of a specific list.

Advantages of this technique to help evaluate a collection are as follows:

- A wide range of lists is available.
- Many lists are selective and include informative annotations.
- Lists of this nature are frequently updated and revised.
- Lists can be compiled to meet the needs of a collection.

- Searching lists is a comparatively easy way to evaluate a collection.
- Most compilations have been prepared by competent professional school librarians or subject specialists.

This technique also has some disadvantages for evaluating a collection:

- Some items may be out of print.
- The cost of the list may outweigh the benefit of its use.
- No single list can cover every subject or need.
- Bibliographies cover materials for all ages and may have limited usefulness for evaluating a collection established to serve a specific age group.
- This approach does not give credit to titles in the collection that could be equal to or better than those the list recommends.

In schools where teachers use textbooks or curriculum guides that include bibliographies of recommended resources, librarians can measure their collections against the recommended titles. Teachers appreciate having lists of titles that are available in the school library, along with the call numbers of the materials. Creating such lists for teachers can also alert you to gaps in the collection and simultaneously provide teachers with an opportunity to suggest alternate materials. A limitation of this approach is that titles listed in textbooks and curriculum guides may be out of print. However, newer materials may provide the same content.

Examining the Collection Directly

A physical examination of materials can reveal the size, scope, and depth of a collection. An assessment of the timeliness of materials and their physical condition can help identify which items need to be mended, repaired, bound, replaced, removed, or discarded. An examiner can be a member of the school library staff or an outsider. The latter is usually someone knowledgeable about materials on a specific subject.

School library staff can examine the collection on two levels. The more cursory approach is to examine only the shelves while asking yourself questions. Are some shelves consistently empty? Is that a sign of popularity or improper distribution? Are teachers giving assignments that call for those materials? Does the collection development policy provide for adequate coverage in this area? Do some shelves have materials that are seldom used? Have students turned to electronic forms for this information? This cursory approach takes little time and can indicate a section of the collection that calls for more careful study.

A more in-depth approach is a systematic review of the collection. One examines the materials while considering the collection development policy. If users' needs have changed, a policy change is imperative. For subjects that have low priority in a collection, infrequently used materials are probably unnecessary. Knowledge of the collection policy and the extent to which materials are added, withdrawn, or replaced can help the librarian establish goals for the review program.

Selection criteria such as those presented in Chapter 7, "General Selection Criteria," can guide these decisions. Ideally, such a review is an ongoing process. It is easy to check the physical condition of books and periodicals when users return them. More time is required to check damage to software or audiovisual materials.

Advantages of directly examining a collection include the following:

- A cursory examination can be accomplished quickly.
- School librarians considering resource sharing can readily identify a collection's weaknesses and strengths.
- Reviewing a collection on a systematic and ongoing basis ensures that both the collection policy and the collection are responsive to school goals and user needs.
- Establishing criteria for decisions about relegating, repairing, binding, replacing, and discarding materials facilitates and standardizes those processes.

Some disadvantages of this technique include the following:

- One must consider any materials that are being circulated during the examination study.
- The process, unless computerized or focused on one aspect of the collection, is time consuming and requires trained personnel.
- If one does not consider the collection development policy and the rate of growth, individual items, rather than the collection as a whole, will be evaluated.
- Resources available through cooperative efforts are not considered. If a library is participating in a resource-sharing program where another collection is responsible for collecting on a specific subject, those materials will not appear in the examination.
- People who are knowledgeable about the school program, as well as a subject area, may be difficult to locate and expensive to hire.

Age Analysis

One method of examining the collection is to estimate the age of the information in the materials. This can be done by selecting a random sample of materials and then computing the average copyright date.

The advantages of utilizing the age analysis technique are as follows:

- Others can easily understand the result.
- It is possible to match the result with anecdotal information, such as noting that the average age of the materials in the collection is 25 years and then recalling what was happening in the world at that time.

Disadvantages of this technique of evaluating a collection are as follows:

- It is difficult for one number to represent an entire set of materials. Sometimes it is better to use one number for fiction and another number for nonfiction.
- One must consider how old is too old for a children's collection. Presently, no standard guidelines determine the appropriate age for children's collections.

Compiling Comparative Statistics

Although the limitations of quantitative methods were discussed earlier in this chapter, there are reasons for collecting these types of data. For example, comparing data collected at various times of the year reveals patterns of use. State and federal agencies, professional associations, and accrediting agencies typically request circulation statistics.

Several types of statistics can be used with local, state, and national policymakers. Statistics can be collected about the following aspects of the collection: size, growth rate (volumes added within a given period of time), expenditures for materials, and collection overlap (how many individual titles are held in common among two or more collections). Advantages of using comparison of statistics to evaluate a collection include the following:

- If records have been kept, statistics are easy to compile.
- If the application is clearly defined, it is easy to understand and compare the statistics.
- The method relates directly to the users in the case of requests filled or not filled.

Disadvantages of using this technique for collection evaluation include the following:

- Standard definitions of the content or quantity of a unit are lacking.
- It is difficult to count nonprint items and sets of materials.
- Significance may be difficult to interpret.
- Possible inaccuracy or inconsistency in data collection and recording exists.
- Statistics are usually non-applicable to a library's goals and objectives.

The gathering of statistics is commonly used to compare one collection with another, to examine subject balance within a collection, and to decide whether to share resources or to allocate monies. When using data for comparative purposes, the participating agencies need to agree on the definition of each statistical component and use identical measurement methods. You will need to learn what your district or state considers a statistical component and which data-collecting methods are used.

If the collections in your district or state are being compared, data must be gathered in the same way. You should check for the district's or state's guidelines. Are you to use a volume or title count? If you are to count each volume of an encyclopedia set or each record in an album, the total size of the collection may be distorted. Some districts with centralized processing may count an item as it appears in its main entry. For example, because each school may have a separate main entry, a school that owns a kit containing two videos, five books, and a teacher's guide might record one kit; another school with only one of the videos and one of the books might record two items, a book and a video. An encyclopedia set cataloged as one item would count as one title. A multivolume set in which each volume is separately cataloged would be recorded as the number of individual titles.

Automated catalog systems use barcodes, generally with each volume having an individual barcode. If an item in a kit can be checked out separately, each item would have a separate barcode. However, if the intent is for the kit to be checked out with all items included, one barcode is used for the kit. It is relatively easy to determine the number of volumes in a collection when the items are separately barcoded.

The use of online databases to access titles that are not physically in the school library can also complicate the counting of volumes and titles. Although the materials may not be physically in the school library, they are accessible, and the library budget is being used to purchase their accessibility.

When information is to be used for allocating funds, there is an advantage to having uniform data about the quantity of materials accessible to each student. One could argue that several students can use an encyclopedia set; however, circulating materials, such as kits, are usually checked out to one person at a time. Data that include both a title and a volume count reveal more about the accessibility of materials than does a volume count alone. This dual procedure accounts for duplicate titles that can serve more people for a specific item but records the limit of the total resources available.

Statistics about unfilled requests can help determine what materials to add to a collection. It is a good idea to record requests by students and teachers for information or specific items not in the collection. You can then use these records when making selection decisions.

Applying Standards

In this procedure, the collection is compared to quantitative and qualitative recommendations that various standards, guidelines, or similar publications list. The issuing body may be professional associations, such as the AASL and the AECT, who jointly published *Information Power: Guidelines for School Library Media Programs* (American Association of School Librarians & Association for Educational Communications and Technology, 1988). These guidelines, which focus on qualitative standards and a planning approach based on the needs of individual media centers, note that "Quantitative descriptions are limited in value because the quantitative characteristics of programs vary in relation to needs and program activities. They are, by no means, the sole criteria by which individual programs should be evaluated" (p. 115). The guidelines provide qualitative and quantitative descriptions of state-of-the-art schools, which provide a basis for comparison of performance standards. AASL's *Empowering Learners: Guidelines for School Library Media Programs* (American Association of School Librarians, 2009) notes that the scope and size of each school library depends on the needs of the patrons of the library. However, tools such as reports and surveys from state and national programs can be used to benchmark a school library collection (p. 40). AASL also conducts a national survey of school librarians entitled *School Libraries Count!* The survey includes statistics on library collections, as well as total expenditures per student (American Association of School Libraries, 2011).

Accreditation agencies, such as the Southern Association of Colleges and Schools, are another source of standards. Typically such standards include basic criteria for evaluation of materials, level of financial support, size and condition of the collection, and access to materials. Accreditation agency standards are based on resources or inputs, such as the amount of money spent per student.

Advantages for evaluating your collection by applying standards include the following:

- The guidelines generally are relevant to a school library and the school's goals and objectives.
- Educators usually accept standards and guidelines and consider them authoritative.
- They can be used in persuasive ways to solicit support.

Disadvantages of applying standards to evaluate a collection include the following:

- The recommendations may be stated so generally that a high degree of professional knowledge and judgment may be needed to interpret the statements.
- Knowledgeable people may disagree about the application and interpretation of the statements.
- Minimum standards may be perceived as sufficient.

Use-Centered Measures

Use-centered measures can be used to determine whether, how often, and by whom materials are used. Circulation studies, in-house studies, user opinion surveys, shelf-availability studies, and analysis of interlibrary loan studies focus on the users and the use of materials.

Circulation Studies

Analysis of circulation data can help you examine the collection as a whole, or any part of it, in terms of publication data, subject, or user group. You can use this information to identify (1) low-usage materials, which may be ready to be removed from the collection; (2) high-usage materials, which may be titles to duplicate; (3) patterns of use in selected subject areas or by format; and (4) materials favored by specific user groups.

The advantages of using circulation studies for evaluating a school library collection include the following:

- Data are easily arranged into categories for analysis.
- Flexibility in duration of study and sample size is possible.
- Units of information are easily compiled.
- Information is objective.
- Data can be readily available with automated circulation systems.
- Types of users can be correlated with the types of materials they use.

Disadvantages of using this technique to evaluate a collection include the following:

- In-house use is excluded, thus under-representing actual use.
- It reflects only materials found by users and does not record whether the user did not locate a desired item or whether the collection did not have that item.
- Bias may be present because of inaccessibility of heavily used materials.
- The method is not suitable for noncirculating collections, such as periodicals.

One can use the evidence from circulation statistics to show how well the collection supports the curriculum. Increased circulation of reading for pleasure may result from the introduction of whole language or reading motivation programs. By documenting this increase, a librarian could justify an increased budget allocation for fiction. New school librarians can use this technique to identify which courses and teachers make extensive use of which sections of the collection. By identifying weak areas of the collection, teachers and librarians can work together to identify materials to fill those gaps.

In-House Use Studies

In-house studies can focus on either the use of noncirculating materials or on the users of materials within the school library. During these studies, users are asked not to shelve materials. This allows the library staff to record use of the materials before returning the items to the shelves. You can also request that a database vendor provide you with statistics on how many times students from your school accessed a particular database. However, this service might add an additional charge to your database subscription.

Advantages of collecting data on in-house use of materials include the following:

- Types of users can be correlated with the types of material they use.
- A circulation study combined with the in-house use study about the same part of the collection provides more in-depth information about the use of that section.
- The method is appropriate for noncirculating materials.
- It can help one determine which journals to keep and for how long, which databases meet students' needs, areas in which students need help in developing search strategies, and gaps in the collection.

Disadvantages of this evaluation technique include the following:

- Users' cooperation is needed.
- If conducted during a high- or low-use period, results may be biased.
- Circulating items will not be included, and this may create bias.
- The method does not reflect a student's failure to locate and find desired information.

User-Opinion Surveys

A survey of users and user groups requires soliciting verbal or written responses through interviews, questionnaires, or a combination of methods. User opinions can be gathered informally to help identify users' needs. Examples of informal surveys include asking students as they check out materials whether they found what they wanted and recording their answers.

A formal survey is more systematic and thorough. The formal approach involves a series of steps: identifying the objectives, selecting and designing the data collection technique, developing and testing the instrument, selecting the sample (the subgroup of the population), collecting and analyzing the data, and interpreting the results. Questions that could be addressed in a formal survey given to teachers include the following:

- Do your students have available resources to complete their projects and assignments?
- Do students have adequate resources for pleasure reading?
- Is there a variety of formats to support the learning styles of your students?
- Is there a balanced collection with a wide range of views on controversial topics?
- Is there sufficient access to electronic information and databases to meet your information needs and the needs of your students?
- Does the school library have adequate resources to support your curriculum?
- Does the school library have appropriate professional development materials?

Whether using a written questionnaire or conducting interviews, one can use carefully worded questions to identify the strengths and weaknesses of the collection as perceived by the users. The questions should be directed to specific goals, which may or may not be of significance to the user. Formulating questions that solicit the type of information that you need can be time consuming. Interviews, which take longer to administer, can provide more in-depth information. However, the length of time involved may mean that fewer individuals participate in the process. The results of either type of survey can provide the basis for making changes in the collection development policy.

Advantages of using user-opinion surveys to evaluate a collection include the following:

- The survey can be developed to relate directly to the needs of users and to the goals and objectives of the collection.
- The information collected may reflect current interests.
- A survey can be used for most types of users.

Disadvantages of this technique of evaluation include the following:

- The method requires aggressive seeking of opinions.
- Those polled may be passive about participating or lack a point of comparison.
- Users' interests may be narrower than the collection development policy.
- Designing written questionnaires for young children may be difficult.

Shelf-Availability Studies

To determine whether users are finding specific works they seek, users can be interviewed or handed a brief questionnaire that asks them to identify titles they could not find. These data can help identify titles the library does not own, titles for which the library needs duplicate copies, items that have been improperly shelved, and insufficient directions for locating materials. One may also learn that the user had an incomplete or inaccurate citation, copied the call number incorrectly, or did not know where to locate the materials. This information about the collection and the user identifies areas that call for corrective action and changes.

Advantages of using shelf-availability information to evaluate a collection include the following:

- The method identifies failures that users face in trying to find materials.
- Data on possible changes in library policies and procedures are provided.
- The method can be used repeatedly to measure changes in library performance.

Disadvantages of using this technique include the following:

- User cooperation is required.
- Staff time in planning and collecting data is involved.
- The needs of non-users are not identified.
- Users may not remember titles.

Using a simple questionnaire, a librarian can have students indicate what they are looking for and whether they find it. The results can indicate areas of the collection that need strengthening or areas where circulation is high and duplicate copies may be needed. Staff members may need to follow up on the survey by determining whether students had the wrong call number or whether materials were shelved incorrectly.

Analysis of Interlibrary Loan Statistics

Interlibrary loan requests represent materials people did not find in the collection and sought to obtain from other sources. Analyzing these requests can identify subject or format weaknesses in the collection, identify specific titles needed, and monitor resource-sharing agreements. You should compare analyses of subject areas with similar analyses of acquisition and circulation data to identify areas of heavy use or lack of materials. The results must be evaluated in terms of the collection development policy and existing resource-sharing agreements involving interlibrary loan.

Advantages of analyzing interlibrary loan requests to evaluate a collection include the following:

- The data are often readily available. For example, statistics on requests for periodical titles are usually kept to avoid copyright infringement.
- The items are needed by at least one person.
- Requests may indicate weaknesses in the collection.

Disadvantages of this evaluation technique include the following:

- The significance of the data may be difficult to interpret because it represents the request of only one person.
- Needs of users who personally go to other collections and skip making interlibrary loan requests are not identified.

Records of interlibrary loan requests can be analyzed to identify titles that patrons request. The results can be analyzed in terms of frequently sought subjects in which materials need to be added to a collection. Analysis of requests for articles can reveal heavily used periodicals the collection may need.

Simulated-Use Studies

Information about the use of a collection can be gathered without directly involving users. These simulated situations include citation studies and document delivery tests.

Citation Studies

This method can be used if users of the collection utilize other libraries. If students write term papers or do independent projects, school librarians can check the bibliographies of student papers or projects to identify titles cited that are not holdings of the school collection.

Advantages of evaluating a collection by examining citations include the following:

- Lists are easily obtained from the students' project bibliographies.
- The method relates directly to users.
- The procedure is easy to apply.
- This method identifies works not in the collection.

Disadvantages of utilizing this method include the following:

- The value is limited if students use only the collection being evaluated.
- Citations are limited to the subject of the paper, a small portion of the total collection.
- The method is limited by the number of students who write papers.

Document Delivery Tests

This technique is similar to the shelf-availability study; however, members of the library staff, rather than users, perform the searching. It also carries the citation study a step further. It helps determine whether the collection includes a specific title, whether one can locate the item, and how long it takes to do so. The purpose of document delivery tests is to assess the capability of a library to provide users with the items they need at the time they need them. A typical approach is to compile a list of citations that reflects users' needs and determine the time it takes to locate each item.

Advantages of using tests of document delivery to evaluate the collection include the following:

- Objective measurements of the capability of the collection to satisfy user needs are provided.
- Data can be compared between libraries if identical citation lists are used.

Disadvantages of this evaluation method include the following:

- A representative list may be difficult to create.
- Because library staff members perform the searches, the test understates the problems users encounter.
- To be meaningful, tests need to be repeated or compared with studies conducted in other libraries.

Logs can be kept of interlibrary loan requests to record the requested item, the date of the request, the date the item was available to the requestor, and the response time (days between request and availability). The same type of information can be recorded about the response time for a teacher requesting a title for purchase. Further information can be obtained by asking whether the requestor still needs the item.

COLLECTION MAPPING

In recent years collection mapping has been one of the most popular evaluation techniques used by school librarians. It can involve some of the methods already described. Collection mapping is a visual display of the strengths and weaknesses of a library collection. Sometimes the entire collection is mapped, while in other instances specific areas of the collection are mapped. When mapping only a specific area of the collection, these maps are sometimes called *emphasis maps* or *mini-maps*. Some school librarians try to select one area of the collection each year and create a mini-map project for that area. Often the areas selected correspond with particular areas of the curriculum; therefore it is important to have knowledge about the curriculum. Frequently curriculum mapping is performed prior to collection mapping. To make certain that a collection meets the needs of a school a librarian should relate the collection mapping to local, state, and national standards.

Different ways are available to develop procedures for collection mapping and to graphically present a collection. Today most OPAC systems can create reports that list each item by Dewey number or by copyright date. These reports can be used to create collection maps. Although it has an older copyright date, Loertscher's (1996) book *Collection Mapping in the LMC: Building Access in a World of Technology* can be helpful in

Jane Doe Middle School Student Enrollment = 439 January 2012		
Category	**Number of Books**	**Average Age of Books**
000 General	157	2002
100 Philosophy	142	1995
200 Religion	158	1999
300 Social Science	997	2006
400 Language	153	2000
500 Pure Science	1803	2007
600 Applied Science	1892	2009
700 The Arts	512	1997
800 Literature	304	1992
900 History/Geography	1087	2007
Biography	1601	2002
Fiction	2049	2003
Short Stories	667	2000
Reference	330	2002

Total number of Books = 11852
Books per Student = 27
Average Age of Categories (Sections of the School Library) = 2002

Figure 12.1. Collection map

learning about several collection mapping techniques. Some of the articles and websites listed at the end of this chapter have additional information about collection mapping.

Figure 12.1 is a sample of a collection map for a middle school. This map provides a graphic representation of the number of books in the collection and the average age of the books. When analyzing the results of this collection map, it can be noted that the number of books per student (27) is adequate. Generally a school library should have at least 10 books per student. Also, since the collection map was made in 2012 we can also conclude that the average age of the sections of the school library collection (2002) could be newer, but it is not nearly as old as many school library collections. The sections that have older average ages (Philosophy, Religion, and Literature) are generally those where the age of the materials is not as important as in other sections, such as Pure Science, Applied Science, and History or Geography. This is a collection that has most likely been weeded on a regular basis, and newer titles have been added. Since reference materials also need to be current the librarian might consider weeding next items in the Reference section and replacing them with more current titles. The librarian will need to find out from teachers and students how frequently the print reference titles are being used. It may be a better expenditure of funds to purchase some of the reference titles online than in print format.

Other media formats (e-books, videos, DVDs, electronic databases, etc.) should also be included in a collection map. Quality components, such as condition of the materials, diversity of formats, cultural representation, and diversity of reading levels can also be used in a collection mapping project. There are methods to determine what percentage should be recommended for each area of the collection and how well a particular collection is meeting those needs.

Advantages of creating a collection map include the following:

- A collection map can be read and understood fairly easily.
- A collection map can show the strengths and weaknesses of the collection.
- It can be used to indicate areas that need weeding.
- It can demonstrate areas of excellence and areas of need.
- A collection map can be used to develop collection goals.
- Collection mapping can be used to support the curriculum.
- A collection map can be used as a tool to request funding for specific needs.

Disadvantages of collection mapping include the following:

- The process of creating a collection mapping project can be time consuming.
- Knowledge of the curriculum and research assignments must be obtained in order to ascertain curriculum needs.
- Assistance might be needed to analyze the results of a collection map.

VENDOR SERVICES

Several vendors provide online collection analysis services that make it easy to analyze a library collection. One such service is provided by Follett Library Resources' *Titlewave,* which can quickly identify areas of a school library collection that are strong and areas that need weeding. In order to receive such a service the MARC records from a school library must be downloaded and submitted online to the vendor, who then compares the records with a standard based on award-winning library collections. Reporting on a school's collection areas is immediate, and there is no charge for entry-level reports. However, some vendors charge for more in-depth reports that evaluate certain aspects of the collection. OCLC also provides a *WorldCat Collection Analysis*™, which allows libraries to analyze their collections against other WorldCat institutions.

CONCLUSIONS

Several techniques can be used to evaluate school library collections. The methods are usually categorized under collection-centered or use-centered approaches. It is important to use both qualitative and quantitative measures when evaluating a school library collection. Generally two or more methods are used together to obtain meaningful results. In recent years collection mapping, graphically representing a collection, has been used to demonstrate the strengths and weaknesses of a collection. Some vendors also provide online free collection analysis to school libraries.

The collection evaluation process provides an opportunity to work with students, teachers, and administrators to ensure that a collection meets their needs. Their involvement can lead to understanding why certain decisions are made.

REFERENCES

American Association of School Librarians. (2009). *Empowering learners: Guidelines for school library media programs.* Chicago: American Library Association.

American Association of School Librarians. (2011). *School libraries count!* Retrieved from http://www.ala.org/ala/mgrps/divs/aasl/researchandstatistics/slcsurvey/slcsurvey.cfm

American Association of School Librarians & Association for Educational Communications and Technology. (1988). *Information power: Guidelines for school library media programs.* Chicago: American Library Association.

Baker, S.L., & Lancaster, F.W. (1991). *The measurement and evaluation of library services* (2nd ed.). Arlington, VA: Information Resources Press.

Doll, C.A., & Barron, P.P. (2002). *Managing and analyzing your collection: A practical guide for small libraries and school media centers.* Chicago: American Library Association.

Everhart, N., & Curtis, D. (2001). Turning data into dollars: The Baltimore school library renaissance story. *Knowledge Quest, 30*(2), 58–62.

Loertscher, D. (1996). *Collection mapping in the LMC: Building access in a world of technology.* San Jose: Hi Willow.

ADDITIONAL READINGS

Adamich, T. (2010). Florida power-library schools and the role of quality library catalogs and collections in 21st century student achievement. *Technicalities, 30*(2), 13–16.

Cisnek, M.P., & Young, C.L. (2010). Diversity collection assessment in large academic libraries. *Collection Building, 29*(4), 154–161.

Cox, E. (2010). Assessing student evaluations of resources: Approximation of expertise. *Knowledge Quest, 38*(3), 14–17.

Enochs, E.L. (2010). Features of elementary school library poetry collections: A collection analysis study. *School Libraries Worldwide, 16*(2), 64–79.

Greiner, T., & Cooper, B. (2007). *Analyzing library collection use with Excel.* Chicago: American Library Association.

Griffin, G.G. (2011). Steps for evaluating a fifth grade science collection. *Library Media Connection, 29*(5), 26–27.

Howard, J.K. (2010). Information specialist and leader—taking on collection and curriculum mapping. *School Library Monthly, 27*(1), 35–37.

Hyöodynmaa, M., Ahlholm-Kannisto, A., & Nurminen, H. (2010). How to evaluate library collections: A case study of collection mapping. *Collection Building, 29*(2), 43–49.

HELPFUL WEBSITES

Arizona State Library, Archives and Public Records. (n.d.). *Collection assessment & mapping.* Retrieved from http://www.lib.az.us/cdt/collass.aspx

Follett Library Resources. (2006). *TITLEWAVE, TitleWise, TitleMAP, TitleCheck & QuizCheck.* Retrieved from http://www.flr.follett.com/intro/titleservices.html

Lamb, A., & Johnson, L. (2010). *Library Media Program: Collection mapping.* Retrieved from http://eduscapes.com/sms/program/mapping.html

OCLC. (2011). *WorldCat Collection Analysis™: Resource evaluation, comparison and planning.* Retrieved from http://www.oclc.org/collectionanalysis/

Ethical Issues and the Collection

School librarians continually use decision-making skills when dealing with the various processes of collection development. Numerous collection development issues exist in school libraries today. Issues such as intellectual freedom and copyright have been present in school libraries for many years, but others, like the use of Internet filtering and allowing students to use social networking sites in school, are more recent. In order to make both sound and ethical decisions regarding these issues, library policies and procedures must be in place.

Ethical responsibilities are encountered not only with the selection of materials, but also with other processes of collection development: the acquisition of materials and equipment, students' access to materials, preserving and maintaining the collection, circulating materials, and evaluating the collection. This chapter discusses some issues and ethical responsibilities that involve decisions on the part of school librarians. For some of the issues, there are definite legal and ethical guidelines, but in other instances there may be more than one acceptable opinion about an issue. Therefore, a beginning librarian should reflect on some of these issues and try to read some of the items listed in "Additional Readings" or "Helpful Websites" at the end of the chapter. At the end of this chapter are scenarios involving intellectual freedom, confidentiality, access equality, the use of Internet, and copyright. As you study them, bear in mind the very real possibility that you may one day face such situations.

PROVIDING ACCESS

Access to information involves both intellectual and physical access. Intellectual access addresses students' rights to hear, read, and view information; to receive ideas; to express ideas; and to develop skills to receive, examine, analyze, synthesize, evaluate, and use information. Physical access refers to an environment that permits the unimpeded location and retrieval of information. This involves provision of adequate library staff, access to the library during and after regular school hours; supplying a broad range of resources to meet students' needs in terms of learning styles and linguistic and cultural diversity; use of interlibrary loan; and access to computerized information networks or databases. The school librarian's commitment to intellectual freedom and sensitivity to individual needs influence the extent of intellectual and physical access that is provided to students, teachers, and administrators.

Intellectual freedom is a principle upon which almost all library collections are based. However, when collections are to be used by children or teens, the concept of intellectual freedom becomes much more controversial. Two questions that need to be considered are as follows:

- How does the concept of intellectual freedom apply to children and young adults?
- Should there be limits on students' rights to read, view, and listen? If so, who has the right to impose those limits?

Minors' Rights and Intellectual Freedom

The information you make available to students reflects the value you place on intellectual freedom and students' rights. In the United States, the First Amendment serves as the basis of intellectual rights. Intellectual freedom is the basis of the First Amendment's three major sections: freedom of religion, freedom of expression, and freedom of association. These three rights have been topics of controversy and court cases. A young person's intellectual rights can be viewed as legal rights, as well as ethical rights. The application of the First Amendment to minors generally arises in matters dealing with public education, particularly in court cases concerning censorship.

How does the First Amendment apply to young people and to intellectual freedom? Moshman (1986) edited a book on the intellectual rights of children in which he addresses this subject. He lists the following legal intellectual rights as they apply to children:

- *Free expression*—Government may not control a child's right to form or to express ideas.
- *Freedom of nonexpression*—Government may not require a child to adopt or express belief in a particular idea.
- *Freedom of access*—Government may not restrict children's access to ideas and sources of information.
- *Free exercise of religion*—Government may not restrict children from acting according to their religious beliefs.
- *Distinction of child from adult*—Limiting First Amendment rights must be based on compelling reasons by showing that harm would occur because the children in question are less competent than the typical adult (p. 27).

How have the courts interpreted the rights of minors? The representative court case for young people's First Amendment rights is *Tinker v. Des Moines* (1969). This is the first time the Supreme Court declared a government action unconstitutional because it violated minor students' rights to freedom of expression. The Supreme Court said:

> School officials do not possess absolute authority over their students. Students in school as well as out of school are "persons" under our Constitution. They are possessed of fundamental rights which the State must respect, just as they themselves must respect their obligations to the State. (*Tinker v. Des Moines*, 1969)

In 2007 the *Tinker v. Des Moines* ruling was attacked by the U.S. federal government in *Morse and the Juneau School Board et al. v. Frederick* when the Supreme Court ruled that a school board can place restrictions on certain areas of speech (in this case, glorification of illegal drugs) within a school environment.

Another important U.S. Supreme Court ruling dealing with young people's rights is *Board of Education, Island Trees, New York v. Pico* (1982). In this case the Court ruled that a board of education cannot simply remove books from a school library because of the ideas, values, and opinions expressed in them.

An excellent discussion of some of the Supreme Court cases that deal with students' rights appears in Lukenbills' (2007) article "Censorship: What Do School Library Specialists Really Know?" In this article the authors also report on the findings of a study to determine the knowledge levels of a sample of school librarians concerning what they know about court rulings that affect students' First Amendment rights and how the librarians support the rulings. Some of these cases are summarized in Table 13.1.

Librarians tend to take one of two positions in response to the question "What intellectual rights do children have?" One position, the protector, assumes that adults know what is best for children, what will harm them, what information they need, and how their needs should be met. The other position, the advocate, assumes an open stance, perceiving children as capable of defining both their information needs and their resource needs. The first position strives to protect students from themselves, from others, and from ideas. The second strives to help students identify, evaluate, retrieve, and use information.

Barriers to Access

Common barriers to access include inequality of access. Inequality is caused by fiscal limitations; physical limitations of materials, equipment, and individuals; design of resources, such as interactive retrieval systems; attitudes and practices regarding reference and interlibrary loan services; and censorship.

Inequality of Access

We are increasingly aware of inequality in accessing computer-based information. These inequalities result from factors such as the following:

- More software tends to be designed to appeal to boys, rather than girls; however, in recent years more girl interests have been incorporated into software.
- Wealthy school districts continue to own more computers than less wealthy ones.
- The technology gap between wealthy and poor schools and wealthy and poor homes is widening.
- Minority students may have less computer experience.
- Schools without librarians may have computers, but lack trained personnel who are able to assist students in effective computer use.

Neuman (1990) recommends actions to meet the challenge, including the following:

- Look for software that appeals to girls and balance it with the software provided primarily for boys' interests.
- Provide adaptive input and output devices (e.g., guarded keyboards for students with physical impairment and large print monitors for students with visual impairment) designed for students with disabilities.
- Ensure equitable scheduling.
- Explore ways to use new technologies to promote equity.

TABLE 13.1. SUPREME COURT CASES RELATING TO PUBLIC SCHOOLS

Case Name	Case Cite/Year	Topic	Court Ruling
Tinker v. Des Moines Independent Community School District	393 U.S. 503 (1969)	First Amendment—Freedom of Speech	Seminal case involving students who were expelled after wearing black armbands to school in symbolic protest of the Vietnam War. The U.S. Supreme Court held that "students do not shed their constitutional rights at the schoolhouse gate" and that the First Amendment protects public school students' rights to express their social and political views
Board of Education v. Pico	457 U.S. 853 (1982)	First Amendment—Removal of controversial books from school library	The U.S. Supreme Court held that the school board's attempt to remove controversial books from the school library was unconstitutional. The Court stated that "the right to receive ideas is a necessary predicate to the recipient's meaningful exercise of his own rights of speech, press, and political freedom"
Hazelwood School District v. Kuhlmeier	484 U.S. 260 (1988)	First Amendment—Removal of content considered controversial from school materials	The U.S. Supreme Court held that a school principal acted reasonably after he removed pages dealing with controversial issues from school materials. The Court concluded that "educators do not offend the First Amendment when exercising editorial control over the style and content of student speech in the school-sponsored expressive activities so long as their actions are reasonably related to legitimate pedagogical concerns"
United States, et al. v. American Library Association, Inc., et al.	539 U.S. 194 (2003)	First Amendment—The Internet	The U.S. Supreme Court upheld the Children's Internet Protection Act, which requires libraries receiving federal funds for their Internet access, to install filters so that neither adult or children patrons can access materials that are considered obscene, child pornography, or "harmful to minors"

Fiscal Limitations

Budgetary constraints limit available resources, including personnel. Lack of a materials and equipment replacement plan encourages librarians to hold onto out-of-date materials and equipment. School librarians who automate circulation and cataloging systems or expand software and online services without outside funding are likely to have fewer funds available for books and audiovisual materials.

Physical Limitations

Physical barriers to access limit the use of resources and restrict the number of people who can use them. The physical environment of the school library can create limitations: lack of seating and work space, shelving beyond people's reach, lack of electrical outlets for equipment, or an insufficient number of terminals. Provisions for people with disabilities are discussed in Chapter 15, "Special Groups of Students." Barriers created by administrative decisions include rigid schedules, limited hours for use, restrictive circulation and interlibrary loan practices, and limited student pass systems. Inappropriate or missing catalog subject headings can also inhibit access to resources.

Inadequate Design of Resources

Another aspect of access is the effectiveness of interactive information retrieval systems for children. Jacobson (1991) calls for an evaluation of exactly how children use these systems; such research reveals whether software is properly designed. She describes the challenge:

> There are clearly many issues to be explored in evaluating information retrieval systems in youth services. Until recently, designers seem to have assumed that products initially developed for adults also would meet the needs of children and young adults. But unlike paper-based systems, electronic systems are fluid in nature. They can be adapted and modified; they also can be developed specifically for targeted user groups. Researchers and practitioners have a unique opportunity to influence this process by communicating their concerns to product developers. Certainly, the potential for truly responsive systems is worth the effort. (Jacobson, 1991, p. 112)

This situation has dramatically improved in recent years since there are now vendors who produce retrieval systems that are designed for children. Publishers, producers, and vendors can benefit from librarians alerting them to areas that need materials or improvements. Generally they are eager to receive input from librarians. Regional library and education associations can collect comments and suggestions or sponsor a workshop on this topic at a conference.

Internet

Before the 1990s, the majority of censorship challenges dealt with materials that were housed in the school library. However, with increased access to the Internet in school libraries, one of the main targets of censorship has been the use of the Internet.

The Internet is very different from other resources in the school library in that it is composed of a huge number of resources, many of which provide rich research materials for students. However, the Internet also provides access to numerous sites that a school librarian would not consider useful or appropriate for students' use in the school library. Initially, the choice was an all-or-nothing proposition for school librarians: either provide access to the Internet or don't provide it. Because of the possibility of accessing inappropriate sites (particularly those that were sexually graphic), many parents, organized groups, and legislators challenged access to the Internet in school libraries (or anywhere in the school).

The Communications Decency Act (CDA), hotly debated in 1998, was an unsuccessful federal legislative attempt to legislate safe Internet use. Its original intent was to protect children from inappropriate websites, but its broad wording potentially deprived adults of nonsexual information in areas such as science, health, and art. The U.S. Congress, however, was successful in passing the Children's Internet Protection Act (CIPA) and the Neighborhood Children Internet Protection Act (NCIPA) to address concerns about access to offensive Internet materials in schools and libraries. These acts went into effect on April 20, 2001. They place certain requirements on schools or libraries that receive support from federal grants or the E-rate program, a program that makes technology more affordable for eligible schools and libraries. School personnel are required to certify that they have an Internet safety policy in place and that they have Internet filters to block materials that might be harmful to minors. Schools must also adopt and enforce a policy to monitor the activities of minors. Even before these laws were passed most schools with Internet access had an Internet safety or acceptable use policy. In some schools this policy is sent home for parents to sign, while in other schools parents are notified about the policy and if they do not want their children to have Internet access at school, then it is the parents' responsibility to contact the school.

Many commercial companies have produced filters for the Internet, which, according to the companies, eliminate objectionable materials. A problem with some of the filters is that they do not always work as intended, for they sometimes block potentially educational sites while permitting access to other inappropriate sites. Software programmers, however, have continually improved the filters and have made them much more sophisticated. The filters can now allow administrators to determine categories of materials to block and to allow various levels of access determined by user passwords. They also allow librarians to override a blocked site.

Many states and school districts have passed legislation dealing with the use of filters on individual computers in schools. Other districts and some states have moved to proxy servers (on external computers) that filter all files before they arrive at individual computers. Some Internet service providers (ISPs) also offer a filtering service for a small fee in addition to their regular Internet service fee.

Much controversy in recent years has been about the use of social networking sites in schools. The American Library Association addressed the issue in *Minors and the Internet Interactivity: An Interpretation of the Library Bill of Rights* (American Library Association, 2009) by noting if children and young adults are not allowed to use these sites, they will not learn safe online behavior. These sites are used in many school districts to make it possible for students to work in groups and to create and exchange information on the web. It is important for school librarians to advocate for the use of Web 2.0 in their schools, and to join with teachers, administrators, and parents in teaching students to use the tools and resources in responsible and safe ways.

Regardless of whether a filter on each computer or a proxy server controls Internet access, whether there is open access to the Internet, or whether students are allowed to use Web 2.0 tools, it is important that a school have a written Internet policy or an acceptable use policy (AUP) that includes parental consent on the use of the Internet. It is essential

COMPUTER AND INTERNET STUDENT ACCEPTABLE USE POLICY
ANYWHERE SCHOOL DISTRICT

Introduction:

The District provides computers, networks and Internet access to support educational excellence and to enhance the curriculum and learning opportunities of all students and staff. The District believes that access to Internet resources is valuable to the student and to the overall learning process to prepare students for future success. However, the District requires that reasonable controls for lawful, appropriate and efficient use of this technology be implemented.

Computer and Internet Use – Rules for Students:

The following rules are intended to provide general guidelines but do not elaborate all required or prohibited activities by users. Failure to comply with these rules may result in loss of computer and Internet privileges, disciplinary action or legal action.

- Student use of District computers, network or Internet services is a privilege, not a right. Unacceptable use may result in suspension or revocation of privileges as well as other disciplinary action.
- Student access to the District's computers, networks or Internet services are for educational purposes consistent with the educational mission, instructional goals and curriculum of the school.
- The user is responsible for his/her actions when utilizing school computers, network, and/or Internet services. Examples of unacceptable use that are prohibited include, but are not limited to the following:

  Accessing, downloading, forwarding, scanning, posting or publishing inappropriate materials that are abusive, offensive, vulgar, sexually explicit, threatening, discriminatory, harassing and/or illegal;

  Using school computers, networks, and/or Internet services to engage in any illegal activities and/or activities that violate any of the District policies or rules;

  Copying or downloading copyrighted materials without permission of the owner;

  Copying materials from the Internet and representing the work product as your own (plagiarism);

  Copying or downloading software without the permission of the system administrator or District;

  Utilizing school computers, network and/or Internet for non-school related purposes;

  Malicious use of the school computers, network and/or Internet, including uploading viruses or other hacking activities; and

  Accessing chat rooms, social network sites, or other streaming media without specific authorization from the supervising teacher or the District.

Privacy:

The District retains custody, control, and supervision of all computers, networks and Internet services owned or leased by the District. The District reserves the right to monitor all computer activities and students have no expectation of privacy while using school computers.

Loss or Damage:

The student and/or the student's parent/guardian are responsible for compensating the school for any loss or damage incurred by the school related to violations of school policies, rules or guidelines.

Acknowledgement:

I have read the Computer and Internet Student Acceptable Use Policy and agree to comply with the policies set forth herein. I further understand that any violations of the policy and/or rules outlined may result in revocation of computer, network and/or Internet privileges and may also result in further disciplinary or legal action.

____________________ Signature of Student

____________________ Date

Figure 13.1. Computer and Internet student acceptable use policy

that school librarians be well acquainted with any policies (state, district, or school) that relate to Internet access in their school libraries. Several items that should be addressed in an Internet or AUP are as follows:

- A statement addressing the educational uses and advantages of Internet access in the school
- The responsibilities of teachers, administrators, and library staff
- The responsibilities of students
- The role of parent(s) or guardian(s)
- A code of conduct describing how the Internet should be used in the school
- A description of acceptable and unacceptable uses of Internet
- A description of network etiquette
- A description of the consequences for violating the policy, including first offenses and loss of the privilege of using the Internet
- A statement regarding the need to maintain personal safety and privacy while accessing the Internet
- A statement regarding the need to comply with copyright fair use guidelines
- A statement explaining that the use of the Internet is a privilege and not a right
- A signature form that will be signed by the Internet user (and usually by a parent or guardian)
- Assurance that the policy will be enforced
- A disclaimer absolving the school or school district from responsibility
- A statement that the policy is in compliance with state and federal telecommunication rules and regulations

You can find some actual Internet policies of school districts by searching online. Some of these are listed at the end of the chapter under "Helpful Websites." Ideally you should have your Internet policy examined by a lawyer. Many school districts have consulting lawyers for such tasks.

The agreement form that users are asked to sign before using computers or the Internet in a school should be clearly written and easy to understand. Figure 13.1 is a sample student use form that could be utilized in a school.

Copyright

As respecters of creative contributions, school librarians have a responsibility to ensure that copyright laws are honored. These professional responsibilities include educating teachers and students about fair use guidelines and the copyright laws, placing copyright notices near copy machines and computers, identifying copyrighted materials, and monitoring the use of copyrighted materials. Chapter 8, "Criteria by Format," describes copyright regulations for various formats. The fair use guidelines can be found on websites listed under "Helpful Websites" at the end of this chapter. Copyright guidelines for resource sharing are discussed later in this chapter under "Acquisition of Materials and Equipment."

SELECTING MATERIALS

Some of the most important ethical decisions made by librarians are in the selection of materials. All selection policies should uphold the principle of intellectual freedom for all the users of the library collection. The *Code of Ethics of the American Library Association* addresses this topic: "We uphold the principles of intellectual freedom and resist all efforts to censor library resources" (American Library Association Council, 2008).

Selection and Censorship

What is the difference between selection and censorship? Selection is by nature exclusive. In choosing materials to include in the collection, the school librarian excludes the materials not chosen. Selection and censorship can be differentiated. Selection is a process of choosing among materials. The choices are relative as one item is compared with others. In choosing materials, the librarian strives to give each item fair consideration and makes a concerted effort to suppress personal biases. In censorship, an individual or a group attempts to impose certain values on others by limiting the availability of one or more items. By examining definitions of selection and censorship, one can see how censorship creates barriers to intellectual freedom and how selection can promote intellectual freedom.

Reichman (1993) describes the differences between selection and censorship by explaining that selection is conducted by trained professionals who are familiar with resources and choices, as well as being guided by meeting educational purposes. Censors, on the other hand, look for reasons to exclude materials from a collection.

Censorship can be described in terms of who is doing the questioning, which materials they are questioning, what is being questioned in those materials, and how the questions are handled. Policies and procedures to guide these situations are described in Chapter 6, "Selection."

Common objections to materials include sexuality (including sexual orientation), profanity, obscenity, immorality, witchcraft, nudity, occultism, and violence. Less frequently cited reasons include incest, mental illness, and slavery. Censors state family values and the immaturity of students as reasons for their challenges. The list of those who initiate challenges is long. Individuals include parents and other members of students' families, teachers, students, principals, and other school administrators, school support staff, community members, school library supervisors, library support staff, and even librarians. Groups include school boards, local government officials, and organized groups who share political or religious beliefs.

School Librarians and Personal Biases

Unfortunately some school librarians' choices are colored by their personal values, rather than commitment to intellectual freedom. Setting aside one's biases or special interests when making selections for a school library collection is not easy for some librarians. However, it is necessary that this be done if school librarians are to follow American Library Association's (ALA) *Code of Ethics*, which states that "We do not advance private interests at the expense of library users, colleagues, or our employing institutions" and that "We distinguish between our personal convictions and professional duties and do not allow our personal beliefs to interfere with fair representation" (American Library Association, 2008).

Knowing one's self is a prerequisite for selection. School librarians should be aware of their own biases and preferences so that personal prejudices do not inadvertently affect selection decisions. A school librarian with a strong belief in higher education may be tempted to purchase more college-oriented materials than items for vocational courses. A librarian who advocates online searching as a major teaching tool may be overzealous in budgeting for online services. A librarian whose hobby is cinema may buy numerous materials about movies and equipment for movie production. College preparatory materials, online databases, books on cinema, and movie production equipment are all worthy resources; however, the librarian's personal interests should not unduly influence selection decisions.

When you next visit a school library, examine the collection. Can you detect any bias on the selector's part? Does this indicate the need to involve others in the selection process? One purpose of the collection is to fulfill the needs of everyone in the school. If you sense that your personal views may be outweighing your professional judgment, seek other people's opinions.

Providing Balance in a Collection

Some people define a balanced collection as one that contains materials that represent all sides of various issues. Advocates of this position express the belief that young people should learn to gather and evaluate information; they believe these skills are necessary to preserve democracy. Opponents argue that students need to be directed or guided to materials selected by adults to reflect the adults' beliefs and values.

Another debate centers on whether it is possible to objectively present any controversial subject. Would oversimplification and generalization result? Attempting to be objective may put constraints on the writer who is well informed about an issue and cares about the outcome. Authors who attempt to present both sides may become bogged down in phrases such as "some experts believe." Fortunately, many writers achieve objectivity while stimulating curiosity.

A more realistic goal of collection development is to maintain objectivity by including works that present differing views. Some students may not be aware of the wide range of viewpoints that exist about a particular subject. School librarians should encourage students to seek many sources of information and not stop at the first source encountered.

When examining materials about controversial subjects, you should consider not only content, but also presentation. Excluding relevant facts is only one way to slant information. Word choice and connotations, use of visuals, vocal inflection, or filming techniques may be used to elicit emotional responses.

One benefit of a balanced collection containing many diverse viewpoints is that there will be materials on hand to counter criticism of controversial works. For example, one can anticipate questions about contemporary works on creation science, sexuality, birth control, and homosexuality. One response to critics is to refer them to works that present a different perspective on adolescents' problems. To address this situation, some librarians may select works that reflect traditional, conservative, or various religious views.

Popularity versus Literary Merit

To achieve balance within a collection, librarians must grapple with the conflict between popular appeal and literary value. At one end of this spectrum is a collection that includes only popular items lacking literary merit. At the other end is a collection that contains classic works of little or no interest or relevance to many young people. Proponents on both sides argue vehemently, generating lively debate in conversations and in print. Some say that appeal is more important than quality; others promote the role of libraries in preserving and providing quality materials.

The issue of demand selection versus literary selection cuts across the boundaries of content, format, reading level, and intellectual freedom. You may want to ask yourself some questions. Should the school librarian purchase popular material that contains racial, ethnic, or sexual stereotypes? Should one buy mostly visual materials and software because fewer students seem to read today?

Some people argue that if children do not find items they want in the library, they leave with a negative attitude about libraries that endures for life. Others argue that a school librarian's professional responsibility is to motivate young people by exposing them to materials that will aid the development of their literary and aesthetic tastes. Many people feel that responding to readers' requests encourages reading. Their position is that children will reach a saturation point with a series and will then turn to school librarians for recommendations. Others argue that limited budgets demand that librarians encourage readers to explore worthy works that are less advertised.

An ongoing debate centers on the inclusion of series titles from so-called *fiction factories*, where hired writers complete a prepared character and plot outline (often referred to as *formula writing*). The debate, active since the 1920s, when the series in question were Nancy Drew and The Hardy Boys, is a prime example of the demand-versus-quality issue. Similar debates center on the widely advertised Junie B. Jones or Amelia Bedelia series for younger readers, Captain Underpants and Star Wars series books, the young adult Gossip Girl series, and the popular Redwall series, which are just a few of the numerous series on display in mall bookstores. As a school librarian you will need to decide whether to include series books in your collection and how to determine which series titles to include.

The issues concerning series apply to other materials as well. Comics, materials from the popular culture, and materials based on popular television programs are a few examples. Should comics be in the collection? Are there differences in value among *Peanuts* or *Green Lantern* comic books and comic books that are based on classics? Are these materials more or less valuable than graphic novels or nonfiction presented in comic book form?

Those who say comics have a place in the collection call for clear guidelines for selection. These criteria address the visual art, social values, potential use for language development, and quality of the story.

ACQUISITION OF MATERIALS AND EQUIPMENT

From whom to purchase materials and equipment can also involve ethical decisions. In many cases there may be more than one jobber or vendor who can provide the material or the equipment that a school librarian has selected to purchase. Since vendors are in the business to make money, it is possible that they can entice librarians to purchase items from them. Such enticements might involve personal gifts or free dinners. Although these enticements might occur through the mail, more often they occur at conferences. At conferences vendors frequently offer special luncheons or dinners to customers or potential customers. They may also provide gifts, such as tote bags or candies, at their exhibits. However, one must be careful not to let the acceptance of meals or gifts influence the selection of vendors to furnish the needs of a school library. This is why having a policy for acquisitions and following that policy is so important. Purchases should be made for appropriate reasons: good quality of items, savings for the library, and excellent vendor service record, not because the librarian is able to personally gain from doing business with particular vendors.

School librarians also have ethical responsibilities to the businesses with whom they deal. These include paying bills on time, not over-encumbering funds, and not asking for special favors or non-library funding from the vendors. It is always wise to have written agreements made between the vendor and the school so both parties are well aware of their ethical obligations.

If a school librarian is involved in resource sharing and obtains some materials through interlibrary loan, then there are some ethical decisions and obligations that must be considered. Most of these issues deal with the amount of copying and number of interlibrary loans that can be made. The National Commission on New Technological Uses of Copyrighted Works (CONTU) provides guidelines for interlibrary loans. The guidelines describe the procedures that need to be followed to comply with copyright laws. You should become familiar with copyright laws; pleading ignorance cannot be used as a legal defense. You, as a school librarian, have an ethical responsibility to stay informed about copyright laws and guidelines and to keep a file of information that can be used by the teachers in your school.

If your school is purchasing access to online databases, there are license agreements that need to be signed and should be followed. If your school shares funding for the databases with other schools in the district, then making a single copy of an article for another school is considered an intralibrary loan and is allowable. However, making copies for school libraries that do not share in the funding of the online databases is neither legal nor ethical.

MAINTAINING AND PRESERVING THE COLLECTION

Ethically, school librarians have many responsibilities in the area of maintaining and preserving collections. With tight educational budgets it is imperative that we take good care of the materials and equipment in the school library. Librarians should train children and teachers on the proper care of materials and equipment. Copy machines should be available to cut down on possible destruction of materials when students are in need of information that is in noncirculating materials, and if economically feasible a security system can be installed to alleviate the loss of materials. Making certain that proper lighting and humidity control is maintained is also a maintenance responsibility as is weeding or deselecting materials to maintain an atmosphere of care and order. Additionally, properly disposing of weeded materials is an ethical obligation. Giving deselected materials that contain inaccurate information to classrooms or community organizations is not ethical.

CIRCULATING THE COLLECTION

Besides treating all users fairly when enforcing circulation rules, the major ethical concern in the area of circulation is confidentiality. ALA's *Code of Ethics* addresses this important principle of librarianship by noting that "We protect each library user's right to privacy and confidentiality with respect to information sought or received and resources consulted, borrowed, acquired or transmitted" (American Library Association Council, 2008). Almost all states have confidentiality laws that apply to libraries. Some of the state laws include school libraries, while others do not. Whether or not you live in a state that has passed legislation on the confidentiality of school library circulation records, it is important to try to protect the privacy of students and teachers. Displaying overdue lists of materials by linking them to student names is not ethical. Supplying information about a student or a teacher's reading habits is also not appropriate. If a person asks who has a particular book checked out, it is not ethical to provide that information, but you may tell the person requesting that information that you will try to *recall* the material. Such a recall will let the person who has the material checked out know that someone else is requesting the use of that particular item.

Sometimes there may be legitimate reasons to share information about the materials that a child has checked out of the library. In the lower grades teachers or parents may need to help students locate the books they have checked out. However, the privacy rights of older students, particularly teenagers, should be protected, and any circulation issues should be discussed directly with these students. If you fear that a student may be checking out information that might be used to injure themselves or someone else, then obtaining some guidance from the school administrator or guidance counselor is warranted.

The USA PATRIOT Act (commonly known as The Patriot Act) passed by the U.S. Congress in 2001 and renewed in 2006 can impact the confidentiality of school library records. The law made it possible for government agents to access library records without possible cause and without notifying patrons. Under the law, the government can have access to user circulation information for all types of materials, as well as Internet history logs (websites visited), e-mail messages, and student projects. The Patriot Act expands the ways in which law enforcement officials may track Internet usage and conduct computer network surveillance. Librarians are not allowed to tell anyone of the agents' actions.

Placing materials on restricted shelves and only allowing certain students to check out the items or requiring a parental signature to let a student see restricted materials also infringes on the intellectual freedom of patrons by restricting access to information. Additionally, if a student is checking out a book that a librarian thinks may be too difficult or may contain advanced information, it may be appropriate to provide some reading guidance, but the final decision on whether to check out a book should rest with the student.

EVALUATING THE COLLECTION

Ethical decisions also need to be made in the evaluation of the collection. It is the responsibility of a school librarian to make certain that the collection is meeting the needs of the users. This can be done by one or more of the various methods discussed in Chapter 12, "Evaluation of the Collection." Evaluation should be done in light of the policies in place and the goals of the library. Evaluation should not be done to weed out controversial materials. On the other hand, materials should be added to the collection when evaluation provides evidence of a need. When the curriculum in a school changes, then a school librarian should reevaluate the collection and purchase appropriate materials to support the curriculum. Failing to do so is not meeting the needs of users.

PROFESSIONAL RESPONSIBILITIES

As professionals, school librarians' responsibilities for intellectual freedom and access extend to collection activities other than selection. As selectors, school librarians need to be aware of their own biases. As managers of the collection, they need to ensure adequate funds to support the collection. As respecters of the creative contributions of authors, illustrators, and producers, librarians need to ensure the enforcement of copyright practices. Commitments to intellectual freedom and balance in the collection come into play in all of these areas.

A school librarian's professional responsibilities include obtaining funding that will support and strengthen a collection. This may mean presenting facts about the collection, noting its condition, anticipating replacement costs, informing those who make the budget decisions of the average costs of materials, deciding how much of the budget should go toward the purchase of online databases, or seeking outside funding through grants.

SCENARIOS

Think about how you would handle the following situations and discuss them with your colleagues:

1. A school board member removes books from a high school library because a citizen said the books contain offensive language. Neither the citizen nor the board member has read the books in question.
2. A student who rides a bus to school tells you that he does not have Internet access at home and he has no study hall period in which to complete a research assignment that his social studies teacher has made.
3. The principal checks out some books that have gay and lesbian characters in them. He fails to return them, but offers to pay for them.
4. Your library clerk tells a high school parent that the parent's daughter is checking out books about abortion.
5. One of your teachers is checking out numerous DVDs and returning them the following morning. You suspect that she is making copies of the DVDs at home.
6. The band director is using a copy machine in the school library to make copies of a piece of music that is going to be played by students at an upcoming school concert.
7. A high school teacher comes into the school library after school hours and tries to access pornographic websites.
8. A parent comes into your middle school library and asks that you restrict her son from checking out any graphic novels.
9. The site-based council informs you that they want the materials budget to be spent on online databases this year, with no new purchases of print materials.
10. The assistant principal, whose hobby is antiques, has requested 15 books on various types of antiques and antique collecting.
11. A parent comes to the library to inform you that her family is moving and she needs a list of all the books checked out by her high school son so she can make certain all books that have been checked out are returned before the family moves.
12. Two high school students come to the library and ask you to help them obtain some interlibrary loan materials that will describe how to build a bomb.

CONCLUSIONS

Ethical situations and potential dilemmas of collection development are inescapable. School librarians need to be prepared to face these dilemmas, whether they involve challenges to materials in the library, equality of access to needed information, or protecting the intellectual freedom rights of young people. Every school librarian should be familiar with the *Code of Ethics of the American Library Association* and be ready to support the principles on which librarianship is based. It is important to have written policies and procedures for any potential collection development issue that might be encountered.

Considering possible scenarios that involve ethical issues and discussing professional responsibilities with other professionals will help prepare school librarians for the real situations that occur in their schools.

REFERENCES

American Library Association. (2009). *Minors and Internet interactivity: An interpretation of the Library Bill of Rights.* Retrieved from http://www.ala.org/ala/issuesadvocacy/intfreedom/librarybill/interpretations/ALA_print_layout_1_552631_552631.cfm

American Library Association Council. (2008). *Code of ethics of the American Library Association.* Retrieved from www.ala.org/ala/oif/statementspols/codeof ethics/codeofethics.htm

Jacobson, F. F. (1991). Information retrieval systems and youth: A review of recent literature. *Journal of Youth Services in Libraries, 5*(1) 109–113.

Lukenbill, W. B., & Lukenbill, J. F. (2007). Censorship: What do school library specialists really know? A consideration of students' rights, the law and implications for a new education paradigm. *School Library Media Research, 10.* Retrieved from http://www.ala.org/ala/mgrps/divs/aasl/aaslpubsandjournals/slmrb/slmrcontents/volume10/lukenbill_censorship.cfm

Morse and the Juneau School Board et al. v. Frederick, 551 U.S. 393 (1970).

Moshman, D. (1986). Children's intellectual rights: A First Amendment analysis. In D. Moshman (Ed.), *Children's Intellectual Rights* (pp. 25–38). San Francisco: Jossey-Bass.

Neuman, D. (1990). Beyond the chip: A model for fostering equity. *School Library Media Quarterly, 18*(3), 158–164.

Reichman, H. (1993). *Censorship and selection: Issues and answers for schools.* Chicago: American Library Association; Arlington, VA: American Association of School Administrators.

Tinker v. Des Moines Independent Community School District, 393 U.S. 503 (1969).

ADDITIONAL READINGS

Adams, H. R. (2008). *Ensuring intellectual freedom and access to information in the school library media program.* Westport, CT: Libraries Unlimited.

Adams, H. R. (2008). The materials selection policy: Defense against censorship. *School Library Media Monthly Activities, 24*(7), 28.

Adams, H. R. (2010). Libraries and intellectual freedom in developing countries. *School Library Monthly, 26*(10), 47–48.

Adams, H. R. (2011). The Intellectual Freedom Manual: A guide to protecting minors' rights in a school library. *School Library Monthly, 27*(5), 52–53.

Adams, H. R. (2011). Solo librarians and intellectual freedom: Perspectives from the field. *Knowledge Quest, 40*(2), 30–35.

Allmang, N. (2009). Audiobooks on iPods: Building a program for a research library. *College & Research Libraries News, 70*(3), 173–176.

Barber, R. (2011). My experience with library censorship and some suggestions. *Library & Media, 39*(1), 11–13.

Bogel, G. (2009). School librarian's bill of responsibilities and the ALA core competencies.

Butler, R. P. (2009). *Smart copyright compliance for schools: A how-to-do-it manual.* New York: Neal-Schuman.

Chmara, T. (2009). *Privacy and confidentiality issues: A guide for libraries and their lawyers.* Chicago: American Library Association.

Chmara, T. (2010). Minors' first amendment rights: CIPA & school libraries. *Knowledge Quest, 39*(1), 16–21.

Chmara, T. (2012). Privacy and e-books. *Knowledge Quest, 40*(3), 62–65.

Cornog, M., & Perper, T. (Eds.). (2009). *Graphic novels beyond the basics: Insights and issues for libraries*. Santa Barbara, CA: Libraries Unlimited.
Flowers, M. (2010). Libraries catch up with the twentieth century. *Young Adult Library Services, 9*(1), 35–37.
Fredrick, K. (2011). Creative commons goes to school. *School Library Monthly, 28*(1), 25–27.
Gras, M., & Floyd, S. (2010). Filtering Texas style: An interview Michael Gras and Scott Floyd. *Knowledge Quest, 39*(1), 31–39.
Hill, R. (2010). The problem of self-censorship. *School Library Monthly, 27*(2), 9–12.
Lincoln, M. (2009). Ethical behavior in the information age. *Knowledge Quest, 37*(5), 34–37.
Maycock, A. (2011). Issues and trends in intellectual freedom for teacher librarians: Where we've come from and where we're heading. *Teacher Librarian, 39*(1), 8–12.
Riehl, D. (2007). Students' privacy rights in school libraries: Balancing principles, ethics and practices. *School Libraries in Canada (Online), 26*(2), 32–42.
Scales, P.R. (2009). *Protecting intellectual freedom in your school library: Scenarios from the front lines.* Chicago: American Library Association.
Scales, P.R. (2010). The blame game. *School Library Journal, 56*(1), 16.
Scales, P.R. (2010). *Protecting intellectual freedom in your school library*. Chicago: American Library Association.
Simpson, C. (2007). The debate over graphic books. *Library Media Connection, 25*(5), 6.
Simpson, C. (2008). Interlibrary loan of audiovisuals may bring a lawsuit. *Library Media Connection, 26*(5), 26–28.
Simpson, C. (2010). *Copyright for schools: A practical guide.* Santa Barbara, CA: Linworth.
Simpson, C. (2011). *Copyright catechism II: Practical answers to everyday school dilemmas.* Santa Barbara, CA: Linworth.
Stripling, B., Williams, C., Johnston, M., & Anderton, H. (2010). Minors & Internet interactivity: A new interpretation of the LBOR. *Knowledge Quest, 39*(1), 38–45.
Wu, H., Chou, C., Ke, H., & Wang, M. (2010). College students' misunderstandings about copyright laws for digital library resources. *The Electronic Library, 28*(2), 197–209.

HELPFUL WEBSITES

American Library Association. (2008). *Code of ethics of the American Library Association.* Retrieved from http://www.ala.org/ala/issuesadvocacy/proethics/codeofethics/codeethics.cfm
American Library Association. (2011). *The censor: Motives and tactics.* Retrieved from http://www.ala.org/ala/issuesadvocacy/banned/challengeslibrarymaterials/essentialpreparation/censormotives/index.cfm
American Library Association. (2011). *Copyright: Fair use legislation.* Retrieved from http://www.ala.org/ala/washoff/WOissues/copyrightb/fairuseleg/fairuselegislation.htm
American Library Association. (2011). *Intellectual freedom issues.* Retrieved August 28, 2006, from http://www.ala.org/ala/oif/ifissues/Default883.htm
Federal Communications Commission. Consumer & Governmental Affairs Bureau. (n.d.). *Children's Internet Protection Act.* Retrieved from http://www.fcc.gov/cgb/consumerfacts/cipa.html
Janney Elementary School Library. (2010). *Acceptable use policy.* Retrieved from http://teacherweb.com/DC/janney/Cybrary/h3.aspx
Lamb, A., & Johnson, L. (2010). *Information access & delivery: Intellectual freedom.* Retrieved from http://eduscapes.com/sms/access/cdfreedom.html
Monroe Community School Corporation. (2007). *Policy 2521 IV. Student access to networked information resources.* Retrieved from http://www.mccsc.edu/policy.html
National Council of Teachers of English. (2011). *NCTE position statements on censorship and intellectual freedom.* Retrieved from http://www.ncte.org/positions/censorship

North Dakota State Library. (2011). *Examples Internet acceptable use policies.* Retrieved from http://www.library.nd.gov/internetacceptableusepolicies.html

Scholastic. (2011). *Using technology: Why have a technology policy in your school library?* Retrieved from https://www.scholastic.com/librarians/tech/techpolicy.htm

Schrader, A. M. (2009). *Internet access policies: School libraries.* Retrieved from http://www.ualberta.ca/~aschrade/internet/school.htm

U.S. Copyright Office. (2011). *Copyright.* Retrieved from http://www.copyright.gov/

Chapter 14 The Curriculum

A major purpose of the collection is to support the school curriculum. The collection should be comprised of a variety of materials that can be used for inquiry-based learning and for the needs and interests of its users (American Association of School Librarians, 2009).

The wide range of instructional programs and practices in a school creates many demands upon its library collection. To be well versed about instructional programs, a school librarian must understand the school's approaches to education, be knowledgeable about the curriculum, and be aware of any educational trends that might affect the curriculum. At the time of the writing of this book the adoption of the Common Core State Standards (CCSS) by most of the U.S. states has had a great impact on the curriculum of schools. The CCSS provide a clear and consistent understanding of what students are expected to learn in their K-12 education in order to be prepared for success in college and careers. This state-led initiative is coordinated by the National Governor's Association for Best Practices (NGA Center) and the Council of Chief State School Officials (CCSSO). The CCSS themselves were developed in collaboration with teachers, administrators, and other education experts and were built upon the strengths and lessons of state and international standards. They include rigorous content and the application of knowledge through high order skills (National Governors Association for Best Practices Council & Chief of State School Officers, 2011a).

School librarians are able to help teachers align their instructional focus by providing the necessary technology to locate curriculum-relevant primary sources. Since the CCSS emphasize reading in content areas school libraries must also provide an abundance of nonfiction materials that support the curriculum. This may involve some shifts in budget allocations to make certain that the necessary technology and nonfiction print materials are available.

THE SCHOOL'S PURPOSE

A look at a high school mission statement can illustrate the complexity of demands for educational support. Some high schools serve a single, overriding purpose. Sometimes this purpose is expressed in the name of the institution, with adjectives such as "vocational," "technical," "preparatory," or "alternative." For some schools the purpose is narrowly defined, and thus the role of the school library program can be relatively narrow in scope. More often a high school serves more than one purpose. A multipurpose or comprehensive high school exerts varied demands on the library collection and presents added challenges to the school librarian. In some comprehensive high schools, the purposes may not be clearly defined, which may lead to problems for budget allocations.

In order to determine the type or purpose of a school one should ask the following questions. Is the school a comprehensive high school with both academic and practical courses and departments? Is it a vocational school emphasizing specific job-related courses? Is the school a performing arts or technical school offering special programs for talented students? Is there a nontraditional or an alternative program? A school librarian needs to consult with administrators, teachers, curriculum coordinators, and students to learn about the school's purposes and programs. The school board's annual report to the community can also offer additional insight into the purposes of the school and its place in the district's overall education plan.

Middle schools and elementary schools also have mission statements. Like high schools, some of these schools have specific purposes that can affect a school library's program and collection. For instance, the Mary E. Nicholson Elementary School #70 in Indianapolis has the following mission statement: "Our mission is to inspire excellence in education in a culturally diverse environment through developing creativity in the arts" (Mary E. Nicholson Elementary School, n.d.). The school's library website notes that they have a unique video and book collection that highlights their position as an elementary performing arts school.

A school's purpose has implications for the collection. Each of the schools described requires different sources in its collection. Some general materials, such as ready reference works, may be in the collections of all the schools. In the case of a relatively expensive multi-volume work, such as *The New Grove Dictionary of Music and Musicians* (Oxford University Press, 2003) all schools may not need to own a copy; however, a school that emphasizes performing arts may want its own copy. The full text of the hardback version (plus other music reference tools) is also available by subscription at *Grove Music Online*.

EDUCATIONAL PROGRAM

A school achieves its purpose through its educational program, the curriculum. The curriculum may be in response to mandated standards of the school district or state, professional organizations, and even federal government issues. The standards may call for specific content, establish sequencing of experiences, prescribe the teaching methods, and define the learner. If a school is teaching to specific standards that have been established by the state, such as the CCSS, it is essential that you obtain copies of those standards for each of the subject areas and grade levels taught in your school. You need to make certain that you have the print and nonprint resources available to support the teaching of all standards in your state or school district.

Most schools develop curriculum plans to meet the school's purpose or particular standards. A typical curriculum plan includes a statement of goals and objectives, the content teachers must cover, the organization (or sequencing) of that content, teaching strategies designed to meet the objectives or organizational requirements, and a program for evaluation. Curriculum plans may emphasize one or more of these elements. Each element of the curriculum plan has implications for the library program and its collection.

You should examine the curriculum plans for your school. This may be a time-consuming task since curriculum plans vary in scope, and there may be plans for all subject areas. Some plans are comprehensive, covering all educational programs; others cover specific subjects or specific learning situations. Curriculum plans may be general or give very specific directives to teachers. The general approach outlines the broad tasks of the school and identifies the teachers' responsibilities. More specific curriculum plans prescribe when, how, to whom, with what, and under what conditions teachers are to function. Specific plans may also offer more direct practical information for the school librarian than the general curriculum. However, both types of plans will be helpful guides for deciding material purchases for the school library collection.

An analysis of a curriculum plan can indicate what content or subject matter is required or recommended, when and to what depth it will be covered, and how it will be presented. If several classes will be studying the same unit simultaneously, you most likely will need to have duplicate copies of some materials. In other cases, the school librarian can work with teachers to decide whether certain units can be taught at different times of the year. The curriculum plan might indicate why a unit is recommended for a specific time and whether altering its sequence would be detrimental to the learning process.

Many school staff goes through an involved process of curriculum planning and present their curriculum in a graphic representation called a *curriculum map*. Generally all members of the teaching staff, including the school librarian, participate in the planning. Curriculum maps present data about implemented curriculum, using data collected from individual teachers. These may then be integrated into grade levels or subject areas. The maps offer a scope of what is taught, the sequence of the content taught, the processes involved, and the assessments that are utilized to evaluate student learning. By reviewing curriculum maps educators can determine if there are redundancies or gaps in the curriculum, as well as documenting the relationship of components of the curriculum with intended student learning outcomes. The maps also can help identify interdisciplinary opportunities. Curriculum maps are reviewed and updated on a regular basis. For further information about curriculum mapping, including website links to actual curriculum maps, refer to listings under "Helpful Websites" at the end of this chapter.

RANGE OF COURSE OFFERINGS

To explore a school's unique demands on its collection, you should examine the range of courses the school offers. A high school may offer basic courses in art, computer education, dance, drama, foreign languages, health, humanities, language arts, library media, mathematics, music, physical education, safety and driver education, family and consumer services, science, and social studies. The social studies department may offer anthropology, economics, global studies, and history. History courses may include African, Asian, U.S., and world history. The school may offer courses in agribusiness, natural resources, business, health occupations, industrial occupations, marketing, public-service occupations, and technology. Additional courses may be designed to meet the needs of exceptional students, including gifted students and students with disabilities.

The state department of education in each state most likely has lists of approved courses. This information may be available through the department's website or obtained from the principal or curriculum coordinator.

If a collection is to support a wide variety of courses, it must provide some level of coverage for all subjects. Again, you will need to ask some questions. Is the subject covered at an introductory, advanced, or remedial level? Are there honors courses? Do honor students have access to a nearby college collection? Has a shift in the local population created a need for materials that present concepts in simple English or bilingual formats? How are the subjects organized or approached? For example, is art history taught as a separate course, or is it integrated into a study of humanities?

Extracurricular groups and programs create demands for specific subject materials. A debate society needs timely information and opinions on controversial issues. A drama club needs plays, information about costumes, and ideas for set designs. After school programs require information about crafts and sports.

New programs or changes in organization create new demands. An example is the case of an actual school district in which it was decided to open a centrally located high school library to serve students from all schools in the district during after school hours and on Saturdays. School librarians from various schools took turns overseeing the school library. They found that the reference collection needed to expand in order to meet the needs of students from diverse programs. In another community, students in adult education programs began meeting in a high school during evening hours. They had access to the high school library. Although the students used some of the materials that daytime students used, they also needed materials to support additional subjects taught in the adult education programs; thus other resources were added to the collection.

SPECIAL PROGRAMS AND EVENTS

Often schools initiate special programs that will influence the school library collection and activities. Usually these occur after much discussion and planning at the district level. It is important for school librarians to be involved in these discussions. Sometimes the programs are long term, lasting several years; in other cases a program may be in place for only a year or two. Examples of such programs are literature-based reading programs and electronic reading programs.

In a literature-based reading program, trade books (the types of books found in libraries and bookstores in contrast to instructional textbooks) are used to teach reading to students. In these programs large amounts of print materials must be made available to teachers and students. If a literature-based reading program is used across disciplines, as is usually the case, then these materials must include both fiction and nonfiction materials. Often these programs are set up around thematic units developed by individual teachers or more frequently by grade-level faculty. It is essential that a school librarian be aware of these themes and the teachers' plans to use library materials in thematic units. Figure 14.1 is a sample of a form that could be used to maintain records of units taught each year. The school library collection may not be adequate to support the themes the teachers select; thus, the librarian may need to order special materials. Sitting in on grade-level curriculum planning sessions will enable you to know in advance what types and quantities of materials might be needed (frequently sets of particular titles are used in literature-based reading programs). Such a program will greatly affect the monetary demands on the school library budget. It is advisable that you address this topic as early as possible. A meeting with school administrators and faculty may make it possible to

Unit Theme:	**Grade:**	**Teacher:**
Objectives:		
Information Literacy Skills:		
Student Considerations:		
Resources Required	**Call # or Source**	**Evaluative Comments**

Figure 14.1. Unit resource form

shift textbook funds to the school library budget to meet the needs of the literature-based reading program.

Another program that has had great impact on school library collections and programs is the use of electronic reading programs, such as *The Accelerated Reader* (produced by Renaissance Learning) and *Scholastic Reading Counts* (produced by Scholastic). In these programs, students read specific books with designated reading levels and take computer tests on those books. Thus, there is much pressure on the school librarian to have specific titles in the library and to have them labeled with reading levels. This may not make it possible for the school librarian to purchase other materials that are needed by the curriculum or that would be of particular interest to students. Also, a librarian may have a philosophical problem with labeling books that teachers say are to be read by only certain students. These programs exist with much controversy about them including their effects on student reading and their impact on collections in school libraries. It is important for you to be aware of these programs and the controversy. If there is discussion about initiating such a program in your school, you should participate in the discussions. Share your views on the programs and the ways that they might impinge on both students and the school library collection.

Only a few of the special programs that have been introduced into schools have had significant effects on school library collections. Whenever there is discussion at your school about initiating a new program, be prepared to share your views by participating in discussions and serving on committees.

Schools often hold special events that need to be supported by the school library resources. Examples of such events are author visits, science fairs, and participation in Battle of the Books. For such events you will often need to collaborate with classroom teachers to plan the event and provide the necessary library resources.

EDUCATIONAL REFORMS AND TRENDS

An educational reform that often affects school libraries is the initiation of block scheduling in high schools or middle schools. Numerous models are used for block scheduling. Block scheduling typically involves having classes meet on only certain days of the week, but for longer periods of time than in the traditional class period scheduling. This type of scheduling can also have an impact on the school library. Teachers whose students have not been doing research requiring the school library collection may find that by using block scheduling they are able to have large blocks of time that can be used beneficially in the school library. Thus, the school librarian may need to order materials to fit those research needs.

The increase in the number of students who are being home schooled is another educational trend that can affect school libraries. In recent years some school districts have partnered with parents of home-schooled students so that the students can take part in various school activities and use some of the public school facilities and resources. Thus, there can be increased demand for the resources in a school library. In some cases the home-schooled students follow a different curriculum so additional materials may need to be added to the collection.

With the increased pressure from high-stakes testing, school librarians have been asked to take on an additional role in reading. While school librarians have always had responsibility in motivating students to read, this additional role includes helping teach specific reading skills, such as comprehension, predicting, and synthesizing. The American Association of School Librarians has developed a reading tool kit for school librarians to assist with this role. It can be found at <http://www.ala.org/ala/mgrps/divs/aasl/aaslissues/toolkits/slroleinreading.cfm>. Several articles about the role of school librarians in teaching reading and motivating students to read are listed in "Additional Readings" at the end of this chapter.

Recently there has also been resurgence in emphasis on science, technology, education, and math (STEM) in K-12 schools. School librarians have been called upon to support STEM learning. With the national emphasis on science literacy skills, school librarians have an opportunity to strengthen their collaboration efforts with science and math teachers. Some interesting and beneficial articles on this topic are listed in "Additional Readings" at the close of the chapter.

Other educational trends or reforms that can affect the school library program and collection include site-based management, school choice, distance education, inclusion, and school-to-work programs. You should become knowledgeable about educational trends and issues and consider how they impact school libraries.

ASSESSMENT OF STUDENT LEARNING

With the introduction of national and state standards in the 1980s and 1990s, several states began to develop their own state-wide student tests. National assessment programs were also implemented, with the National Assessment of Educational Progress (NAEP), which is sometimes referred to as the nation's report card. Like the adoption of the CCSS, it will be up to states to develop a common assessment system that will make it possible to allow comparisons across states and to provide information to support more effective teaching and learning (National Governors Association for Best Practices Council & Chief of State School Officers, 2011b). High academic standards and accountability have become the emphasis in education, and much pressure from the new standardized tests has been put on both teachers and students. These tests and the standards upon which they are based have greatly affected curriculum.

Some educators disagree with the emphasis on standardized testing; they have advocated alternative assessments of student learning, such as performance-based learning experiences that involve higher order of thinking skills. The use of student projects and portfolios of students' works are two alternative assessments that are sometimes utilized in schools.

No matter what type of assessment of student learning is used in a school, school librarians need to work collaboratively with classroom teachers to ensure that the resources needed to prepare the students for assessment are available. Many of the standardized tests emphasize information skills; thus, school librarians should work with classroom teachers to make certain students can fulfill the learning standards summarized in *Empowering Learners: Guidelines for School Library Media Programs* (American Association of School Librarians, 2009). These standards include inquiring, thinking critically and gaining knowledge; drawing conclusions, making informed decisions, applying knowledge to new situations, and creating new knowledge; sharing knowledge and participating ethically and productively as members of a democratic society; and pursuing personal and aesthetic growth. The full text of the learning standards can be found at <http://www.aasl.org/ala/mgrps/divs/aasl/guidelinesandstandards/learningstandards/standards.cfm>.

School libraries and school librarians have also been affected by the recent trend of standardized testing, student learning, and accountability. Many school districts have cut budgets for any programs that cannot demonstrate that they are directly affecting student test scores. The school library profession has become much more proactive and has been demonstrating their impact on student learning through research studies and positive public relations. You should be aware of the findings of such studies and share them with teachers, administrators, and parents. Citations for some of the studies are listed under "References" in Chapter 4, "The School Library Program."

DISTRIBUTION OF LEARNING MATERIALS

Another factor influencing subject- and program-oriented materials is the location of the materials themselves. When departmental libraries or resource centers are established to support particular subject areas, their relationships to the collection housed in the school library must be determined. Are the centers' materials purely instructional? Are the materials considered part of the school library collection, but housed conveniently near the classrooms?

Another pattern of housing occurs when materials are stored in the classroom or teaching areas where they are used most frequently. For instance, cookbooks might be housed in a family and consumer services classroom or materials on woodworking could be in a woodworking shop. A tour of the school helps you identify the distribution pattern. If materials are not housed in the school library, you need to determine who is responsible for them. You may need to ask some additional questions. What are the circulation procedures? Who is responsible for inventory, maintenance, and control? Have the materials been entered on the OPAC? Are separate funds used to buy these materials, or are they purchased with school library funds?

PROFESSIONAL COLLECTION

You will also need to provide professional resources for staff members in your school. Staff members include people with teaching responsibilities, as well as those who work with students in other ways: administrators, guidance counselors, social workers, nurses, speech therapists, aides, secretaries, and technical staff. The portion of the collection designated to fulfill these people's needs is usually called the *professional collection.* Frequently a professional collection is housed in a specified area in the school library; other times the collection is in a separate room, such as a teacher workroom. The professional collection should be placed in a location that is convenient for teachers and where it can get adequate exposure.

As is true with the rest of the collection, a variety of formats and resources should be available. If the collection does not contain the materials the school staff needs for their professional duties, then the school librarian should know where one can obtain those materials.

Some of the resources that compose a professional collection should relate to the student standards for the various subjects. If a school is participating in special programs, such as block scheduling, literature-based reading, or distance education, then the materials dealing with those programs should be in the professional collection.

Resources for Particular Grade Levels

Resources are also available that will assist teachers at the various grade levels. People who are responsible for preschoolers will find Barbara Taylor's *A Child Goes Forth: A Curriculum Guide for Preschool Children*, 10th edition (Prentice Hall Career & Technology Division, 2003) to be a helpful guide for selecting materials and activities for young children. *A to Zoo: Subject Access to Children's Picture Books*, 8th edition (Libraries Unlimited, 2010) by Carolyn W. and Rebecca L. Thomas can assist preschool and primary-level teachers in locating picture books about particular topics.

Teachers in elementary or middle schools that utilize thematic units for instruction will especially appreciate a subscription to *Book Links: Connecting Books, Libraries, and Classrooms* (American Library Association), which reviews old and new materials for individual units and provides suggestions for using the materials with children. *Weaving the Literacy Web: Creating Curriculum Based on Books Children Love* (Redleaf Press, 2005) by Hope Vestergard provides information relating to book-based webbing with young children. Cora M. Wright's *More Hot Links: Linking Literature with the Middle School Curriculum* (Libraries Unlimited, 2002), which is arranged by categories and curriculum areas, is another useful source for teachers using thematic units or literature across the curriculum.

Literature and Genre Materials

Survey books about children's and young adult literature can be helpful to teachers and school librarians as they work with students in classrooms and in the school library. *Huck's Children's Literature in the Elementary School,* 9th edition (McGraw-Hill Humanities/Social Sciences/Languages, 2006) by Barbara Kiefer, Janet Hickman, and Susan Hepler is a classic survey of children's literature. More recent titles relating to Huck's book are *Charlotte Huck's Children's Literature*, 10th edition (McGraw Hill, 2010) by Charlotte S. Huck and Kiefer and *Charlotte Huck's Children's Literature: A Brief Guide* (McGraw Hill, 2010) by Huck, Cynthia A. Tyson, and Kiefer. A smaller book focusing on literary aspects is Rebecca J. Lukens's *A Critical Handbook of Children's Literature*, 9th edition (Allyn & Bacon, 2012). The second part of each chapter in Donna and Saundra Norton's *Through the Eyes of a Child*, 8th edition (Prentice Hall, 2010) includes activities on how to use each genre of children's literature in the classroom, while the first part deals with the books themselves. Carol Lynch-Brown and Carl M. Tomlinson's *Essentials of Children's Literature*, 7th edition (Allyn & Bacon, 2011) interweaves the history of each genre with the selection and evaluation of such materials. Their chapter on multicultural and international literature is particularly useful. Catherine Barr and John T. Gillespie's *Best Books for Children: Preschool Through Grade 6*, 9th edition (Libraries Unlimited, 2012), their *Best Books for Middle School and Junior High Readers*, 2nd edition (Libraries Unlimited, 2011), the authors' *Best Books for High School Readers*, 2nd edition (Libraries Unlimited, 2009), and their *Best Books for High School Readers, Supplement to the 2nd edition* (Libraries Unlimited, 2011) are all useful tools that include lively annotations for numerous titles.

Elementary classroom teachers dealing with the genre of picture books will find over 200 books organized into categories in Patricia J. Cianciola's *Informational Picture Books for Children* (American Library Association, 2000). *Popular Series Fiction for K-6 Readers: A Reading and Selection Guide*, 2nd edition (Libraries Unlimited, 2008) by Rebecca L. Thomas and Catherine Barr, covers selected series books, which are annotated and arranged alphabetically by the series name.

You will want to include award-winning books in your collections for teachers to use. *Newbery and Caldecott Awards: A Guide to the Medal and Honor Books* (American Library Association, 2011) provides annotations for all the winning and honor titles since the inception of the awards. Other books that are award-winning titles can be found in Chapter 15 "Special Groups of Students."

Teachers interested in working with particular genres will find *Genreflecting: A Guide to Popular Reading Interests*, 6th edition (Libraries Unlimited, 2005) by Diana Tixier Herald and Wayne A. Wiegand valuable as it contains over 5,000 titles. Herald's *Teen Genreflecting*, 2nd edition (Libraries Unlimited, 2003) is a well-organized resource that can be used as a reading advisory tool for middle school and high school students. Christine Meloni's *Teen Chick Lit* (Libraries Unlimited, 2009) provides a bibliography of over 500 titles of the genre, with annotations and grade levels included. Ruth Nadelman Lynn's comprehensive guide *Fantasy Literature for Children and Young Adults*, 5th edition (Libraries Unlimited, 2005) can be especially helpful in recommending titles for young readers. Although it does not cover recent titles *Junior Genreflecting: A Guide to Good Reads and Series Fiction for Children* (Libraries Unlimited, 2000) by Bridget Dealy Volz, Lynda Blackburn Welborn, and Cheryl Perkins Scheer describes titles for upper elementary and middle school students.

Specific Subject Areas

A few books are designed to connect literature and specific subject areas. These books are especially helpful to teachers who want to have their students use school library resources. Lynda G. Adamson has written several books that connect literature to history. Her most recent book *Thematic Guide to Popular Nonfiction* (Greenwood, 2006) groups nonfiction books into themes, such as "American Dream" and "Race Relations." *Gotcha Good!* (Libraries Unlimited, 2008) by Kathleen A. Baxter and Marcia A, Kochel includes high-interest nonfiction books for grades 3–8 intended to get children excited about reading. Melissa Rabey's *Historical Fiction for Teens* (Libraries Unlimited) lists over 300 annotated titles of historical fiction that are organized by subgenres and themes. Carol M. and John W. Butzow's *Science Through Children's Literature: An Integrated Approach*, 2nd edition (Libraries Unlimited, 2000) includes 30 instructional units that integrate children's literature into science activities.

Teachers and school librarians who work in schools that specialize in the fine arts have other needs. Titles such as *Halliwell's Film Video and DVD Guide 2008*, 23rd edition (HarperCollins, 2007) and the website *Contemporary Drama Service* <http://contempo

rarydramanewsletter.contemporarydrama.com/public/item/203194> might be useful resources for such teachers and school librarians. *Television Production*, 2nd edition (Libraries Unlimited, 2004) by Keith Kyker and Christopher Curchy is an excellent choice for teachers or school librarians who teach television production in secondary schools.

Journals produced by professional organizations provide worthwhile information. Many carry reviews and produce bibliographies. Titles you might consider for a professional collection are *Language Arts, School Talk*, and *English Journal* (National Council of Teachers of English), *American Music Teacher* (Music Teachers National Association), *Educational Leadership* (Association for Supervision and Curriculum Development), *History Teacher* (Society for History Education), *Journal of Geography* (National Council for Geographic Education), *Journal of Family & Consumer Services* (American Association of Family & Consumer Sciences), *Journal of Physical Education, Recreation & Dance* (American Alliance for Health, Physical Education, Recreation, and Dance), *Teaching Children Mathematics, Mathematics Teaching in the Middle School*, and *Mathematics Teacher* (National Council of Teachers of Mathematics), *Reading Teacher* and *Journal of Adolescent & Adult Literacy* (International Reading Association), *Science* and *S B & F Science Books and Films* (American Association for the Advancement of Science), *Science & Children, Science Scope,* and *The Science Teacher* (National Science Teachers Association), and *Social Studies and the Young Learner* and *Social Education* (National Council for the Social Studies). Several of the associations have journals specific to either elementary, middle, or high schools so you should select the journals that are most appropriate for the level of your school.

CONCLUSIONS

A school librarian is responsible for ensuring that a collection meets a school's curricular and instructional needs. To carry out this responsibility, one must be knowledgeable about the purpose of the school and the curriculum. A school librarian should be aware of conditions for use of materials, including who will use the resources and for what purposes. As curricula and teaching methods change, librarians must reevaluate items in the collection in terms of how effectively the resources contribute to the teaching and learning process. Standardized testing, educational reforms, extracurricular activities, special events, and programs adopted by a school can also affect a school library collection.

School librarians should provide a professional collection for the school staff so classroom teachers are able to obtain materials that support their instruction. They should have a budget that can be used to purchase some of the resources described in this chapter. Through cooperative efforts, teachers and school librarians can make selection decisions that will meet the school's curricular needs.

As school librarians get caught up in the day-to-day administrative activities and are busy coping with technological advances, they should not forget that the common goal shared by educators is to create an effective environment for the educational experience.

REFERENCES

American Association of School Librarians. (2009). *Empowering learners: Guidelines for school library media programs*. Chicago: American Library Association.

Mary E. Nicholson Elementary School. (n.d.). *About us.* Retrieved from http://www.70.ips.k12.in.us/index.php?id = 7888

National Governors Association for Best Practices Council & Chief of State School Officers. (2011a). *About the standards.* Retrieved from http://www.corestandards.org/about-the-standards

National Governors Association for Best Practices Council & Chief of State School Officers. (2011b). *Frequently asked questions.* Retrieved from http://www.corestandards.org/frequently-asked-questions

ADDITIONAL READINGS

Anderson, C. (2009). The five pillars of reading. *Library Media Connection, 28*(2), 22–25.

Bateman-Whitson, J. (2011). From refuse to refuge: Create a game plan for your library to encourage reading. *Knowledge Quest, 39*(4), 16–21.

Beckham, S. (2011). Promoting the joy of reading without killing it. *Knowledge Quest, 39*(4), 50–54.

Bishop, K. (2011). *Connecting libraries with classrooms: The curricular roles of the school librarian* (2nd ed.). Santa Barbara, CA: Linworth.

Carter, B. (2007). Leading forward by looking backward. *Library Media Connection, 25*(4), 16–20.

Clark, R. C. (2011). Readicide—killing the love of reading in our schools. *Knowledge Quest, 39*(4), 6–9.

Cregar, Elyse. (2011). Browsing by numbers and reading for points. *Knowledge Quest, 39*(4), 40–45.

Diekema, A. R., Leary, H., Haderlie, S., & Walters, C. D. (2011). Teaching use of digital primary sources for K-12 settings. *D-Lib Magazine, 17*(3/4). Retrieved from http://www.dlib.org/dlib/march11/diekema/03diekema.html

Donham, J. (2010). Enduring understandings—where are they in the library's curriculum? *Teacher Librarian, 38*(1), 15–19.

Eecegovac, Z. (2012). Letting students use Web 2.0 tools: To hook one another on reading. *Knowledge Quest, 40*(3), 36–39.

Fiefer, C. (2011). Achieving a standard of reading excellence in Kansas. *Knowledge Quest, 39*(4), 60–67.

Fontichiaro, K. (Ed.). (2009). *21st-century learning in school libraries.* Santa Barbara, CA: Libraries Unlimited.

Franklin, P., & Stephens, C. G. (2009). Use standards to draw curriculum maps. *School Library Media Activities Monthly, 25*(9), 44–45.

Frazier, D. (2010). School library media collaborations: Benefits and barriers. *Knowledge Quest, 39*(4), 34–36.

Friesen, S. (2010). Uncomfortable bedfellows: Discipline-based inquiry and standardized examinations. *Teacher Librarian, 38*(1), 8–14.

Glass, K. T. (2007). *Curriculum mapping: A step-by-step guide for creating curriculum year overviews.* Thousand Oaks, CA: Corwin Press.

Hanks, L. Q. (2011). Updating the professional collection at the Dan River Middle School Library. *PNLA Quarterly, 75*(2), 41–46.

Hill, R. (2011). Common Core curriculum and complex texts. *Teacher Librarian, 38*(3), 42–46.

Howard, J. K. (2010). Information specialist and leader—taking on collection and curriculum mapping. *School Library Monthly, 27*(1), 35–37.

Hughes-Hassell, S., & Harada, V. H. (2007). *School reform and the school library media specialist.* Westport, CT: Libraries Unlimited.

Jaeger, P. (2012). Complex text, reading, and rigor using technology to support the dramatic changes in the Common Core State Standards. *Library Media Connection, 30*(5), 30–32.

Jaeger, P. (2012). Transliteracy—new library lingo and what it means for instruction. *Library Media Connection, 30*(2), 44–47.

Kelsey, M. (2011). Compel students to read with compelling nonfiction. *Knowledge Quest, 39*(4), 34–39.

Kimmel, S.C. (2011). The school library: A space for mathematical thinking, learning, and sharing. *Library Media Connection, 30*(3), 26–28.

Klock, J. (2010). Building novel connections in an increasingly standardized world. *Teacher Librarian, 38*(2), 15–18.

Kramer, P.K. (2011). Common Core and school librarians: An interview with Joyce Karon. *School Library Monthly, 28*(1), 8–10.

Lamb, A., & Johnson, L. (2011). Nurturing a new breed of reader: Five real world issues. *Teacher Librarian, 39*(1), 56–63.

Loertscher, D.V., & Marcoux, E. (2010). The Common Core Standards: Opportunities for teacher-librarians to move to the center of teaching and learning. *Teacher Librarian, 38*(2), 8–14.

Mardis, M. (2009). You've got the hook: Droppin' science on school libraries and the future of learning. *Library Media Connection, 28*(3), 10–13.

Mardis, M., & Howe, K. (2010). STEM for our students: Content to co-conspiracy? *Knowledge Quest, 39*(2), 8–11.

Mayer, M.W., & Williams, M. (2011). Personal programming. *Knowledge Quest, 39*(4), 68–73.

McLean, L. (2010). Cook up curriculum with Content Clips. *Knowledge Quest, 39*(2), 47.

Mcllvain, E. (2010). NSDL as a teacher empower point: Expanding capacity for classroom integration of digital resources. *Knowledge Quest, 39*(2), 54–63.

Meloni, C. (2009). *Teen chick lit.* Santa Barbara, CA: Libraries Unlimited.

Montiel-Overall, P., & Jones, P. (2011). Teacher and school librarian collaboration: A preliminary report of teachers' perceptions about frequency and importance to student learning. *Canadian Journal of Information and Library Science, 35*(1), 49–76.

Moreillon, J. (2009). Reading & the library program: An expanded role for the 21st-century SLMS. *Knowledge Quest, 38*(2), 24–30.

Nelson, C. (2011). Educate the masses, educate yourselves: The school librarian and educational technology. *Library Media Connection, 29*(5), 18.

Pfeiffer, C. (2011). Achieving a standard of reading excellence in Kansas. *Knowledge Quest, 39*(4), 60–67.

Schultz-Jones. (2010). School librarians, science teachers, + optimal learning environments. *Knowledge Quest, 39*(2), 12–17.

Small, R.V., & Arnone, M.P. (2011). Creative reading: The antidote to readicide. *Knowledge Quest, 39*(4), 12–15.

Solley, K. (2011). Accelerated Reader can be an effective tool to encourage and bolster student reading. *Knowledge Quest, 39*(4), 46–49.

Tinkle, C. (2009). Reading for meaning: Synthesis. *School Library Media Activities Monthly, 25*(7), 49–51.

Torrise, M.L. (2010). Role of the library media specialist in greening the curriculum: A community-based approach to teaching 21st century skills outside the school library through practice of urban agriculture. *Library Media Connection, 28*(4), 18–20.

Van Orden, P.J., & Strong, S. (2007). *Children's books: A practical guide to selection.* New York: Neal-Schuman.

Vardell, S.M. (2008). *Children's literature in action: A librarian's guide.* Westport, CT: Libraries Unlimited.

Zmuda, A., & Harada, V.H. (2008). *Librarians as learning specialists: Meeting the learning imperative for the 21st century.* Westport, CT: Libraries Unlimited.

HELPFUL WEBSITES

American Association of School Librarians. (2011). *School librarian's role in reading toolkit.* Retrieved from http://www.ala.org/ala/mgrps/divs/aasl/aaslissues/toolkits/slroleinreading.cfm

American Association of School Librarians. (2011). *Standards for the 21st-century learner.* Retrieved from http://www.ala.org/ala/mgrps/divs/aasl/guidelinesandstandards/learningstandards/standards.cfm

Bertland, L. (n.d.). *Resources for school librarians: Information skills instruction.* Retrieved from http://www.sldirectory.com/libsf/resf/libplans.html

Carvin, A. (n.d.). *Trends in education reform.* Retrieved from http://www.edwebproject.org/edref.html

Common Core State Standards Initiative. (2010). *Common standards.* Retrieved from http://www.corestandards.org/

Core Knowledge Foundation. (2011). *Core knowledge.* Retrieved from http://www.coreknowledge.org/ccss

Education World. (2011). *Curriculum mapping.* Retrieved from http://www.educationworld.com/a_curr/virtualwkshp/curriculum_mapping.shtml

Education World. (2011). *National standards.* Retrieved http://www.educationworld.com/standards/national/

H.W. Wilson. (n.d.). *School-libraries.net: Web pages created by school librarians.* Retrieved from http://www.school-libraries.net/

New South Wales Department of Education and Training. (2011). *School libraries & information literacy.* Retrieved from http://www.curriculumsupport.education.nsw.gov.au/schoollibraries/index.htm

TeachingBooks.net LLC. (2011).*Welcome to TeachingBooks.net.* Retrieved from http://www.teachingbooks.net/home/

Wisconsin Department of Public Instruction. (2009). *Library media programs and connecting the curriculum.* Retrieved from http://www.dpi.state.wi.us/imt/lmcctc.html

Chapter

Special Groups of Students

One of the primary purposes of school libraries is to meet the needs of all students in a school. Thus, it is important to understand and address the needs of special groups of students. Trends in our society and in public education in the past few decades have resulted in many more students designated as having special needs. Some of these trends include the mainstreaming or inclusion of students with disabilities; acknowledgment that gifted and talented students have specific needs; an increase in ethnic and cultural diversity in the population, including the addition of large numbers of families whose first language is not English; a decrease in some student reading test scores; recognition of gay and lesbians in society; and the inclusion of preschool programs in some public schools.

Although each person is unique, some students are part of groups sharing characteristics that require special consideration in the collection. Meeting the needs of special groups of students affects selection of resources, as well as accessibility of materials. Consideration of the needs of these students can also impact circulation policies.

STUDENTS WITH DISABILITIES

People with special needs based on disabilities may not only be students, but also teachers and staff members. Not until the author of this book had a paraplegic teacher join the faculty at the high school where she was a librarian did she realize the physical access problems in the school's library. School librarians should have as one of their goals to ensure that students, teachers, and staff members with disabilities have access to both print and electronic resources. The following discussion provides basic information about different types of disabilities and identifies resources that can be helpful to librarians, teachers, other staff members, parents, and caregivers.

Two pieces of national legislation of particular relevance for this discussion are the Education for All Handicapped Children Act of 1975 (Public Law 94-142), now called the Individuals with Disabilities Education Act (IDEA), and the ADA (Public Law 101-336).

IDEA addresses the needs of the child and calls for an individualized education program (IEP) based on each child's needs. School librarians should cooperate with teachers to learn about the methods teachers are using for IEPs in order to offer support. *Building the Legacy* produced by the National Dissemination Center for Children with Disabilities (NICHY, 2010) is a training curriculum intended to help all persons involved with children with disabilities understand and implement IDEA 2004, the United States' special education law. All parts of the modules are available in both English and Spanish. Other books dealing with special education and IEPs include *The Special Educator's Survival Guide* (Jossey-Bass, 2004) by Roger Pierangelo, *Special Education and the Law: A Guide for Practitioners*, 2nd edition by Allan G. Osborne and Charles J. Russo (Corwin Press, 2006), and *The Every Day Guide to Special Education—A Handbook for Teachers, Parents and Other Professionals,* 2nd edition (The Legal Center for People with Disabilities and Older People, 2008).

Information about the characteristics of disabilities and the materials recommended to meet the needs of people with disabilities can guide collection activities. The characteristics of a specific disability, however, might not apply to everyone with that disability. Also, many children have needs identified with more than one type of disability.

In working with these students, you have a responsibility to learn about the different characteristics and the implications for resources. School staff members can help. Teachers can describe students' behavior management programs, abilities, and learning styles. The school librarian can learn which disabilities call for modifications or adaptations and how to implement them. Specialists at the district or state level can also provide information and advice.

The Association for Library Services to Children (ALSC) recommends several books that deal with children with disabilities. The resources, which include working with autistic children, providing disability etiquette tips, including families with special needs, and mainstreaming services in school and public libraries, are particularly useful for teachers and librarians. The website that lists and annotates the resources is listed at the end of the chapter under "Helpful Websites."

Other sources of information are national organizations and clearinghouses. The U.S. Council for Exceptional Children (CEC) provides information about education for both children with disabilities and gifted children. CEC provides suggested resources and professional development opportunities, advocates for appropriate governmental policies, and sets professional standards. The Canadian CEC assists educators, support personnel, and parents who work with special students. They also provide professional development and blogs, as well as helping develop responsible legislation. The National Information Center for Children and Youth with Disabilities (NICHCY) is a central source of information on disabilities in children and youth, IDEA, and how NCLB relates to children with disabilities. They also provide research-based information on effective educational practices. The home pages for these organizations are listed under "Helpful Websites" at the end of this chapter. Journals of interest to adults working with special education children include *Exceptional Children, Teaching Exceptional Children,* and *Teaching Exceptional Children Plus* (CEC), and *Exceptional Parent Magazine* (Exceptional Parent).

Not only do school librarians need to know the materials in the collection that are appropriate for children with disabilities, but they also have a responsibility to be aware of the resources available in the community. These may include rehabilitation agencies, information agencies, and other educational or recreational programs. For example, some communities have recreation areas designed to accommodate wheelchairs or to provide information that children can learn through a variety of senses. In one such recreational area, trails provide easy access to picnic areas, a fishing pier, and nature paths. Along the trails, information stations use models, large charts, printed information, and recorded messages to point out items of interest. Messages written in Braille encourage people to feel an object or to smell it. Sheltered eating areas provide spaces for wheelchairs interspersed at the picnic tables. School librarians should make information about such facilities available and suggest them as possible destinations for field trips.

Formats and Assistive Technologies

Students with special needs use the same range of formats that other students use, but in some cases alternatives or adaptations are necessary. For instance, paperback books are ideal for students with upper extremity weakness. Students with cognitive disabilities may find audio, video, toys, and multimedia formats useful. Large print books and magazines are helpful to students with visual disabilities.

In recent years many technologies have been adapted to assist persons with special needs. Frequently these technologies are referred to as *assistive technologies*, which are defined by the Technology-Related Assistance for Individuals with Disabilities Act, 1988, U.S. Public Law 100-407 as "any item, piece of equipment or product system, whether acquired commercially, off the shelf, modified, or customized, that is used to increase or improve functional capabilities of individuals with disabilities" (University of Iowa. Iowa Center for Assistive Technology Education and Research, n.d.). In *Assistive Technology: Access for All Students*, 2nd edition (Pearson, 2011) authors Lawrence A. Beard, Laura Bowden Carpenter, and Linda Johnston discuss the most recent assistive technology for students who require special accommodation. A chapter on universal design is included in the book. *ATNetwork: Assistive Technology . . . Tools for Living* (AT Network, 2010) is a website that provides a variety of information and resources about assistive technologies.

Autism

Students diagnosed with autism are becoming increasingly prevalent in schools. Autism is a complex developmental brain disorder with different levels of severity. One percent of children in the United States have been diagnosed with an autism spectrum disorder. The rate of increase in recent years has been 10–17 percent annually. It is the fastest growing serious development disability in the United States, surpassing juvenile diabetes and childhood cancer. Boys are generally four times more likely to be diagnosed with autism than girls. Currently in the United States one of 70 boys is diagnosed with autism (*Autism Speaks*, 2011).

The increase in autism in young people is a growing challenge for schools. In some school districts the lower functioning autistic students are educated in special schools or classes with special education teachers. However, higher functioning students are usually placed in regular classrooms, and the extra services needed by the students are brought to the classroom. In the United States schools must first consider the option of inclusion in a regular classroom. School librarians should use the same types of instructional strategies for autistic children as those used by special education teachers. Chapter 5 of Kay Bishop's *Connecting Libraries with Classrooms: The Curricular Roles of the Media Specialist,* 2nd edition (Linworth, 2011) discusses several strategies that can be used in the school library to help meet the needs of autistic students. A list of resources for professionals and for students is included in the book. Some websites that contain resources about autism, including books for professionals, books for teens, and books for children are listed in "Helpful Websites" at the end of this chapter. Articles that discuss how school librarians can help meet the needs of students with autism can be found under "Additional Readings."

Visual Impairment

Persons who have vision problems may require special types of materials. Some people with partial sight can use regular print materials, whereas others need large print materials. One cannot make the assumption that large print materials are appropriate for all students with partial sight. Low-vision aids, handheld magnifiers, or closed circuit televisions can magnify standard print materials. Trained students can use Braille books, games, and outline maps. A blind person can read printed materials by using optical machines that allow users to feel sensation on their fingertips. For others, taped materials may be most useful.

Students with visual disabilities can participate in all school library activities. Useful pieces of equipment include rear projection screens, which permit students to get close to the screen without blocking images; tape recorders; speech compressors, which eliminate pauses between words and thus reduce the time needed to access recorded materials; talking calculators; and computers with voice recognition software.

People with visual and other physical disabilities can use audiobooks (talking books), textbooks, and magazines (available in English and other languages, including Spanish). Talking books are a free service of the National Library Service for the Blind and Physically Handicapped (NLS), part of the Library of Congress. Arrangements can be made through a local public library. Titles can be found in plaintext catalogs and bibliographies obtained from the NLS, or they can be downloaded online. Information on the books can be found in the print and online versions of *Braille Book Review* (1932–) and *Talking Books Topics* (1935–) from the NLS. These titles are available free to the blind or people with other disabilities. In 1998 the titles in the audiobooks program became available in digital format.

In 1999 the Library of Congress introduced the Web-Braille service, which offers many books in electronic format, as well as some music scores, and all Braille magazines produced by NLS. Because of copyright laws, access to Web-Braille is limited to NLS patrons and eligible institutions that provide services to the blind. Links to Web-Braille books are included in the NLS online catalog.

The Complete Directory of Large Print Books and Serials (Grey House, 2010) lists adult, juvenile, and textbook titles and indicates the type size and the physical size of each book, as well as full contact information on publishers, wholesalers, and distributors. The American Foundation for the Blind develops, publishes, and sells useful books, pamphlets, periodicals, videos, and electronic materials for students and professionals. They also publish the *Journal of Visual Impairment and Blindness*.

The American Printing House for the Blind (APHB) publishes Braille books, magazines, and large print texts, as well as materials in recorded and computer disk formats. They also produce an online monthly newsletter, which includes brief reviews of new recreational books in Braille.

Deafness or Hearing Impairment

Young people with hearing impairments have difficulty hearing spoken language, and as a result they often have difficulty understanding written and spoken language and abstract concepts. Visual formats are useful for these students. The visuals should be large and present a single, distinct concept or idea. Illustrations and print should be immediately recognizable. Language patterns and sentence structures need to be simple. Repetition and reinforcement are helpful.

Captioned videotapes, CD-ROMs, and DVDs are useful for persons with hearing impairments. These materials can be obtained free through a loan program of open-captioned materials provided by the Described and Captioned Media Program (DCMP), whose services are available through the National Association of the Deaf and are funded by the U.S. Department of Education. The materials can be found on the DCMP website, which lists captioned media that can be borrowed by deaf and hearing impaired people. Check with your local educational television station for information about captioned programming and the equipment necessary to receive it.

You can provide materials to students who have learned sign language. Books, videotapes, and other materials in sign language are available from the Alexander Graham Bell Association for the Deaf and Hard of Hearing online bookstore. Weston Woods produces audiovisual adaptations of several children's books with sign language narration. These materials are intended for young children who cannot yet read captioned media. The American Speech-Language-Hearing Association publishes the newsletter *The ASHA Leader*, which includes articles for persons working with the deaf and hard of hearing. It can be accessed online at <http://www.asha.org/leader.aspx>. School librarians who take a course in sign language can greatly increase rapport with students who are deaf or have hearing impairments.

Other Disabilities

Other students who are officially identified through an assessment process include learning disabled (LD), emotionally disturbed (ED), behavior disordered (BD), or mentally retarded (MR). Learning disabled children may have difficulty acquiring and storing information, but their visual and auditory senses are fully functional. Students with behavior disorders may have several behavior problems, including depression, unusual behavior in normal circumstances, and chronic misbehavior such as aggressiveness. Students with intelligence quotients (IQs) below 70 are considered mentally retarded and may have low adaptive behaviors. Students with brain injuries and other health impairments may also have physical disabilities that require special attention. It is important that all these students have school library privileges although in some cases it may require special education teachers or teacher assistants to accompany the students to the library. Table 15.1 lists the disabilities that are included in federal education law.

School librarians should include in their collections materials appropriate for all students, including those with disabilities. The students should be guided to the materials that will fit their special needs and interests. For instance, children who are mentally retarded will need materials that are simple and sequential. Librarians may need to modify assignments and materials when teaching library skills to students with disabilities.

One of the most important ways of serving students with disabilities is to provide books and other materials that deal with disabilities. School library collections should include not only nonfiction resources about disabilities, but also fiction titles in which persons with disabilities occur as main or minor characters. All students with disabilities need to see themselves represented in books and other library materials. Additionally, other students need to be exposed to materials that have in them persons with disabilities so they can better understand their peers with handicaps. Mason Crest Publishers has produced *Kids with Special Needs: IDEA* (2010–2011) an entire series of books (11-volume

TABLE 15.1. CATEGORIES OF DISABILITY IN FEDERAL EDUCATION LAW

Federal Disability Term	Alternative Terms	Brief Description
Learning disability (LD)	Specific learning disability (i.e. aphasia, dyslexia)	A disorder related to processing information that leads to difficulties in reading, writing, and computing; the most common disability, accounting for half of all students receiving special education.
Speech or language impairment	Communication disorder (CD)	A disorder related to accurately producing the sounds of language or meaningfully using language to communicate.
Mental retardation (MR)	Intellectual disability, cognitive impairment	Significant limitations in intellectual ability and adaptive behavior; this disability occurs in a range of severity.
Emotional disturbance (ED)	Behavior disorder (BD). emotional disability	Significant problems in the social-emotional area to a degree that learning is negatively affected.
Autism	Autism spectrum disorder (ASD), Pervasive developmental disorder (PDD, PDD-NOS)	A disorder characterized by extraordinary difficulty in social responsiveness; this disability occurs in many different forms and may be mild or significant.
Hearing impairment	Deaf, hard of hearing (DHH)	A partial or complete loss of hearing.
Visual impairment	Low vision, blind	A partial or complete loss of vision.
Deaf-blindness		A simultaneous significant hearing loss and significant vision loss.
Orthopedic impairment (0I)	Physical disability	A significant physical limitation that impairs the ability to move or complete motor activities.
Traumatic brain injury (TBI)		A medical condition denoting a serious brain injury that occurs as a result of accident or injury; the impact of this disability varies widely but may affect learning, behavior, social skills, and language.
Other health impairment (OHI)		A disease or health disorder so significant that it negatively affects learning; examples include cancer, sickle-cell anemia, and diabetes.
Multiple disabilities		The simultaneous presence of two or more disabilities such that none can be identified as the primary disability; the most common example is the occurrence of mental retardation and physical disabilities.
Developmental delay (DD)		A nonspecific disability category that states may choose to use as an alternative to specific disability labels for identifying students up to age 9 needing special education.

set) on youth with special needs. The books, which are geared for ages 10 and up, address the challenges and triumphs of youth with special needs, including physical, mental, and emotional disabilities.

GIFTED AND TALENTED STUDENTS

As any parent of a gifted or talented child knows, gifted students also have special needs. Often these needs are not addressed in public schools as some school systems spend most of their special monies on programs that help students who are physically or learning disabled. Yet many gifted students have problems adjusting to school, perhaps because of boredom, feeling uncomfortable about their abilities, or being seen by other students as misfits. Gifted students can also have learning disabilities, and some of them perform far below their abilities. Gifted and talented students will be many of our future leaders in society so it is important to address their educational needs.

At one time gifted students were identified only though IQ tests. But educators in recent years have moved to an expanded definition of giftedness in which intelligence is seen as multifaceted. The U.S. federal definition of gifted and talented students that is currently used can be found in the Elementary and Secondary Education Act and is as follows: "Students, children, or youth who give evidence of high achievement capability in areas such as intellectual, creative, artistic, or leadership capacity, or in specific academic fields, and who need services and activities not ordinarily provided by the school in order to fully develop those capabilities" (U.S. Congress, 1988).

Some school programs that deal with gifted and talented students involve enrichment activities that are not included in the regular curriculum and others concentrate on higher level thinking skills, such as problem solving and critical thinking. With either type of program library resources are frequently needed, and often teachers of gifted and talented students work closely with school librarians to assist the students in conducting independent research projects.

Many professional organizations deal with gifted and talented students. The National Association for Gifted Children (NAGC) deals specifically with the needs of gifted students and publishes *Gifted Child Quarterly*. Prufrock Press is the leading producer of materials in gifted education. They also publish three periodicals: *Gifted Child Today Magazine, Journal for the Education of the Gifted,* and *Journal of Advanced Academics.*

Gifted and talented students frequently use school library resources to pursue their special interests and talents. It is especially important that they learn to access, evaluate, and use information so they can work independently. School librarians can help assist these students obtain the literacy skills that they need to be successful in their research.

It is also essential that school librarians develop collections that meet the needs of the gifted and talented students. Good reading advisory can be especially helpful to gifted students and can lead them to quality literature. These students should be introduced to the classics. Knowing the interests of gifted and talented students is important to matching the students to appropriate materials. Research has shown that gifted students have particular preferences for certain genres: fantasy, science fiction, humor, and series books, such as *The Chronicles of Narnia* (Carter, 1982; Cavazos-Kottke, 2006; Chrisman & Bishop, 1985; Jackson, 1999). Thus, it is important to include in a collection challenging materials in these genres.

Just as is true for other special needs youth, gifted and talented students need to see themselves in books and to gain self-understanding and social understanding. *Gifted Books, Gifted Readers: Literature Activities to Excite Young Minds* (Libraries Unlimited, 2000) by Nancy J. Polette is a valuable resource for selecting books and activities for these students. Judith Wynn Halsted's *Some of My Best Friends Are Books: Guiding Gifted Readers*, 3rd edition (Great Potential Press, 2009) contains a bibliography of recommended reading for gifted students. *Hoagies' Gifted Education Page* <http://www.hoagiesgifted.org/reading_lists.htm> has numerous links to bibliographies of books recommended for gifted and talented students.

DIVERSITY AND STUDENTS

Multicultural materials support individual needs as well as the curriculum. These materials help students learn about people whose backgrounds are different from their own. Seeing their culture represented in materials helps raise the self-esteem of members of minority groups. It is important for the school librarian to be aware of the diversity of a school's population and to make certain that materials are available to meet those students' needs. If there are large numbers of non-English-speaking students in the school population, the library needs to have materials available in languages other than English.

The topic of multicultural materials can raise heated debate. Questions center on a few issues:

- *Definition of multicultural materials:* Does it include books from or about other nations? How does it define a cultural group? Should Vietnamese, Cambodian, Chinese, and Japanese materials all be labeled "Asian American" when the differences between these cultures are significant?
- *Background of authors:* Who is qualified to write about ethnic and cultural experiences? Should only those who are actually members of a culture write about that group? Can an author successfully write about a culture if he or she has gained insight into it through extensive research or experience in the culture?

Because you will want to select high-quality multicultural materials to include in your collection, a third issue, the quality of the literature, deserves your special attention as a school librarian. It is important to remember that the standards for any good literature also apply to multicultural and international literature. However, additional criteria should be considered:

- The materials should be culturally accurate. This includes the illustrations in a book as well as text.
- Ethnic materials should contain authentic dialogue and depict realistic relationships.
- The materials should avoid racial and cultural stereotyping. Characters should be regarded as distinct individuals.
- The materials should not contain racial comments or clichés.
- Details in a story should help the reader gain a sense of the culture.

Several resources address multicultural materials. Sherry York's *Ethnic Book Awards: A Directory of Multicultural Literature for Young Readers* (Linworth, 2005) is a comprehensive listing of the award-winning titles of several multicultural awards.

York's *Booktalking Authentic Multicultural Literature: Fiction, History and Memoirs for Teens* (Linworth, 2008) is a valuable resource for school librarians to help promote cross-cultural understanding. Donna E. Norton's *Multicultural Children's Literature: Through the Eyes of Many Children,* 3rd edition (Prentice Hall, 2008) can help school librarians evaluate and select multicultural literature for children and young adults. *Across Cultures: A Guide to Multicultural Literature for Children* (Libraries Unlimited, 2007) by Kathy East and Rebecca L. Thomas is arranged thematically and includes annotations, programming ideas, and activities for 150 multicultural titles.

The following sources can help you select African American titles for your collection. *The Coretta Scott King Awards Book: 1970–2009* (American Library Association, 2009) edited by Henrietta M. Smith features annotations of winning and honor titles, as well as biographies of their authors and illustrators. The website *Black Books Galore* (2011), which can be found at <http://www.blackbooksgalore.com/> has additional information about African American children's books.

The Pura Belpré Awards: Celebrating Latino Authors and Illustrators (American Library Association, 2006) edited by Rose Z. Trevino covers the first 10 years of the Pura Belpré Awards. It annotates the award-winning titles and provides biographies of the authors and illustrators. Another helpful resource for selecting Latino titles for your collection and using them in lessons is *Celebrating Cuentos: Promoting Latino Children's Literature and Literacy in Classrooms and Libraries* (Libraries Unlimited, 2010) edited by Jaime Campbell Naidoo. Isabel Schon's *Recommended Books in Spanish for Children and Young Adults: 2004–2008* (Scarecrow, 2008) is an essential selection aid for purchasing materials in Spanish.

Recent selection tools for Native American Indian materials are more difficult to locate. Sherry York's *Children's and Young Adult Literature by Native Americans: A Concept Guide for Librarians, Teachers, Parents, and Students* (Linworth, 2003) covers titles in print for fiction, folklore, drama, poetry, and nonfiction. An older source *Through Indian Eyes: The Native Experience in Books for Children* (American Indian Studies Center, 1998) includes critical evaluations of books by and about Native Americans. Some additional resources for Native American books for children and young adults are listed in "Helpful Websites" at the end of this chapter.

Reviews of new print and nonprint resources, as well as articles about multiculturalism can be found in *MultiCultural Review: Dedicated to a Better Understanding of Ethnic, Racial and Religious Diversity.* This quarterly journal published by the Goldman Group is designed for educators and librarians at all levels.

Sources that are particularly helpful for international materials include *Crossing Boundaries with Children's Books* (Scarecrow, 2006) edited by Doris Gebel and *Bridges to Understanding: Envisioning the World Through Children's Books* (Scarecrow, 2011) edited by Linda Pavonetti. *Bookbird: A Journal of International Children's Literature* is a refereed journal published quarterly by the International Board on Books for Children. It features articles of interest on international literature for children, including themed issues and news of children's literature awards around the world.

Bibliographies of multicultural materials for the groups discussed, as well as for Asian Americans, can be found on several Internet sites. Some of the sites are listed under "Helpful Websites" at the end of this chapter. Additionally the websites for some awards that are given for books that deal with minorities are also listed. These lists can be helpful selection aid resources since the winning titles are some of the best books published about the represented minorities. It is important for school librarians to purchase these books and give these award-winning titles the recognition that they deserve.

POOR AND RELUCTANT READERS

Poor or reluctant readers have always been a challenge to teachers and school librarians who teach literature appreciation and encourage reading. The poor reader reads below capacity. This is not a reflection of that person's potential to read. A reluctant or a resistive reader is one who has the skills needed to read, but prefers not to read. Sometimes these students are referred to as aliterate. Books with high appeal and appropriate reading levels can help these students. The phrases *high interest/low vocabulary* (hi-low) or *high interest/low reading level* (HILRL) are often used to describe these works. Some helpful criteria for evaluating such books include:

- Cover should be catchy and attractive
- Good blurb
- Appropriate format with an appealing balance of text and white space
- Clear writing without long, complex sentences or sophisticated vocabulary
- Direct and simple narrative
- A few well-defined characters
- Use of dialogue and action
- Well-organized, direct information
- Repetition of main points
- Illustrations to explain the text
- Humor when appropriate
- Presented in chronological order

The topic of reluctant readers has been addressed in library literature during the past few years. *Connecting with Reluctant Teen Readers* (Neal-Schuman, 2006) by Patrick Jones, Maureen L. Hartman, and Patricia Taylor provides ideas on the types of books that will entice teens to read. Lists of over 600 books, series, and magazines are included. Orca Book Publishers in Victoria, British Columbia published *Orca Currents: Middle-School Fiction for Reluctant Readers* (2010), which includes 46 paperback resources and a resource guide. Michael Sullivan has researched the problem of aliteracy among boys. His book, *Connecting Boys with Books 2 Closing the Reading Gap: What Libraries Can Do* (American Library Association, 2009) can help school librarians learn about the books that boys like to read. His first reading advisory title *Serving Boys Through Reading Advisory* (American Library Association, 2009) emphasizes nonfiction titles and boy-friendly categories of genre fiction. Each year the Young Adult Library Services Association (YALSA) selects Quick Picks for Reluctant Young Adult Readers. The website for this lists, as well as other lists for reluctant readers can be found under "Helpful Websites" at the end of this chapter. Books that often appeal to reluctant and resistive readers include graphic novels, series books, and picture books for older readers.

Unfortunately some educators equate reading only with books. Some even think of reading as only the reading of fiction. In reality, today's youth are doing much reading in formats other than books. Magazines, newspapers, and comics are appealing not only to reluctant or resistive readers, but also to teenagers in general. It is important to remember that the time that students spend on computers and playing video games also involves reading. If we want to motivate students to read, we must first find out their interests, including what they are reading. We can then be more successful in matching their interests to reading materials.

Criteria for selecting books for ESL (English as a Second Language) students include some of the same considerations. According to McGaffery (1998, p. xiv), these books should have the following:

- An appealing format
- Appropriate reading and content levels
- Appropriate illustrations
- Accurate text and illustrations
- Access to information through an index
- A glossary of terms
- Bibliographies for further exploration

ESL books need to be representative of the culture they describe and effectively explain that culture. Although the book does not contain recent titles *Book Bridges for ESL Students: Using Young Adult and Children's Literature to Teach ESL* (Scarecrow, 2002) by Suzanne Elizabeth Reid is a valuable resource for both librarians and teachers.

GAY OR LESBIAN STUDENTS

For the most part school library services for gay and lesbian students have been grossly inadequate. Internet filtering on school library computers has seriously affected these students' capabilities to access information about their sexual orientation, and some school librarians are hesitant to include gay literature in their collections because they fear controversy and book challenges. Yet without vital books and resources, gay students can often end up in high-risk situations. Having information available on gays and lesbians can not only provide the information needs of lesbian, gay, bisexual, and transgender (LGBT) students, but it also can discourage the teasing and harassing of LGBT students that exist at many schools. Reading gay-themed books can help LGBT students realize there are other young people like them. Students, including young children, living in families with gay or lesbian parents should be able to see their families represented and accepted in literature.

A growing number of quality gay-themed titles are available, so it should not be difficult to find materials to purchase. *Lesbian and Gay Voices* (Greenwood, 2000) by Frances Ann Day is a valuable resource that contains more than 275 titles of books that are appropriate for young readers and that feature lesbian and gay characters. *Serving LGBTIQ Library and Archive Users: Essays on Outreach, Services, Collections, and Access* (McFarland, 2011) edited by Ellen Greenblatt contains information on library services to lesbian, gay, bisexual, transgender, intersexed, and questioning (LGBTIQ) youth, as well as collection assessment for this population. Carlisle K. Webber's *Gay, Lesbian, Bisexual, Transgender and Questioning Teen Literature: A Guide to Reading Interests* (Libraries Unlimited, 2010) is a valuable reference addition to a school library collection. Each annotated entry is followed by suggested grade levels, awards and honors, and keywords.

OTHER SPECIAL GROUPS OF STUDENTS

Other special groups of students can benefit from materials geared to their needs and interests. Some of these groups include students with attention deficient disorders (ADH) and students with serious or chronic illnesses, such as cerebral palsy or HIV/AIDS. Nonfiction materials on all of these conditions should be available in a school library collection. Additionally, all of these students need to see themselves represented in fiction materials.

Transient students include children and teenagers who live in campgrounds, on migrant farms, in homeless shelters, or with foster parents. Mobility often is accompanied by poverty, hunger, and exposure to violence. Often there is a lack of stability in the lives of transient students, as well as a lack of consistency in their education. It is especially important to make these students welcome in the school library. Materials and library programs to help these students become aware of their value to society can be beneficial in lowering their anxieties and building their self-esteem. In many instances, circulation policies may need to be adapted for these students.

In recent years there has been a growing population of preschool children in our schools. This means that we, as school librarians, should educate ourselves about how children learn in the early years. These children should be welcomed into the library with storytelling programming and learning experiences relating to the care of books. If preschool children are present in your school, your collection should include appropriate age-level books, with sturdy library binding.

Attention to student dropout populations is another recent issue, both for educators and for society in general. These students are referred to as *at-risk youth*. Some characteristics that contribute to students dropping out of school include low family income, weak family cohesiveness, parental apathy, frequent family mobility, low self-esteem, conflict with other students, poor academic achievement, and behavior problems in school. One of the major deficits of students who are not doing well in school is the lack of reading skills. School librarians can help with the dropout problem by providing materials that support students' various learning styles, reading levels, and interests. Keeping a school library open after school so at-risk students can obtain tutoring or homework help is another way to help with dropout prevention. It is extremely important to make the library a safe and welcoming environment for all students, and to be particularly supportive of students who are struggling to fit in with their peers.

Sheila B. Anderson's *Extreme Teens: Library Services for Nontraditional Young Adults* (Libraries Unlimited, 2005) provides tips on building a collection and providing library services to connect with nontraditional young people, including juvenile delinquents, pregnant teens, the homeless, and many others.

CONCLUSIONS

One of the responsibilities of school librarians is to provide materials and services to meet the needs of students, including students who have special needs. Several changes in our society and in education have resulted in many special groups of students in our schools who have needs that impact the school library collection. Such groups include students with physical disabilities, such as sight or hearing impairments; young people with learning disabilities or health problems; gifted and talented students; students from ethnic minority groups; youth whose first language is not English; LGBT students; transient young people; and at-risk students. School librarians should purchase materials that address the needs of all these groups, including books that have these young people as major characters. Additionally, school librarians should provide safe, welcoming environments in their libraries for all these students who often face challenging situations with their peers.

REFERENCES

Autism Speaks (2011). *Facts about autism.* Retrieved from http://www.autismspeaks.org/what-autism/facts-about-autism

Carter, B. (1982). Leisure reading habits of gifted students in a suburban junior high school. *Top of the News, 38* (4), 312.

Cavazos-Kottke, S. (2006). Five readers browsing: The reading of talented middle school boys. *Gifted Child Quarterly, 50*, 132–147.

Chrisman, L. G., & Bishop, K. (1985). Reading preferences of academically talented students at a "parent-controlled" private school: A look at a study and its implications for library media specialists. *School Library Media Quarterly, 13*(3/4), 200–207.

Jackson, T. D. (1999). Reading attitudes, interests, and habits, and their relation to giftedness and gender (Master's Thesis, University of Alberta).

McGaffery, L. H. (1998). *Building an ESL collection for young adults.* Westport, CT: Greenwood Press.

NICHY (2010). Building the Legacy/Construyendo el Legado: *A Training Curriculum on IDEA 2004*. Retrieved from http://nichcy.org/laws/idea/legacy

University of Iowa. Iowa Center for Assistive Technology Education and Research. (n.d.). *Assistive technology glossary*. Retrieved from http://www.education.uiowa.edu/html/icater/AT_glossary.htm

U.S. Congress Public Law 100-297, Title IV, Sec. 4103 (1988).

ADDITIONAL READINGS

Audiobook library website enriches blind users' lives. (2008). *American Libraries, 39*(10), 65.

Berndowski, C. (2009). *Teaching literacy skills to adolescents using Coretta Scott King award winners.* Santa Barbara, CA: Libraries Unlimited.

Bond, G. (2007). Seriously gay and lesbian. *Publishers Weekly, 254*(19), 27, 29, 31.

Brynko, B. (2011). Browse aloud talking websites. *Information Today, 28*(2), 30.

Byerly, G. (2008). Not disabled, but abled—disability websites for children. *School Library Media Activities Monthly, 24*(7), 32–33.

Copeland, C. A. (2011). School librarians of the 21st century: Using resources and assistive technologies to support students' differences and abilities. *Knowledge Quest, 39*(3), 64–69.

Crisman, B. W. (2008). Inclusive programming for students with autism. *Principal, 88*(2), 28–32.

Cummings, E. O. (2011). Assistive and adaptive technology resources. *Knowledge Quest, 39*(3), 70–73.

Evans, M. R. (2007). The digitization of African American publications. *The Serials Librarian, 53*(1/2), 203–210.

Farmer, L.S.J., & Syles, M. (2008). Library services for students with autism. *CSLA Journal, 31*(2), 25–27.

Fisher, D. (2008). Struggling adolescent readers. *Teacher Librarian, 35*(3), 36–37.

Franklin, P., & Stephens, C. G. Managing a collection of multiple formats. *School Library Media Activities, 23*(7), 46–47.

Gleason, C. (2011). Mind the gap: Bridging the divide between non-readers and lifelong readers with hi-low books. *Knowledge Quest, 39*(4), 22–26.

Hanson-Baldauf, D. (2011). The good life: Empowering young adults with intellectual disabilities through everyday life information. *Knowledge Quest, 39*(3), 8–17.

Irwin, M., & Moeller, R. (2010). Seeing different portrayals of disability in young adult graphic novels, *SLMR, 13.* Retrieved from http://www.ala.org/ala/mgrps/divs/aasl/aaslpubsandjournals/slmrb/slmrcontents/volume13/irwin_moeller.cfm

Kim, S.U. (2012). Postsecondary assistance: A research project helps immigrant students plan their education futures. *Knowledge Quest, 40*(3), 49–53.

Krueger, K. S., & Stefanich, G. P. (2011). The school librarian as an agent of scientific inquiry for students with disabilities. *Knowledge Quest, 39*(3), 40–47.

Kurtts, S., Dobbins, N., & Takemae, N. (2012). Using assistive technology to meet diverse learner needs. *Library Media Connection, 30*(4), 22–23.

Lemmons, K. (2009). The International Children's Digital Library enhances the multicultural collection. *School Library Media Activities Monthly, 25*(7), 28–30.

Mason, K. (2010). Disability studies: Online resources for a growing discipline. *College Research Library News, 71*(5), 252–256, 260.

Mates, B. T. (2010). Assistive technologies. *American Libraries, 41*(10), 40–42.

McClary, C., & Howard, V. (2007). From "homosexuality" to "transvestites": An analysis of subject headings assigned to works of GLBT fiction in Canadian public libraries. *The Canadian Journal of Information and Library Science, 31*(2), 149–162.

Moreillon, J., & Cahill, M. (2010). When cultures meet. *School Library Monthly, 27*(2), 27–29.

Perrault, A. M. (2010). Making science learning available & accessible to all learners: Leveraging library resources. *Knowledge Quest, 39*(2), 64–68.

Polette, N. (2009). *Gifted biographies, gifted readers!* Westport, CT: Libraries Unlimited.

Prater, M. A., & Dyches, T. T. (2008). *Teaching about disabilities through children's literature.* Westport, CT: Libraries Unlimited.

Rauch, E. W. (2011). GLBTQ collections are for every library serving teens. *Teacher Librarian, 39*(1), 13–16.

Swarner, S. (2008). Advanced contemporary literacy: An integrated approach to reading. *Teacher Librarian, 36*(1), 26–27.

Tucillo, D. P. (2010). Enduring EMO. *School Library Journal, 56*(10), 42–47.

Wessels, N., & Knoetze, H. E. (2008). *Mousaion, 26*(2), 290–303.

White, B. (2011). The world in words & pictures: How graphic novels can help to increase reading comprehension for students with hearing loss. *Knowledge Quest, 39*(3), 19–25.

Wopperer, E. (2011). Inclusive literature in the library and classroom: The importance of young adult and children's books that portray characters with disabilities. *Knowledge Quest, 39*(3), 26–34.

Wopperer, E. (2011). Multimodal resources for the education of all. *Knowledge Quest, 39*(3), 36–39.

HELPFUL WEBSITES

American Library Association. (2011). *Coretta Scott King Award.* Retrieved from http://www.ala.org/ala/mgrps/rts/emiert/cskbookawards/index.cfm

American Library Association. (2011). *Out in the library: Materials, displays and services for the gay, lesbian, bisexual, and transgender community.* Retrieved from http://www.ala.org/ala/aboutala/offices/oif/iftoolkits/glbttoolkit/glbttoolkit.cfm

Association for Library Service to Children. (n.d.). *Children with disabilities and library programs.* Retrieved from http://www.ala.org/Template.cfm?Section=childrens&template=/ContentManagement/ContentDisplay.cfm&ContentID=165023

Association for Library Service to Children. (2011). *Welcome to the (Mildred L) Batchelder Award home page.* Retrieved from http://www.ala.org/ala/mgrps/divs/alsc/awardsgrants/bookmedia/batchelderaward/index.cfm

Association for Library Service to Children. (n.d.). *Welcome to the Pura Belpré Award home page!* Retrieved from http://www.ala.org/ala/mgrps/divs/alsc/awardsgrants/bookmedia/belpremedal/index.cfm

Association of Jewish Libraries. (2007). *Sydney Taylor Book Award.* Retrieved from http://www.jewishlibraries.org/ajlweb/awards/stba/STBA_Winners.htm

AT Network. (2010). *ATNetwork: assistive technology . . . tools for living.* Retrieved from http://www.atnet.org/

Autism Society. (2008). *About autism.* Retrieved from http://www.autism-society.org/about-autism/

Autism Society of North Carolina. (2011). *Bookstore.* Retrieved from http://www.autismbookstore.com/Merchant2/merchant.mvc

Autism Speaks. (2011). *Resource library.* Retrieved from http://www.autismspeaks.org/family-services/resource-library

Bookshare. (2011). *Books without barriers.* Retrieved from http://www.bookshare.org/

Butte Publications. (2010). *Welcome to Butte Publications.* Retrieved from http://buttepublications.com/

Caldwell, N., Kaye, G., & Mitten, L.A. (2007). *"I" is for inclusion: The portrayal of Native Americans in books for young people.* Retrieved from http://www.ailanet.org/publications/I%20IS%20FOR%20INCLUSION-rev%2010–07.pdf

Canadian Council for Exceptional Children. (2004). *Special education in Canada.* Retrieved from http://www.cec.sped.org/Content/NavigationMenu/AboutCEC/Communities/Canada/default.htm

Chicago Public Library. (2011). *Autism Resources.* Retrieved from http://www.chipublib.org/forkids/kidspages/autism.php

Children's Literature Network. (2011). *Best Native American books for children and young adults.* Retrieved from http://www.childrensliteraturenetwork.org/resource/readlist/favnatv.php

Choice Literacy. (2011). *Multicultural picture books for young children.* Retrieved from https://www.choiceliteracy.com/members/login.cfm?hpage=321.cfm

Council for Exceptional Children. (2011). *About us.* Retrieved from http://www.cec.sped.org/AM/Template.cfm?Section=About_CEC

ICDL. (n.d.). *International Children's Digital Library.* Retrieved from http://en.childrenslibrary.org/

Internet Public Library. (2011). *Native American authors.* Retrieved from http://www.ipl.org/div/natam/

JadeLuck Club. (2011). *Top 10: Best Korean American children's books.* Retrieved from http://jadeluckclub.com/top-10-best-korean-american-childrens-books-ages-2–16/

Jason and Nordic Publishers. (2010). *Welcome to Turtle Books.* Retrieved from http://jasonandnordic.com/

Jessica Kingsley Publishers. (2011). *Home.* Retrieved from http://jkp.com/

Kennedy, E. (2011). *About: Children's books: More Resources for reluctant readers.* Retrieved from http://childrensbooks.about.com/cs/reluctantreaders/a/reluctantreader_2.htm

Kennedy, E. (2011). *Librarians recommend books for boys.* Retrieved from http://childrensbooks.about.com/od/toppicks/a/books_boys.htm

Library of Congress. (2011). *That all may read . . . National Library Service for the Blind and Physically Handicapped.* Retrieved from http://www.loc.gov/nls/index.html

National Dissemination Center for Children with Disabilities. (n.d.). *Welcome!* Retrieved from http://nichcy.org/

National Education Association. (n.d.). *Asian American booklist.* Retrieved from http://www.nea.org/grants/29506.htm

Pacific Rim Voices. (2011). *Papertiger.org.* Retrieved from http://www.papertigers.org/

San Francisco Public Library. (2011). *Our Asian heritage: Children's books on the Asian American experience.* Retrieved from http://sfpl.org/index.php?pg=2000154101

Scholastic. (2011). *How to choose the best multicultural books.* Retrieved from http://www2.scholastic.com/browse/article.jsp?id=3757

Smith, C.L. (2011). *Native American themes in children's & YA books.* Retrieved from http://www.cynthialeitichsmith.com/lit_resources/diversity/native_am/NativeThemes_intro.html

Smith, R.F. (n.d.). *Celebrating cultural diversity through children's literature.* Retrieved from http://multiculturalchildrenslit.com/

SNOW—Special needs opportunity windows. (2011). Retrieved from http://snow.idrc.ocad.ca/

Strauss, C. (2010). *NLS reference bibliographies. Physical handicaps: A selective bibliography.* Retrieved from http://www.loc.gov/nls/reference/bibliographies/awareness.html

Tomás Rivera Mexican American Children's Book Award. (n.d.). Retrieved from http://riverabookaward.wordpress.com/

University of Arizona. College of Education. (2011). *Worlds of words.* Retrieved from http://wowlit.web.arizona.edu/

University of Wisconsin—Milwaukee. Center for Latin American and Caribbean Studies. (2011). *Américas Book Award for Children's and Young Adult Literature.* Retrieved from http://www4.uwm.edu/clacs/aa/index.cfm

Walling, L.L. (2010). *Linda Lucas Walling collection: Materials for and/or about children with disabilities.* Retrieved from http://www.libsci.sc.edu/walling/bestfolder.htm

WETA. (2010). *Reading rockets.* Retrieved from http://www.readingrockets.org/

Whelan, D.L. (2009). The equal opportunity disorder. *School Library Journal, 55*(8), 30–34.

Young Adult Library Services Association. (n.d.). *Quick Picks for Reluctant Young Adult Readers.* Retrieved from http://www.ala.org/ala/mgrps/divs/yalsa/booklistsawards/quickpicks/qphome.cfm

Chapter

16 Fiscal Issues Relating to the Collection

School librarians face the reality that a single collection cannot be comprised of all available resources, nor can it meet all of its users' demands. In meeting this challenge school librarians must address some issues. Among these is the question of ownership versus access. Should a school librarian use funds to purchase an item, or should the librarian obtain a license so patrons can use that item? Other questions deal with technologies. Should one add new formats such as e-books to the collection? How often is it necessary to upgrade the current technology?

Unfortunately in many school libraries there are not enough funds to even purchase basic print materials. Thus, school librarians are faced with the challenge of how to raise additional monies, perhaps through fund raising projects or by applying for grants.

THE BUDGET

Given these situations, how do school librarians plan a budget and allocate funds for acquiring or accessing resources? Very few persons become school librarians because they have a special interest in developing budgets; however, budgeting is an important part of the program administration role of school librarians. Dickinson (2004) notes the budgeting cycle is a three-step process that involves knowledge (having sound understanding of the budget process), planning, and implementation.

Knowledge of the Budget Process

In most schools the principal has a major role in deciding how funds will be dispersed. Some states require that a certain amount of money based on student enrollment be allocated for library resources, but this is generally a minimum amount. In some instances, particularly in schools using site-based management, a school committee also has input into how monies are allocated in the school. In many cases you will be competing with other units in the school for the same funds. Therefore, it is essential that you understand the funding process and are able to clearly communicate in writing the needs of the library, with well-documented costs of the resources that you think need to be purchased for the library.

Planning and Implementing

In order to decide which resources or services to purchase, you should decide on some collection management goals and establish yearly budget priorities. The collection must be assessed to determine how closely the current resources respond to curriculum needs. A collection development plan should then be created to fill any gaps in the current resources. This plan should be reviewed annually. When requesting funds for resources, it is important to include the dollar amount needed to replace old and worn items, in addition to filling any identified gaps.

Budget requests can be presented in various formats, but all budgets should include itemized dollar amounts and justification for the purchase of each item or service. In today's educational setting it is wise to relate justification to student learning and achievement.

Allocation of funds can be based on curriculum areas, subjects, curriculum mapping, formats, and users. Other approaches include historical (how allocations were handled in the past), anticipated loss or replacement, and age of the collection. Allocation of funds also reflects a librarian's stance on the amount of electronic access versus ownership (the more traditional position).

Escalating costs are another factor that school librarians face. The average cost of books continues to increase. However, at the same time the cost of videocassettes, CDs, and DVDs are decreasing. One can consult the April issue of *Publishers Weekly* or the latest edition of the *Bowker Annual Library and Book Trade Almanac* (R.R. Bowker, 1955–) for an annual update on this type of information. Kenney's (2010) article in *School Library Journal* also has recent average book prices for juvenile materials.

It may be possible that the amount of money requested to fully fund the needed resources is not well received; however, it is our responsibility as school librarians to submit a well-justified budget each year. Even if the initial request for funding is not completely fulfilled, that is not a reason to quit asking for funding or to lower the amounts requested. As long as you are basing requests on evidence-based facts, you should continue in your pursuit of requesting funds. It may be necessary for you to become proactive and gather support from others, parents, teachers, and students, who can benefit from the resources that you think should be in the library. Good public relations including attending PTSA meetings, sponsoring extracurricular activities, and presenting staff development workshops will also aid in increasing the chances that the school library program will be funded (Dickinson, 2004, p. 17).

Licensing

In the future and in many school libraries today, licensing or access fees for electronic resources may make up the major portion of the library's non-personnel budget. With the advent of being able to access digital information, rather than obtain outright ownership, school librarians are learning to negotiate licensing agreements. These agreements define appropriate use and specify a given time period. Both the school library as buyer (licensee) and the vendor (licensor) are bound by the negotiated terms. Common issues in licensing electronic resources are the following:

- Resolving the issue of ownership and access.
- Defining how the content may or may not be used (fair use).
- Determining whether the content is to be accessed within the library or remotely.
- Defining who is authorized to use the resource.

When examining access licenses, other practical advice includes:

- Select the clauses in license agreements with which you agree.
- Create a licensing template of those terms.
- Develop a checklist of terms and conditions that are appropriate for your situation.
- Be sure the license follows the copyright laws.
- Avoid licenses that hold the school library liable for each and every infringement by authorized users.
- Avoid non-cancellation clauses.
- Avoid nondisclosure clauses.
- Make certain time limitations are clearly defined.
- Avoid licenses that permit subcontracting to an agent.

Resource Sharing

The basic concept of sharing bibliographic information and collections is not new. However, the advent of telecommunications and other technologies has increased the opportunities to share resources. Although location of information is an important aspect, delivery of the desired items is of greater concern. Changes in technological delivery systems make it possible to address the needs of individual learners more effectively regardless of geographic location. These multi-type library organizations, that is, academic, public, school, and special libraries, establish formal cooperative organizations of independent and autonomous libraries or groups of libraries to work together for mutual benefit. Networks or consortiums are not limited to regions; they can be found within a school system or at the community, county, state, national, and international levels.

The traditional library network was a cooperative in which participating members shared resources on formal and informal bases. These early consortia shared union lists of serials, provided loans through their interlibrary lending (ILL) network, or jointly owned a film collection. The current use of the term *networking* acknowledges the development of online infrastructures through which members are linked to resources through some type of telecommunications connection. The participants include multistate and multi-type libraries.

Successful networks are characterized by a financial and organizational commitment from the members, who agree to perform specific tasks and adhere to specific guidelines. In return, the member library has immediate access through computer and communications technology to databases that originate in the public or private sector. Commonly held beliefs about networks are the following:

- Opportunity to access information is the right of each individual.
- Networks do not replace individual collections; rather, they enhance existing ones and expand their range of services.

- Participating libraries are responsible for meeting the daily needs of their users and for contributing to the network.
- Networking is not free. Costs include equipment, materials, computer time, postage, telephone, copying expenses, and staff time.
- Effective communication among participants is essential.
- Commitment to participation is made at the school district level.
- Local, district, and regional levels of service must be clearly defined.
- School-level personnel need to be notified early in the process and kept informed about plans.
- Decisions must be made as to which services such as bibliographic retrieval, cataloging, or interlibrary loan the network will provide.
- Delivery systems for bibliographic data and information retrieval must be spelled out.
- Remuneration to or from systems must be mutually agreed upon.
- Legislative issues and governance must be agreed upon.

Several states have developed network projects that can be used by school librarians. Wisconsin's BadgerLink is a project begun in 1998 by the Wisconsin Department of Education whose services are available in the state's public, school, academic, and special libraries. They contract with vendors to provide users' access to articles from newspapers and periodicals, image files, specialized reference materials, and websites. INFOhio, a virtual K-12 library, is funded by the state of Ohio. Its resources are available to all of Ohio's K-12 students and teachers. Florida's SUNLINK in partnership with Follett Software Company provides over 30 million titles from 2,750 in K-12 schools in Florida (Follett, 2009). These resources are available to K-12 schools in Florida. These types of projects provide extremely valuable services to their users, including access to electronic materials, interlibrary loan transactions, and cataloging information.

Some states provide funds for databases that can be accessed electronically. To stretch their dollars school libraries need to take advantage of these state-provided databases.

ALTERNATIVE FUNDING

It is a sad time in education when schools are not able to provide the funds to purchase the necessary materials and equipment to support the curriculum of a school and to provide resources for the personal interests of young people. Nonetheless, this is the reality in many communities. Besides fulfilling the major roles of school librarians in recent years, librarians have also needed to develop skills in both fundraising and grant writing.

Fundraising

With rising costs of materials and tightening of budgets, many school librarians have taken up projects for fundraising. While it is possible to sell school supplies out of the school library office or hold garage sales to obtain alternative funding, the author of this book does not recommend such endeavors. Rather, it seems more appropriate to undertake projects that can contribute to the goals of a school library and at the same time raise monies. Sponsoring a book fair is a good example of such a project. Book fairs, however, can be very time consuming so you should solicit the help of parent volunteers or the PTSA organization. While the profits can sometimes be very large for schools with large enrollments or where the economic status of the students is high, in other instances the profit share can be low compared to the amount of time and effort necessary to conduct a book fair. Scholastic and Troll are two publishers who provide book fair materials to many school libraries. Bookstores in a community are sometimes willing to provide materials for a school book fair. If you are a school librarian in a parochial school, you can ask a local religious bookstore if they are interested in collaborating with you on a book fair. Most companies or bookstores that help sponsor book fairs provide either a smaller monetary cash profit, typically 20–30 percent of the sales, or a larger amount if you purchase materials from them with a share of the profits.

Another creative idea for fundraising is to conduct a *read-a-thon* in which students get pledges from family and friends for the number of books that the students read. Students often earn prizes for their fundraising efforts. Local merchants can be asked to provide prizes. Such a project can raise monies for the library while also encouraging reading.

If your school plans an author visit, you should contact a local bookstore to see if they would like to collaborate with you by having multiple copies of the author's books available for sale—providing you with a share of the profits, of course. Most authors are happy to autograph their books, making them even more special to students. Remember to provide adequate time in an author visit for the sale and autographing of the books.

Most of the fundraising projects that you may want to sponsor will take much extra time and effort. Organizing a Friends of the Library group or meeting with the PTSA to share your ideas about fundraising can result in finding able helpers for your projects.

Grant Writing

School librarians can obtain outside funding through grant proposals, with monies coming from local, regional, or national sources. Many of the grant opportunities can be found by searching on the Internet. Some school districts also hire professional grant writers to be in charge of researching possible grants and assisting in the writing of grant proposals. You should be proactive and ask your administrator and classroom teachers to provide you with information on possible grants that could enhance your collection. Do not simply wait for announcements or calls for grant proposals.

Most grants are very specific, and the funds can be used only for specific purposes. Some of the possible funding opportunities include adding new technologies, upgrading technology, purchasing computer software and audiovisual materials, financial support for resource sharing, subscribing to online databases, and improving facilities. Since student reading test scores have been emphasized in recent years several grants provide funding for materials and projects that can improve literacy.

Each grant has its own specifications that must be carefully followed in order for a school library to be considered as a possible recipient of funds. Typical elements in a proposal are the following:

- *Cover sheet*: Brief identification of project, goals, and beneficiaries of the project.
- *Abstract*: Brief summary of project.
- *Table of contents*
- *Introduction*: Description of applicant, purpose, programs, constituents, credibility of organization and its accomplishments, and credibility of proposed program.
- *Needs statement*: Need, support data, and experiences.
- *Goals and objectives*: Intent and anticipated outcomes of the proposed project.

- *Project design*: Plan of action, activities, and methods planned to achieve the project objectives.
- *Budget*: Costs and expenditures for personnel (includes wages, salaries, and fringe benefits) and non-personnel (includes equipment and supplies).
- *Evaluation design*: Plans for determining whether goals are met, assessing process and product, and identifying who will monitor and evaluate.
- *Dissemination*: Identification of what will be reported to whom and how that information will be distributed.
- *Plans for the future*: Outline of how the project will be supported after outside funding runs out.
- *Appendix (you should refer to these items in the narrative)*: Examples of items to include are the mission statement, bibliography, vitae of personnel, and letters of commitment and endorsement.

The Foundation Center <http://foundationcenter.org> established in 1956 is a national nonprofit organization whose mission is to strengthen the nonprofit sector by advancing knowledge about U.S. philanthropy. The center maintains a comprehensive database on U.S. grant makers and their grants. *Fundsnet Services.com* <http://www.fundsnetservices.com> is another useful website that provides grant seekers with opportunities to obtain information on financial resources. The "Additional Readings" and "Helpful Websites" listings at the end of this chapter identify additional sources.

CONCLUSIONS

School librarians face fiscal issues when dealing with their collections. They must have knowledge relating to budgeting processes and how to request the funds needed to administer effective school library programs. Since it is not possible to purchase all available resources that are desired or needed, alternative methods of obtaining materials should be considered. One means of obtaining use of materials is to subscribe to online electronic resources. With such subscriptions, licenses must be negotiated. Many issues should be considered when agreeing to licenses. Some issues include who is authorized to access materials, whether remote access outside of a school is needed, and deciding how content of the materials can be used.

In order to make more materials available to their users, some school librarians participate in resource sharing, which are generally set up through electronic networks with libraries in their own school district or state, or perhaps with other types of libraries. In this way, they are able to provide their users with materials through interlibrary loan. Other means of obtaining the funds needed for a school library collection include fundraising (sponsoring book fairs or read-a-thons) and writing grants.

REFERENCES

Dickinson, G. (2004). Budgeting as easy as 1-2-3: How to ask for—and get—the money you need. *Library Media Connection, 22*(6), 14–17.

Follett. (2009). *Follett Software Company, Florida's SUNLINK partner to offer statewide library union catalog.* Retrieved from http://www.follettsoftware.com/press.cfm?vPress=1890

Kenney, B. (2010). A federal fumble. *School Library Journal, 56*(3), 9.

ADDITIONAL READINGS

Anderson, C. (2011). Free money! *Knowledge Quest, 40*(2), 10–13.

Anderson, C., & Knop, K. (2008). *Write grants, get money*. Columbus, OH: Linworth.

Carpenter, J. (2008). *Library project funding: A guide to planning and writing proposals*. New York: Neal-Schuman.

Edwards, B. (2012). Can-do spirit: Facing the challenges of budget cuts. *Knowledge Quest, 40*(3), 54–57.

Flanders, J. (2010). Grant writing on the web: Resources for finding and securing funding. *College & Research Libraries News, 71*(9), 472–475, 479.

Franklin, P., & Stephens, C. G. (2008). Gaining skills to write winning grants. *School Library Media Activities Monthly, 25*(3), 43–44.

Franklin, P., & Stephens, C. G. (2010). Is L4L worth the effort in a struggling economy? *School Library Journal, 26*(9), 36–37.

Harns, L. E. (2009). *Licensing digital content: A practical guide for librarians*. Chicago: American Library Association.

Johns, S. K. (2011). Your school needs a frugal librarian! *Library Media Connection, 29*(4), 26–29.

Johnson, G. (2009). Greening our libraries: Practical advice for saving the planet and your budget. *Mississippi Libraries, 73*(4), 86–88.

Kachinske, T., & Kachniske, J. (2010). *90 days to success in grant writing*. Boston, MA: Course Technology.

Landau, H. (2010). Winning grants: A game plan. *American Libraries, 41*(9), 34–36.

Landau, H. (2011). *Winning grants: A game plan*. Chicago: American Library Association.

Staines, G. M. (2010). *Go get that grant: A practical guide for libraries and nonprofit organizations*. Lanham, MD: Scarecrow.

Taylor, C. (2010). Thinking out of the box: Fundraising during economic downturns. *The Serials Librarian, 59*(3/4), 370–383.

Vandenbroek, A. (2010). Grant writing without blowing a gasket. *Library Media Connection, 28*(6), 28–30.

HELPFUL WEBSITES

American Library Association of School Librarians. (2011). *Awards & grants*. Retrieved from http://www.ala.org/ala/mgrps/divs/aasl/aaslawards/aaslawards.cfm

Follett Library Resources. (n.d.). *Grants & funding*. Retrieved from http://www.grantwrangler.com/librarygrants.html

Foundation Center: Knowledge to build on. (2011). Retrieved from http://foundationcenter.org

Fundsnet Services.com (2012). *Grants fundraising.com*. Retrieved from http://www.fundsnetservices.com

Grant Wrangler. (2010). *Library grants and resources*. Retrieved from http://www.grantwrangler.com/librarygrants.html

INFOhio: The information network for Ohio schools. (2011). Retrieved from http://www.infohio.org/

The Laura Bush Foundation for America's Libraries. (n.d.). Retrieved from http://www.laurabushfoundation.org/

SUNLINK. (2006). Retrieved from http://www.sunlink.ucf.edu

U.S. Department of Education. (n.d.). *Grants*. Retrieved from http://www2.ed.gov/fund/landing.jhtml

U.S. Department of Education. (n.d.). *Improving literacy through school library grants*. Retrieved from http://www.grantwrangler.com/librarygrants.html

Wisconsin Department of Public Instruction. (n.d.). *What is BadgerLink?* Retrieved from http://www.badgerlink.net/about.html

Chapter 17 Facilities, Digital Resources, and the Learning Environment

School library facilities have an impact on the resources that they house and the utilization of the library collection. As school libraries have added digital resources, there has been a change in the requirements for both physical and virtual space. A primary role of today's school librarian is to provide in those spaces a learning environment where the focus is on helping student learners gain and use media skills ethically and productively.

FACILITIES

Making better use of space in a school library sometimes results in having smaller onsite collections. However, directing students and teachers to the use of items in the physical collection remains critical in a school library. One of the best ways this can be done is through effective signage that is geared toward the age level of the students. When students or teachers enter your school library facility there should be clear, large signs that easily direct them to locate the materials they are seeking. If there are many ESL students in your school, you should consider adding Spanish or another appropriate language to the signs. Although many types of attractive signs can be purchased from library supply vendors, computer-generated signs with clip art or photographs can also be effective. Student volunteers sometimes enjoy creating such signs that can be used to announce award-winning titles or the availability of new digital resources (Sullivan, 2010).

Shelving that is too high for young students to reach needed materials can not only frustrate students as they seek access to materials in a collection, but it also can be a safety hazard if children stand on chairs or climb on shelves to reach desired items. Unstable rotating racks used for paperback books or the removal of all books from one side of such a rack can also cause a safety problem. The needs of students with disabilities must also be considered when placing materials on shelves. Although the suggested maximum bookshelf height is 72 inches, the maximum reach up from most wheelchairs is 54 inches from the floor. Aisles between bookcases should be at least 36 inches for wheelchair accessibility and at least 42 inches if a student in a wheelchair needs to turn and face the opposite bookcase or if other students want to pass a wheelchair in an aisle. Shelves more than 36 inches wide cannot safely hold books without supplementary support. Adjustable shelving makes it possible to more easily accommodate different size materials and shift materials when needed. Slick shelf surfaces like those on metal bookcases make it difficult for book ends and materials to stay in place. Shelves that are overcrowded with books or other materials can also make it difficult for students to remove the desired resources. Mobile shelving can be especially effective in shifting attention to a particular part of the collection.

Setting up displays of library resources in the library or in glass cases in school halls also can draw attention to the materials you want to promote. Using a kiosk with large monitors and looping information on available computer software is an ideal way to introduce students and teachers to new books or materials.

Lighting can not only add ambiance to your school library, but it also can impact the use of materials in a school library. Accent lighting can be used to bring attention to a display of books or to a thematic bulletin board featuring books and other materials. Good lighting in the areas where students read or work on projects makes it easier and more comfortable to use resources. Taking advantage of the sun's natural lighting from windows or skylights can add beauty to the environment and at the same time reduce the need for artificial lighting.

Arrangement of a school library facility should motivate students to learn. Long bookcases of shelves tend to make a library look like an uninviting warehouse. Instead, try using smaller groups of bookcases that are broken up with tables for group work or comfortable chairs for leisure reading. Visiting a successful local bookstore and taking note of their furniture, signage, and display arrangements can give you possible ideas to use in your school library to make the environment more inviting.

DIGITAL RESOURCES

School libraries in the 21st century are not simply warehouses for books and other materials as some may have been in the past. More and more digital resources are being integrated into school libraries and are being utilized by students and teachers for both school assignments and special interests. School librarians are also using digital resources and a wide range of technologies in their instruction. Thus, collections are being vastly expanded to include digital resources and virtual spaces. Digital libraries are now launched from school library websites and can be accessed from classrooms and homes. Databases with numerous resources are available to students online, and e-books and audiobooks are being added to school library networks. In many cases, more than one student is able to access these digital resources simultaneously, a distinct advantage over print materials.

Web 2.0 has also made it possible for many digital resources to be interactive. Setting up book blogs for students to discuss books that they have read or allowing students to use Twitter to find comments made by a favorite author are just a couple examples of how Web 2.0 can be effectively used.

Digital resources also call for an abundance of electrical outlets and careful planning of where computers are placed in a school library. Consolidating the student computers and printers in one area of the library makes it easier to supervise and instruct students as they access digital resources. Laptops and handheld devices need recharging so providing some eight-outlet power sources is appreciated by both students and staff.

Personal Electronic Device Contract

I understand that the use of cell phones, iPods, iPads, MP3 players, or other electronic devices at school is a privilege, and not a right. I understand that if I choose to bring a personal electronic device to school and it is lost, damaged, or stolen, that the school is not responsible and will not reimburse me.

With the exception of the cafeteria, personal electronic devices may not be in use, turned on or visible during customary school hours. I understand that these devices may be used in the classroom as part of a lesson or classroom activity, but only with the prior approval of a teacher or administrator.

I accept that inappropriate behavior or violation of this contract may result in confiscation of equipment, disciplinary action and/or legal action. I also understand the following may occur if this contract is violated:

1st offense—confiscation of the personal electronic device, student warning, and device will be returned at the end of the school day.

2nd offense—confiscation of the device for 24–48 hours, and the student's parent/guardian will be notified.

3rd offense—confiscation of the device until a parent/guardian conference can be scheduled to return the device.

I will accept full responsibility and liability for the results of my actions involving the use of personal electronic devices at school. I release the school from any liability resulting from my use of these devices during school hours.

Student Signature: ______________________

Date: ________________________________

Figure 17.1. Personal electronic device contract

In some school libraries, students are allowed to use their own personal electronic devices, such as laptops, mp3 players, or cell phones to access digital resources. In such cases, it is important that students sign a personal electronic device contract so they understand appropriate use of the devices. The contract should include consequences for inappropriate use. Sometimes such a contract is drafted by a school committee and enforced throughout a school. Figure 17.1 is an example of a possible contract that could be used for personal electronic devices.

LEARNING ENVIRONMENT

Students need to use a variety of informational resources and technologies as they learn to formulate meaningful questions, work on collaborative projects, and create information. *Learning commons* is a term that has been recently used in the school library profession; however, it has been present for the last couple of decades in higher institutions of learning. It refers to transformation from traditional library space to facilities and instruction where students and teachers can master information technology (Mihailidis & Diggs, 2010). *Media literacy* aligns with the learning commons approach. It refers to the ability to exhibit critical thinking skills in relation to information media and technology. Although students in today's libraries have a world of information at their fingertips and are often called *digital natives*, they are still in need of learning how to evaluate resources, problem solve, and use information to appropriately engage with others.

The learning environment in a school library includes not only young people reading books, magazines, and newspapers, but also students who are actively engaged in connecting to resources and persons outside the walls of the school library. Librarians can provide direction to these students by helping them become engaged, safe, and responsible media users in their daily lives.

CONCLUSIONS

Making better use of school library facilities to house and promote the collection is essential. This also includes making certain that students with disabilities have equitable access to materials. The integration of technology and digital resources into school libraries has affected both the physical and virtual space requirements. School libraries continue to change to meet the needs of 21st-century learners. School librarians, in turn, are providing environments where students can develop effective and responsible media literacy skills.

REFERENCES

Mihailidis, P. & Diggs, V. (2010). From information reserve to media literacy learning commons: Revisiting the 21st century library as the home for media literacy education. *Public Library Quarterly, 29*(4), 279–292.

Sullivan, M. (2010). Merchandising your library resources. *Teacher Librarian, 38*(2), 30–31.

ADDITIONAL READINGS

Bolan, K. (2008). *Teen spaces: The step-by-step library makeover* (2nd ed.). Chicago: American Library Association.

Callison, D. (2007). Evaluation criteria for the places of learning. *Knowledge Quest, 35*(3), 14–19.

Cicchetti, R. (2010). Concord-Carlisle transitions to a learning commons. *Teacher Librarian, 37*(3), 52–58.

Corbett, T. (2011). The changing role of the school library's physical space. *School Library Monthly, 27*(7), 5–7.

Erickson, R., & Markuson, C. (2007). *Designing a school library media center for the future* (2nd ed.). Chicago: American Library Association.

Feinberg, S., & Keller, J. R. (2010). *Designing space for children and teens in libraries and public places*. Chicago: American Library Association.

Oswald, J. (2010). Change in the library—for the good. *Library Media Connection, 28*(5), 28–29.

Purcell, M. (2011). The vision: Libraries of the future. *Library Media Connection, 29*(4), 38–39.

Schultz-Jones, B. (2010). School librarians, science teachers + optimal learning environments. *Knowledge Quest, 39*(2), 12–18.

Sinclair, B. (2007). Commons 2.0: Library spaces designed for collaborative learning. *EDUCAUSE Quarterly, 30*(4). Retrieved from http://www.educause.edu/EDUCAUSE+Quarterly/EDUCAUSEQuarterlyMagazineVolum/Commons20LibrarySpacesDesigned/162

Sullivan, M. (2011). *Divine design: How to create the 21st century school library of your dreams*. Retrieved from http://www.libraryjournal.com/slj/home/889642–312/divine_design_how_to_create.html.csp

White, B. (2011). Toward a learning commons: My journey, your journey. *Teacher Librarian, 38*(3), 27–30.

Young, T. E. (2010). Marketing your school library media center: What we can learn from national bookstores. *Library Media Connection, 28*(6), 18–20.

HELPFUL WEBSITES

National Clearinghouse for Educational Facilities. (2011). *Library and media center facilities design—K-12*. Retrieved from http://www.ncef.org/rl/libraries.cfm

National Library of New Zealand. (n.d.). *Library physical environment*. Retrieved from http://schools.natlib.govt.nz/developing-your-library/managing-your-library/library-physical-environment

Partnership for 21st century skills. (n.d.). *21st century learning environments*. Retrieved from http://www.p21.org/documents/le_white_paper-1.pdf

U.S. Department of Justice. (2010). *ADA home page*. Retrieved from http://www.ada.gov/

Wisconsin Department of Public Instruction. (2008). *Classrooms, library media centers, and new technology*. Retrieved from http://dpi.state.wi.us/imt/dsgn-1pg.html

Chapter

Opening, Moving, or Closing the Collection

When student populations shift or there is a change in grade levels served by a school, librarians respond by creating initial collections, combining collections, or closing a collection. The school library might also be moved to a different location within the same school campus. Each situation presents different demands upon school librarians' knowledge and skills. A librarian's human relations skills may be tested in the tensions of these experiences. Emotions can run high when a school is closed or a favorite group or grade level is lost.

CREATING INITIAL COLLECTIONS

The opening of a new school calls for the creation of an initial collection. When a new building is being planned, various patterns of preparation for the initial collection can occur. The optimal time to begin planning is when the building contract is awarded. In an ideal situation, a school librarian and faculty are hired to plan during the year preceding the opening of the building. This procedure has definite advantages. The school librarian can benefit from participating with faculty members as they identify philosophies and goals, create a curriculum, and develop plans. The librarian's major responsibility during the year is to ensure that the desired types of learning environments will be ready on the opening day. The librarian must place orders early enough to allow for delivery, processing, and time to make any necessary substitutions. Admittedly, school districts rarely have the financial resources or educational foresight to provide a whole year of planning.

Even if an entire faculty is not engaged in planning during the year prior to opening a school, the collection needs to be ready on the opening day. If the school's staff has not been appointed, the responsibility often rests with district-level staff. Those planning the new facility need to be aware of the long-range goals and objectives of the district's educational program and the equipment and materials needed for an initial collection. Planners should design flexibility into plans to accommodate changes that may occur in teaching styles, subjects taught, and the needs of unknown users. An example of such flexibility would be to save a portion of the collection budget so it could be spent by the school librarian in the first few weeks of the school year when more information about the users of the collection is available.

Districts follow various patterns for handling orders for a new building. Some districts use one-third of the initial collection budget to buy materials to have on opening day. One third is reserved for recommendations by the principal and professional staff. The remaining one-third is reserved for orders generated by the school librarian, who works with teachers and students to make selections. Other districts spend the entire first year's budget prior to the opening of the school. When making a budget, school district administrators and staff must also consider the cost of licensing electronic resources for the collection.

School districts with recent student population growth patterns may have lists of recommendations for the initial collection or have electronic holdings records of such collections. In some cases, these districts are willing to share or sell their lists. This type of list is designed to cover the broad scope needed by teachers and students in widely varying school communities and may be revised annually. You should contact district school library supervisors to determine if such lists exist in their school districts.

Major book jobbers also offer prepackaged opening day collections. Even though such a package, or any list developed by other school districts, may not address your school's unique needs, there are some advantages to these packages. Current costs are known, out-of-print titles are excluded, time and effort is saved by not having to consider unavailable items, the librarian can add additional materials, and the printout of online orders saves time. Such a list, however, has disadvantages. Direct order items and standing order items will not be covered, items requiring licensing will not be included, and the unique needs of the school may not be met.

General guidelines about the number of items that should be in an initial collection may also be available from the state's school library consultant or state school library association. These guidelines may outline the formats as well as stages of development, from the initial collection to one considered to be excellent.

By using selection aids, one can identify specific titles for a collection. Useful sources include *Children's Catalog* (H.W. Wilson), *Middle and Junior High School Core Collection* (H.W. Wilson), and *Senior High School Library Catalog* (H.W. Wilson). These tools are found in print format as well as online. Additional helpful resources can be found in the "Appendix Resources." The broad scope and coverage of these tools help librarians identify titles to match the wide range of information needs that will be experienced during the opening days of a collection.

SHIFTING OR MOVING COLLECTIONS

Sometimes it becomes necessary to shift or move entire collections. This might occur because of redesigning, remodeling, simply outgrowing space for the present collection, or relocating the entire school library. Moving or shifting a collection is no easy task. Planning is essential in order to avoid many frustrations that can result from such a move.

The following suggestions can help you successfully move a collection with a minimum number of problems:

1. Weed the collection before making a move or shift. There is no reason to move books that are not being used.
2. Read the shelves to ensure that all the books are in order.
3. Measure the floor, wall, and shelf space that will be available for the collection.
4. Make a paper model (to scale) of the school library facility to which you are moving. Be sure to draw in windows, furniture, and cabinets. Also indicate the electrical outlets.
5. Measure and log the amount of space needed for each section of books (as they presently line the shelves). Write in the sections on your paper model, making certain you leave adequate space for each section.
6. Choose sturdy boxes that are not too large for packing the books. Books are heavy, and you may need to move some of them yourself.
7. Pack boxes in reverse order, beginning with the last book on each shelf. When you unpack, the books will be in shelf order.
8. In large letters, label the boxes on the side, identifying which books are in each box. For instance, the easy picture books might be labeled "E AAR-ADA." Consider color coding boxes, using different color marking pens: blue for books that go in the easy section, yellow for fiction, green for nonfiction, and red for computer equipment.
9. Number the boxes and create a database that includes what is inside each box.
10. Put all unpacking supplies (scissors, utility knives, tape, pens, and cleaning rags) in one box. Label it, "Supplies! Open Me First!"
11. Have the movers place all the boxes (in numerical order) near the bookcases where they will be shelved to avoid overlooking a box. If the labels are color coded it will help the movers quickly locate the part of the library where the boxes should be placed.
12. Choose your un-packers carefully and watch closely over their work.
13. Do not fill all the shelves. Leave at least one-fourth of each shelf to allow for expansion.
14. If space allows, do not use the bottom shelves. It is difficult to read the labels on the spines on the bottom shelves. Also, this will again leave room for expansion in individual sections.
15. Do not forget to plan for your online collection as well. Plan the location of computers so they are accessible to electrical outlets and away from the heavy traffic areas. Be sure adequate work surfaces are available next to each computer.
16. Have technicians install and test the equipment, including the computers that house the circulation system.

If these steps are followed when moving a collection, it should avoid many possible problems, but you should also remember to expect the unexpected and not get frustrated with situations that are out of your control.

CLOSING COLLECTIONS

When schools are closed, consolidated, or have attendance districts reorganized, the full impact might not be felt until the formal announcement is made. Someone should be responsible for determining the procedures for removing materials. School librarians must be involved in the planning to avoid confusion and inefficiency.

Consolidation and reorganization of attendance districts can be hot issues calling for special handling by the school librarian. Knowledge about the situation, diplomacy, and tact will help. Perhaps the loss can be turned into a gain for other schools in the district. Planning is the key factor in retaining items that a collection needs, while also preparing for the transfer of other items. Send information about available items, with plans for their transfer, to the receiving school. Assess each of the newly formed collections in terms of their weaknesses and strengths in meeting the new demands.

When schools close, answers to the following questions can guide the planning process. What will be the disposition of the materials, equipment, and furniture? What legal guidelines are there for the disposition of materials and equipment? Are there local constraints? What are the closing deadlines? Will extra help be available?

Once the target date is known, you should create a timeline with specific goals. This information can be posted to alert users and staff so they will be aware of when the school librarian plans to curtail services. Teachers who are moving to other schools can help you by indicating the titles they want available in the other schools. These items should be allocated first so they can be processed into the collections.

You should refer to your policies to see if there are criteria that might relate to the closing of a collection. For instance, does the policy on gift materials provide for transferring the materials to another school? You also need to check to determine if there are additional materials that other regulations or agreements cover. This should be done before deciding on how to dispose of items.

You can provide a list of remaining materials in your library and distribute the list to other schools in the district so librarians can request specific titles. Any items that are not requested will need to be stored, distributed, or discarded. Distribution possibilities include storing materials at an exchange center where they can be examined, or donating the materials to other agencies serving children, such as youth centers. Policies within the district will govern how you can disperse materials; the district may grant approval for sale to other library collections or to individuals.

CONCLUSIONS

Instances occur in which a collection may need to be opened, moved, or closed. In each case, a school librarian will need to follow specific guidelines, as well as be aware of the emotions that may accompany the shifting of a grade level to another school or closing down a school. Early preparations for creating a new collection can make it possible for the school library to be open on the first day that a new school begins operation. Useful selection aids can assist in the selection of an initial school library collection. If a grade level leaves a school or a new grade is added to a school, the collection will need to be assessed and adjusted to meet student and curriculum needs. Following specific guidelines and tips for moving an entire collection can save time and prevent much frustration. When closing an entire collection, it is essential that school librarians follow any existing policies or regulations for the disposition and disposal of resources.

ADDITIONAL READINGS

Bundy, A. (2010). Moving library collections. *Australasian Public Libraries and Information Services, 23*(2), 80.

Fortriede, S.C. (2010). *Moving your library: Getting the collection from here to there*. Chicago: American Library Association.

Information Today. (2010). Getting a move on. *Searcher, 18*(6), 8–11.

Minter, S. (2007). On your mark, get set, MOVE! *Library Media Connection, 25*(7), 44–46.

Stephens, J. (2011). The last of the chicken boxes! *Library Media Connection, 29*(4), 34–35.

Taylor, K. (2000). Reflections on opening a new library media center. *Florida Media Quarterly, 25* (4), 8–9.

Welch, R. (2010). *A core collection for young adults* (2nd ed.). New York: Neal-Schuman.

Wilson, L. (2004). Bringing vision to practice: Planning and provisioning the new library resource center. *Teacher Librarian, 32* (1), 23–27.

HELPFUL WEBSITES

Adcock, D. (n.d.). *Closing—school library media centers.* Retrieved from http://www.lib.niu.edu/1984/il840292.html

American Library Association. (2010). *Moving libraries: ALA library fact sheet 14*. Retrieved from http://www.ala.org/ala/professionalresources/libfactsheets/alalibraryfactsheet14.cfm

Chappell, S. (2006). *Moving library collections: Planning shifts of library collections*. Retrieved from http://libweb.uoregon.edu/acs_svc/shift/

Lamb, A., & Johnson, L. (2010). *Library media program: Collection mapping.* Retrieved from http://eduscapes.com/sms/program/mapping.html

Appendix: Resources

This list identifies books, journals, electronic sources, and organizations useful in dealing with collection matters. In January 2007, books began to be assigned ISBN numbers containing 13 digits, instead of 10. When available, both the 10-digit numbers and the 13-digit numbers are included in this listing. The newer, longer number is preceded with a "13." It should be used when possible for ordering purposes or you may want to include both numbers. For additional resources, see the listings at the end of chapters.

A to Zoo: Subject Access to Children's Picture Books. 8th ed. Carolyn W. Lima and Rebecca L. Thomas. Santa Barbara, CA: Libraries Unlimited, 2010. ISBN 13 978159884061.

Identifies more than 27,000 titles (fiction and nonfiction) for preschoolers through second graders. Titles are grouped in over 1,200 subjects and indexed by author, title, and illustrator. Five sections: subject headings, subject guide, bibliographic guide, title index, and illustrator index.

Abridged Readers' Guide to Periodical Literature. See *Readers' Guide to Periodical Literature.*

Accelerated Reader. Advantage Learning Systems, Inc. Wisconsin Rapids, WI: Renaissance Learning, 2005. ISBN 1594552002, ISBN 13 9781594552007.

Reading comprehension software, reading ability testing software for elementary to high school level. Two CD-ROMs. Includes: one software manual, installation guide, and four reading practice lists. More information about the software and the Accelerated Reading program (http://www.renlearn.com/ar/)

Across Cultures: A Guide to Multicultural Literature for Children. Kathy East and Rebecca L. Thomas. Westport, CT: Libraries Unlimited, 2007. ISBN 13 9781591583363.

Contains listings for more than 400 recent multicultural resources. Arranged by themes. Entries include author, title, publisher, date, ISBN, culture, and grade level.

Adaptive Technologies for Learning & Work Environments, 2nd ed. Joseph Lazzaro. Chicago, IL: American Library Association, 2001. ISBN 0838908047, ISBN 13 9780838908044.

Comprehensive coverage of personal computer hardware basics, keyboard commands, and latest technology for individuals with a range of disabilities. Includes information about accessing the Internet and Intranets and funding adaptive technology.

ALAN Review. Athens, GA: Assembly on Literature for Adolescents, National Council of Teachers of English, 1979–. ISSN 08822840.

Three times per year. Reviews new hardback and paperback titles for adolescents. Special-interest group. Subscription: ALAN Membership, payable to ALAN/NCTE, P.O. Box 10427, Largo, FL 33773 (http://scholar.lib.vt.edu/ejournals/ALAN).

American Book Publishing Record. New Providence, NJ: R. R. Bowker, 1960–. ISSN 00027707.

Monthly. Related Work: *American Book Publishing Record Cumulative*, 1984– (published annually). Compiles titles cataloged by the Library of Congress. Dewey classification arrangement. Provides full cataloging data, LC and DDC numbers, subject headings, and price. Author index.

American Foundation for the Blind.

Produces books, journals, videos, and electronic materials for individuals who are visually impaired and professionals who work with them (http://www.afb.org).

The American Hero in Children's Literature: A Standards-Based Approach. Carol M. Butzow and John W. Butzow. Westport, CT: Greenwood Publishing, 2005. ISBN 1594690049, ISBN 13 9781594690044.

Features more than 30 books exploring the way heroes have influenced American history, the American way of life, the lives of the people, and principles upon which the culture has developed.

American Journal of Health Education. Reston, VA: American Alliance for Health, Physical Education, Recreation and Dance, 1991–. ISSN 19325037.

Bimonthly. Multifaceted resource that aims for the advancement of the health education profession. Priorities of the American Association of Health Education include increasing the amount of available, valid research on health education, creating and fostering dialogue among health education professionals, and promoting related policies, procedures, and standards. Subscription: American Alliance for Health, Physical Education, Recreation and Dance, 1900 Association Drive, Reston, VA 20191 (http://www.aahperd.org/).

American Music Teacher. Cincinnati, OH: Music Teachers National Association, 1951–. ISSN 00030112.

Bimonthly. Covers earliest music history to the latest developments in music technology. Features articles on teaching methods and techniques. Reviews teaching materials, music publications, videocassettes, music software, and other new technology as well as issues and trends (http://www.mtna.org).

American Printing House for the Blind.

"The world's largest source for adapted educational and daily living products—since 1858." Provides educational materials in a variety of formats for visually impaired students (http://www.aph.org/).

American Reference Books Annual. Westport, CT: Libraries Unlimited, 1970–. ISSN 00659959. Also ISBN 1598845934, ISBN 13 9781598845938 (*American Reference Books Annual Edition* 2010, Volume 41).

Reviews print and electronic reference resources published in the United States and Canada. Includes author, title, and subject index (http://www.abc-clio.com/product.aspx?id=2147484177).

Around the World with Historical Fiction and Folktales: Highly Recommended and Award-Winning Books, Grades K-8. Beth Bartleson Zarian. Lanham, MD: Scarecrow, 2004. ISBN 0810848163, ISBN 13 9780810848160.

Guide to approximately 800 highly recommended and award-winning historical fiction books for K-8. Assists teachers and librarians in the selection of high-quality literature (OCLC).

ASHA Leader. Rockville, MD: American Speech-Language-Hearing Association, 1996–. ISSN 10859586. Also, the *ASHA Leader Online.* Available at http://www.asha.org/leader.aspx

Monthly. Full articles are available online. Reports on emerging issues and news of the profession. Subscription: *The ASHA Leader*, 10801 Rockville Pike, Rockville, MD 20852.

Assistive Technology: Access for All Students, 2nd ed. Lawrence A. Beard, Laura Bowden, and Linda B. Johnson. Boston: Pearson, 2011. ISBN 13 9780137056415.

Discusses how assistive technology can be used to meet the needs of students with disabilities. Includes a chapter on universal design.

Assistive Technology Journal. Jeff Jutai, ed. Arlington, VA: Publishing body: RESNA (AT Network). ISSN 10400435. Online at http://resna.org/resna-at-journal/assistive-technology-the-official-journal-of-resna

Quarterly. Rehabilitation Engineering and Assistive Technology Society of North America. Seeks to foster communication among researchers, developers, clinicians, educators, consumers, and others working in all aspects of the assistive technology arena. Subscription: RESNA 1700 N. Moore Street, Suite 1540 Arlington, VA 22209–1903 (http://resna.org/).

ATNetwork: Assistive Technology . . . Tools for Living.

Provides a definition of AT, lists AT laws, devices, and resources (http://www.atnet.org/).

Autism Speaks.

Includes information about the largest autism science and advocacy organization in the United States (http://www.autismspeaks.org/).

AV Market Place: The Complete Business Directory of Audio/Video. Medford, NJ: Information Today, 1989–. ISSN 10440445.

Annual. Lists addresses and services of producers, distributors, production services, manufacturers, and equipment dealers.

AV Market Place, 2011: The Complete Business Directory of Products and Services for the Audio/ Video Industry. 39th ed. Medford, NJ: Information Today, ISBN 1573874078, ISBN 13 9781573874076.

Lists addresses and services of producers, distributors, production services, manufacturers, and equipment dealers.

Best Books for Children: Preschool Through Grade. 9th ed. Catherine Barr and John T. Gillespie. Santa Barbara, CA: Libraries Unlimited/ABC-CLIO, 2010. Series title: Children's and Young Adult Literature Reference Series. ISBN 1591585759, ISBN 13 9781591585756.

Includes brief annotations for 25,000 titles that had two or three recommendations in leading journals. Helps build collections by topic. Provides bibliographic and order information and citations to reviews. Indexes by author and illustrator, title, grade level, and subject.

Best Books for High School Readers: Grades 9–12. 2nd ed. John Thomas Gillespie and Catherine Barr. Westport, CT: Libraries Unlimited, 2009. Series title: Children's and Young Adult Literature Reference Series. ISBN 1591585767, ISBN 13 9781591585763.

Easy-to-navigate resource covering more than 12,000 titles. Includes annotations, plot summaries, reading levels, review citations, and ISBNs. Enables the evaluation of teen literature collections and assists in the creation of thematic and genre-oriented reading lists. Author, title, and subject indexes.

Best Books for High School Readers, Supplement to the Second Edition: Grades 9–12. John Thomas Gillespie and Catherine Barr. Santa Barbara, CA: Libraries Unlimited, 2011. Series title: Children's and Young Adult Literature Reference Series. ISBN 1598847856, ISBN 13 9781598847857.

Enables the evaluations of teen literature collections and assists in the creation of thematic and genre-oriented reading lists. Includes elements such as annotations, bibliographic data, and plot summaries that can aid in curriculum development and recreational reading selection.

Best Books for Middle School and Junior High Readers: Grades 6–9. 2nd ed. John Thomas Gillespie and Catherine Barr. Westport, CT: Libraries Unlimited, 2009. ISBN 1591585732, ISBN 13 9781591585732.

Evaluates teen literature and enables creation of thematic and genre-oriented reading lists. Includes elements such as annotations, bibliographic data, and plot summaries that can aid in curriculum development and recreational reading selection.

Best Books for Middle School and Junior High Readers, Supplement to the Second Edition: Grades 6–9. John Thomas Gillespie and Catherine Barr. Santa Barbara, CA: Libraries Unlimited, 2011. Series title: Children's and Young Adult Literature Reference Series. ISBN 159884783X, ISBN 13 978159158847833.

Evaluates teen literature and enables creation of thematic and genre-oriented reading lists.

Best Books for Young Adults. 3rd ed. Holly Koelling. Chicago: Young Adult Library Services Association, 2007. ISBN 0838935699 (alk. paper), ISBN 13 9780838935699 (alk. paper). Rev. ed. of: *Best Books for Young Adults*/Betty Carter, with Sally Estes and Linda Waddle.

Contains indexed, annotated lists of the best YA books over the past 40 years as well as 27 reproducible book lists that are perfect for collection and curriculum development. Serves as a great resource for all libraries that provide services to teens.

The Best of Latino Heritage, 1996–2002: A Guide to the Best Juvenile Books about Latino People. Isabel Schon. Lanham, MD: Scarecrow, 2003. ISBN 0810846691, ISBN 13 9780810846692.

Lists English in-print books for students in K-12 published in United States. Chapters explore specific Latino countries and cultures, people, history, art, political, social, and economic problems of Latin America and Spain.

BIBZ Selection Tool. Brodart Co.

Web-based service for collection development and ordering. Allows user to search and access relevant titles, build customized bibliographies, select best items, and order online. Includes free full-text reviews from *Kirkus Reviews*. (http://www.bibz.com/)

Black Books Galore! Guide to Great African American Children's Books about Boys. Donna Rand and Toni Trent Parker. New York: John Wiley & Sons, 2001. ISBN 0471437182 (electronic bk), ISBN 13 9780471437185 (electronic bk).

Descriptions of over 600 books. Hundreds of young black heroes, heroines, and positive role models of every age in every category, including board books, story and picture books, fiction, nonfiction, poetry, history, biography, and fables. Includes indexes.

Black Books Galore! Guide to Great African American Children's Books about Girls. Donna Rand and Toni Trent Parker. New York: John Wiley, 2001. ISBN 0471437190 (electronic bk.), ISBN 13 9780471437192 (electronic bk.).

Listings organized by age-level and indexed by title, topic, author, and illustrator. Reflections from famous public figures about their favorite childhood books. Includes bibliographical references and indexes.

Black Books Galore! Guide to More Great African American Children's Books. Donna Rand and Toni Trent Parker. New York: John Wiley, 2001. ISBN 047137525X, ISBN 13 9780471375258, ISBN 0585238944 (electronic bk.), ISBN 13 9780585238944 (electronic bk.).

Features 400 titles and reading plans for historical events, major holidays, and seasons. Descriptions of an additional 200 recommendations. Easy-to-find listings organized by age level. Includes the Coretta Scott King Awards, the Newbery Awards, The Caldecott Awards, and Reading Rainbow selections. Reading interest websites are listed.

Book Bridges for ESL Students: Using Young Adult and Children's Literature to Teach ESL. Suzanne Elizabeth Reid. Lanham, MD: Scarecrow, 2002. ISBN 0810842130, ISBN 13 9780810842137.

Includes basic principles of teaching ESL students; a rationale for using literature in the ESL classroom; using a single work of literature for various activities; the use of picture books for basic-level learners; using fiction and nonfiction works to teach history, math, and science; using multicultural literature; and teaching special populations. Bibliography of recommended literature, activities, suggested materials for classroom use, and lesson plans.

Book Links: Connecting Books, Libraries, and Classrooms. Chicago: American Library Association, 1991–. ISSN 10554742 (http://www.ala.org/ala/aboutala/offices/publishing/booklinks/index.cfm).

Quarterly supplement to *Book List*. Discusses old and new titles. Includes "Quick Tips" with easy to implement classroom ideas, "Classroom Connections bibliographies" that link literature to curricular topics, author profiles and author interviews. Subscription: American Library Association, 50 E. Huron Street, Chicago, IL 60611 (http://www.booklistonline.com/default.aspx?part=booklinks).

Book Review Digest. Bronx, New York: H. W. Wilson, 1905–. ISSN 00067326.

Monthly (except February and July). Quarterly and annual accumulations. "Excerpts from and citations to reviews of more than 8,000 books each year, drawn from coverage of 109 publications" (from website). Available on CD-ROM and online. *Book Review Digest Plus*. Online at http://www.hwwilson.com/Databases/brdig.htm

The Book Review Index. Beverly Baer, ed. Farmington Hills, MI: Gale, 1965–. ISSN 05240581. (Formerly *The Book Report*).

Three times a year. Provides reviews of books, books on tape, and electronic media from a wide range of popular, academic, and professional sources. Subscription: http://www.galegroup.com. Print editions are available.

Book Review Index Online.

An online database of more than 4 million books (http://www.gale.cengage.com/BRIOnline/).

Bookbird: A Journal of International Children's Literature. Toronto, ON, Canada: International Board on Books for Young People, 1962–. ISSN 00067377.

Quarterly. Includes a variety of children's literature topics as well as information on children's literature studies and awards. Subscription: University of Toronto Press-Journals Division, 5201 Dufferin Street, Toronto, ON, Canada, M3H 5T8.

Booklist. Chicago: American Library Association, 1905–. ISSN 00067385. Also *Booklist Online* (http://www.booklistonline.com/)

Semimonthly (22/year). Reviews current books, videos, and software on regular basis. Reviews foreign language materials and materials on special topics in irregular columns. Provides monthly author/title index and semiannual cumulative indexes. Includes *Reference Books Bulletin* with reviews of encyclopedias, dictionaries, atlases, and other books using a continuous revision policy. Subscription: Kable Fulfillment Services, 308 Hitt St., Mt. Morris, IL 61054–7564 (http://www.ala.org).

Books for the Teen Age. New York Public Library, Committee on Books for Young Adults, 1929–. ISSN 00680192.

Annual. In 2009, *Books for the Teen Age* became *Stuff for the Teen Age*. In 2010, *Stuff for the Teen Age* became a blog. Includes book picks for teens by teens, as well as selections from the top 100 teen titles from the previous year. More information: Office of Branch Libraries, New York Public Library, 455 Fifth Avenue, New York, NY 10016 (http://www.nypl.org/voices/blogs/blog-channels/sta).

Books in Print. New Providence, NJ: R.R. Bowker, 1947–. ISSN 00680214.

Annual. Serves as the definitive bibliographic resource with more than 1,879,000 titles of the full range of books currently published or distributed in the United States. Related works include *Subject Guide to Books in Print, Books in Print Supplement, Forthcoming Books, Publishers, Distributors and Wholesalers of the United States*. Also *Books In Print* ON DISC. Various titles available in print, CD-ROM, and online (http://www.booksinprint.com/bip/).

Books in Print Supplement. ISSN 00000310. See *Books in Print*.
Updates the *Books in Print* annual volume and the *Subject Guide to Books in Print* (OCLC).

Books Out Loud: Bowker's Guide to Audiobooks. New Providence, NJ: Grey House Publishing, 1985–. ISSN 00001805.
Annual in two volumes. Covers more than 85,500 audiocassettes. Indexes include title, authors, reader/performer, producer, and distributor.

Books Out Loud 2011: Bowker's Guide to Audiobooks. Bowker Staff, ed. New Providence, NJ: Grey House Publishing, 2011. ISBN 1592376878, ISBN 13 9781592376872.
In two volumes. Formerly *Words on Cassette*. Over 154,000 audiobooks including 56,000 audiobooks on CD. A highly comprehensive tool for collection development. Listings include comprehensive bibliographic resource with information on more than 154,000 audiobooks (http://www.greyhouse.com/bowk_bol.htm).

Booktalking Authentic Multicultural Literature. Sherry York. Columbus, OH: Linworth, 2008. ISBN 158683306, 13 978158633008.
Includes 1,010 booktalks of resources by authors of contemporary fiction for young readers (elementary through middle school). Provides indexes for subject, title, and author/illustrator/translator.

The Bowker Annual Library and Book Trade Almanac. Medford, NJ: Information Today, 1956–. ISSN 00680540.
Includes research and statistics such as average prices of books; news about legislation, associations, and grant-making agencies; lists of distinguished books; and directory information. As of 2009, this annual became *Library and Book Trade Almanac*.

Bowker's Complete Video Directory. New York: R.R. Bowker, 1988–. ISSN 1051290X.
Annual. Identifies more that 169,000 videos, in every format available, for entertainment and/or education.

Bowker's Complete Video Directory, 2011, Vols. 1–4. Bowker Staff, ed. New Providence, NJ: Grey House Publishing, 2011. ISBN 1592377009; ISBN 13 9781592377008.
250,000 selections in four volumes. Indexes include title, subject, genre, cast/director, and others. Coverage includes foreign, Spanish-language, children's, silent, and feature films.

Braille Book Review. Edmund O'Reilly, ed. Washington, DC: U.S. Library of Congress, The National Service for the Blind and Physically Handicapped (NLS), 1932–. ISSN 0006873X.
Bimonthly. Free to individuals with visual impairments and physical handicaps. Describes books for children and adults. Provides title, order code, author, number of volumes, and date of original print edition. Indexed monthly and annually. Includes news of developments and activities in library services. Identifies new Braille books and magazines. Address: U.S. Library of Congress, National Library Service for the Blind and Physically Handicapped (NLS), 1291 Taylor Street, NW, Washington, DC 20011 (http://www.loc.gov/nls/bbr.html).

Bridges to Understanding. Linda M. Pavonetti. Lanham, MD: Scarecrow Press, 2011. ISBN 0810881063, ISBN 13 9780810881068.
Includes nearly 700 listings of annotated books published between 2005 and 2009. Organized geographically by world region and country.

Building Electronic Library Collections: The Essential Guide to Selection Criteria and Core Subject Collections. Diane Kovacs. New York: Neal-Schuman, 2000. ISBN 1555703623, ISBN 13 9781555703622.
Covers collecting, evaluating, and organizing electronic collections. Recommends specific sites with major subject areas. Contains annotated general and major subject webliographies and examples of information mining. Includes a section on resources to support K-12 education.

Bulletin of the Center for Children's Books. Baltimore, MD: The Johns Hopkins University Press, 1945–. (Corporate author: University of Illinois at Urbana-Champaign, Graduate School of Library and Information Science). ISSN 00089036.

Monthly (except August). Summaries and critical evaluations of newly published and forthcoming books for children. Uses codes to indicate level of recommendation. Author/title index in each volume. Subscription: The Johns Hopkins University Press, 2715 North Charles Street, Baltimore, MD, 21218-4363 (http://bccb.lis.uiuc.edu/subscrip.html).

Canadian Books in Print: Author and Title Index. Toronto: University of Toronto Press, 1975–2006. ISSN 00688398.

Annual. Contains more than 52,000 titles and is the complete guide to English-language Canadian books. Supplemented quarterly by *Canadian Books in Print: Update on Fiche*, 1980–. Includes English and French language titles published by predominantly English language Canadian publishers.

CD-ROM Reference Materials for Children and Young Adults: A Critical Guide for School and Public Libraries. Stephen Del Vecchio. Englewood, CO: Libraries Unlimited, 2000. ISBN 1563087111, ISBN 13 9781563087110.

Evaluates new children's references available on CD-ROM. Considers content, usability, design, and extra features.

Charlotte Huck's Children's Literature. 10th ed. Charlotte S. Huck and Barbara Zulandt Kiefer. Boston: McGraw-Hill 2010. ISBN 0073378569, ISBN 13 9780073378565.

This classic text, now in its 10th edition, shows readers how to ensure that K-8 students become lifelong readers. Includes information on the history of children's literature, children's literature genres, and how to evaluate children's literary understanding.

Related work: *Huck's Children's Literature in the Elementary School*.

Charlotte Huck's Children's Literature: A Brief Guide. Charlotte S. Huck, Cynthia A. Tyson, and Barbara Zulandt Ziefer. Boston: McGraw-Hill, 2010. ISBN 0073403830, ISBN 13 9780073403830.

Based on the classic text. Explores the critical skills needed to select and share children's literature in the classroom including researching and evaluation. Provides the reader with evaluative tools, as well as suggestions on how to create and implement curriculum.

Related work: *Huck's Children's Literature in the Elementary School*.

A Child Goes Forth (A Curriculum Guide for Preschool Children). 10th ed. Barbara J. Taylor. Upper Saddle River, NJ: Prentice Hall, 2003. ISBN 0130481165, ISBN 13 9780130481160.

Describes criteria for selecting materials for young children organized around areas of experience critical to a child's development. A relaxed, unstructured, but carefully planned atmosphere is emphasized, along with respect for individuality.

Children's and Young Adult Literature by Latino Writers: A Guide for Librarians, Teachers, Parents, and Students. Sherry York. Worthington, OH: Linworth, 2002. ISBN 1586830627, ISBN 13 9781586830625.

Identifies literature written by Latino authors that is targeted to youth. Bibliographic information and list of additional resources including relevant contact information for publishers and others associated with Latino literature. Genres include novels, chapter books, short stories, folklore, drama, poetry, and nonfiction.

Children's and Young Adult Literature by Native Americans: A Concept Guide for Librarians, Teachers, Parents, and Students. Sherry York. Worthington, OH: Linworth, 2003. ISBN 1586831194, ISBN 13 9781586831196.

A guide to children's books written by Native American authors. Provides bibliographic information on more than 390 books in the areas of fiction, folklore, nonfiction, and poetry. Each entry includes a brief summary, subject headings, reading levels, and awards the work may have received.

Children's Book Review Index. Detroit: Gale Research, 1976–. ISSN 01475681.

Annual. Provides review citations for books recommended for children through age 10. Illustrator and title indexes.

Children's Books in Print. New York: R.R. Bowker, 1969–. ISSN 00693480.

Annual. Two volumes. Children's books for schools and libraries. Related work: *Subject Guide to Children's Books in Print*. ISSN 00000167 (annual). Provides bibliographic and ordering information and uses Sears subject headings, supplemented by LC headings. Excludes textbooks.

Children's Books in Print 2011. New Providence, NJ: Grey House Publishing, 2011–. ISBN 1592377343, ISBN 13 9780835250771.

In its 41st edition, this two-volume set is a vital resource for librarians who work with young readers. Volume 1 contains an index of more than 250,000 books from over 18,000 U.S. publishers. Volume 2 (the author and illustrator index) features more than 223,000 contributors and complete contact information for publishers, distributors, and wholesalers.

Children's Catalog. 19th ed. New York: H.W. Wilson, 2006. ISBN 0824210735 (alk. paper), ISBN 13 9780824210731 (alk. paper).

Three annual supplements. Covers materials for preschool through grade 6. Uses abridged Dewey Decimal Classification. Provides bibliographic and order information, recommended grade level, subject headings, and descriptive or critical annotations. Index lists authors, subjects, titles, and analytical references to composite works. Also available online at http://www.hwwilson.com/print/childcat.cfm.

Children's Catalog: 2009 Supplement to the 19th ed. Anne Price, ed. New York: H.W. Wilson. ISBN 084210735, ISBN 13 97980824210731.

Supplement. Contains over 2,200 additional titles (http://www.hwwilson.com/news/news_9_15_06.cfm).

Children's Core Collection. 20th ed. Anne Price and Marguerita Rowland, eds. New York: H.W. Wilson. ISBN 0824211065, ISBN 13 978084211066.

A definitive collection development resource. Contains more than 10,000 titles including fiction, graphic novels, magazines, and nonfiction works. Paperback supplements: 2011, 2012, and 2013 will contain approximately 2,200 new listings annually and are provided free of charge (www.hwwilson.com/print/childcat.cfm).

Children's Magazine Guide: Subject Index to Children's Magazines and Web Sites. Westport, CT: Greenwood, 1948–. ISSN 07439873. Also *CMG Online* at (http://www.childrensmag.com).

Nine issues per year with an annual accumulation. Indexes more than 60 children's magazines. Identifies wide range of recent articles and websites. Provides name of article, author, magazine, issue date, and number of pages. Aids children, parents, and teachers in easily finding curriculum-specific materials.

Choice Magazine: Current Reviews for Academic Libraries. Middletown, CT: Association of College and Research Libraries, 1963–. ISSN 00094978. Also *Choice Reviews Online* at (http://www.ala.org/ala/mgrps/divs/acrl/publications/choice/index.cfm)

Monthly (except bimonthly July/August). Related works: *Choice Reviews on Cards*. Reviews periodicals, books, nonprint media (films, audiotapes, videos, slides, microforms, software, CD-ROMs, websites, and filmstrips). Annual cumulated index published separately. Subscription: P.O. Box 141, Annapolis Junction, MD 20701, Tel: 240-646-7027, Fax: 301-206-9789 or choicesubscriptions@brightkey.net.

CM Magazine: Canadian Review of Materials. Winnipeg, MB, Canada: The Manitoba Library Association, 1971–. ISSN 12019364.

Weekly online. Electronic reviewing journal. Reviews books, videotapes, audiotapes, and CD-ROMs. Includes news, feature articles, interviews, and web reviews. The magazine is for children, parents, teachers, librarians and professions working with young people. No charge for reading website or receiving their e-mail version, but they ask regular readers for annual contributions to help defray costs. Postal address: CM, 167 Houde Dr., Winnipeg MB R3V 1C6 Canada (http://www.umanitoba.ca/cm).

The Complete Directory of Large Print Books and Serials, 2010. 30th ed. Rev. New Providence, NJ: Grey House Publishing, 2010. ISBN 1592376126, ISBN 13 9781592376124.

Resource to build or manage a large print books or serials collection. Bibliographic information on over 22,500 titles. Lists all active adult, juvenile, and textbook titles. Indicates the type size, physical size of each book, and contact information of publishers, wholesalers, and distributors. Nine indexes including title, author, general reading subject, textbook subject, children's subject, serials subject, and serials title.

Computers in Libraries: Complete Coverage of Library Information Technology. Medford, NJ: Information Today, 1981–. ISSN 10417915.

Monthly. Practical application of technology in community, school, academic, and special libraries. Carries news items and general technical articles designed to provide practical information. Recent topics include e-books, licensing, virtual libraries, fundraising, and web designing. Subscription: Information Today, Inc., 143 Old Marlton Pike, Medford, NJ 08055-8750 or custserv@infotoday.com. Phone: 609-654-6266 or FAX: 609-654-4309 (http://www.infotoday.com/cilmag/).

Connecting Boys with Books: What Libraries Can Do. Michael Sullivan. Chicago: American Library Association, 2003. ISBN 0838908497, ISBN 13 9780838908495.

It has been statistically proven that boys do not read as much as girls. This text provides insight as to why boys are not reading as much, as well as suggestions on how to increase engagement so as to change the statistic. Includes programming ideas and recommendations for librarians on how to better reach this segment of the population.

Connecting Boys with Books 2: Closing the Reading Gap. Michael Sullivan. Chicago: American Library Association, 2009. ISBN 13 9780838909799.

Discusses what boys like to read and programming ideas. Includes an index.

Connecting Libraries with Classrooms: The Curricular Roles of the Media Specialist. 2nd ed. Kay Bishop. Worthington, OH: Linworth, 2011. ISBN 1598845993, ISBN 13 9781598845990.

Provides school librarians with guidelines to help them assume active roles in school library media centers. Includes collaboration, subject areas, special groups of students, and educational trends such as distance-learning. Closely matches the new AASL or NCATE Standards.

Connecting with Reluctant Teen Readers: Tips, Titles, and Tools. Patrick Jones, Maureen L. Hartman and Patricia Taylor. New York: Neal-Schuman, 2006. ISBN 1555705715, ISBN 13 9781555705718.

Hands-on guide to define and woo reluctant readers. Lists more than 600 books, series, and magazines with tips on types of books that will entice teens to read. Includes helpful resource lists, booktalking scripts, and reading surveys.

The Consumer Information Catalog. Washington, DC: Consumer Information Center, General Services Administration, 1977–. Available online at http://www.pueblo.gsa.gov/catalog.pdf.

Quarterly. Free. Delivers useful consumer information from federal agencies to the public. Subscription: Consumer Information Center-R, P.O. Box 100, Pueblo, CO 81002 (http://www.pueblo.gsa.gov).

Consumer Reports. Yonkers, NY: Consumers Union of the United States, 1942–. ISSN 00107174.

Monthly (December issue is annual buying guide issue). Provides evaluative comparisons of equipment including emerging technologies. Available online. Subscription: Consumers Union, Customer Service, P.O. Box 2109, Harlan, IA 51593-0298 (http://www.consumerreports.org).

Contemporary Drama Service.

Provides sources for one-act comedies, melodramas, and musicals for students (http://contemporarydramanewsletter.contemporarydrama.com/public/item/203194).

The Coretta Scott King Awards Book 1970–2009. 4th ed. Henrietta M. Smith, ed. Chicago: American Library Association, 2009. ISBN 0838935842, ISBN 13 9780838935842.

Provides annotation and biographical information about works by African American authors and illustrators for the designated award or honor books. Includes example of each winning illustration. Includes a subject index which may assist with curriculum planning.

Critical Handbook of Children's Literature. 9th ed. Rebecca J. Lukens. Boston: Allyn & Bacon, 2012. ISBN 10 0137056389, ISBN 13 9780137056385.

Provides readers with examples of quality children's literature to aid in the book selection process. Explains the essential literary elements of literature and suggestions applying these elements to additional readings that are reflective of the current time.

Crossing Boundaries with Children's Books. Doris Gebel, ed. Lanham, MD: Scarecrow, 2006. ISBN 0810852039, ISBN 13 9780810852037.

An annotated bibliography that is organized geographically and includes more than 700 works from 73 countries. Tool for promoting diversity and international understanding. Sponsored by the United States Board on Books for Young People. Includes bibliographical references and indexes.

Described and Captioned Media Program. National Association of the Deaf, 1447 E. Main St., Spartanburg, SC 29307. 800-237-6213 (voice) 800-237-6819 (TTY). Also *CMP Media Program* (online), *CMP En Español* (online), and *Captioned Media Program 2001–2002 Catalog.* (Formerly *Captioned Films/Videos Program*).

A free-loan library that has more than 4,000 described and caption media titles available to members. Created to promote and provide equal access to information for those with auditory or visual impairments (http://www.dcmp.org/).

Developing Library and Information Center Collections. 5th ed. G. Edward Evans and Margaret Zarnosky Saponaro. Westport, CT: Libraries Unlimited, 2005. ISBN 1591582199, ISBN 13 9781591582199.

Provides a comprehensive overview, including needs assessment, development policies, the selection process, an overview of publishing, print and electronic serials, other electronic materials, government information, audiovisual materials, acquisitions, distributors and vendors, fiscal management, collection evaluation, resource sharing, collection protection, legal issues, censorship, and intellectual freedom, with focus on the issues and processes of collection development.

Directory of Video, Computer and Audio Visual Products. (Former title: *Directory of Video, Multimedia, and Audio-Visual Products*). Fairfax, VA: International Communications Industries Association, 1953–. ISSN 08842124.

Provides photographs and specifications for video, projection systems, accessories, audiovisual products. Includes glossary, membership directory, indexes by product, company, and InfoComm International Association (ICIA) directory.

Education: A Guide to Reference and Information Sources. 2nd ed. Nancy P. O'Brien, ed. Reference Sources in Social Sciences Series. Englewood, CO: Libraries Unlimited, 2000. ISBN 1563086263, ISBN 13 9781563086267, ISBN 0585333629 (electronic bk.), ISBN 13 9780585333625 (electronic bk.).

Contains nearly 500 entries. Annotations describe sources in educational technology, multilingual or multicultural education, curriculum, instruction, content areas, educational research, and others. Topics covered are from a wide range of topics including educational technology and multicultural education. Author, title, and subject index.

Educational Leadership. Alexandria, VA: Association for Supervision and Curriculum Development, 1943–. ISSN 00131784. Also online at (www.ascd.org)

Eight times a year. Online version has selected full-length articles and several abstracts of articles. Reviews professional books. Subscription: ASCD, 1703 N. Beauregard Street, Alexandria, VA 22311.

Educational Media and Technology Yearbook. Vol. 35. Michael Orey, V. J. McClendon and Robert Maribe Branch. Westport, CT: Libraries Unlimited, 2010. ISBN 1441915028, ISBN 13 9781441915023.

Published annually in cooperation with, and cosponsored by the Association for Educational Communications and Technology and the American Society for Training and Development, Media Division. Educators Guides (annuals) available from Educators Progress Service, 214 Center Street, Randolph, WI 53956. Phone: 888-951-4469. Describes current developments and trends in the field of instructional technology. Highlights the major trends of the previous year and advances in online learning. It identifies instructional technology-related organizations and graduate programs across North America. Includes mediagraphy of journals, books, ERIC documents, journal articles, and nonprint resources. See also *FreeTeachingAids.com* at http://www.freeteachingaids.com/index.html.

Titles include:

Elementary Teachers Guide to FREE Curriculum Materials

Middle School Teachers Guide to FREE Curriculum Materials

Secondary Teachers Guide to FREE Curriculum Materials

Educators Guide to FREE Videotapes Elementary/Middle School Edition

Educators Guide to FREE Videotapes Secondary Edition

Educators Guide to FREE Films, Filmstrips, and Slides

Educators Guide to FREE Internet Resources-Elementary/Middle School Edition

Educators Guide to FREE Internet Resources-Secondary Edition

Educators Guide to FREE Science Materials

Educators Guide to FREE Social Studies Materials

Educators Guide to FREE Guidance Materials

Educators Guide to FREE Family and Consumer Education Materials

Educators Guide to FREE Health, Physical Education and Recreation Materials

Educators Guide to Free Multicultural Materials

El-Hi Textbooks and Serials in Print, 2011, New Providence, NJ: Grey House Publishing, 2011. ISBN 1592376959, ISBN 13 9781592376957.

Indexes over 195,000 textbooks and has additional resources such as reference books, periodicals, maps, tests, teaching aids, and audiovisuals. Titles are listed and cross-referenced in subject, title, author and series indexes. Entries include title, author, grade, publication, date, educational level, price, ISBN, related teaching materials. Includes publisher, wholesaler, and distributor index, with complete contact information.

Encyclopedia of Software Engineering. 2nd ed. John J. Marciniak, ed. New York: John Wiley & Sons, 2002. ISBN 0471377376, ISBN 13 9780471377375. Online at http://onlinelibrary.wiley.com. Online ISBN 9780471028956.

Over 500 entries covering 35 taxonomic areas. Includes entries that define terms according to Institute of Electrical and Electronic Engineers standards. Topics include the Internet and web engineering. Biographical section includes over 100 personalities who have made an impact in the field.

English Journal. Urbana, IL: National Council of Teachers of English, 1912–. ISSN 00138274. Online at http://www.jstor.org/journals/00138274.html.

Bimonthly. Reviews young adult literature, films, videos, software, and professional publications. Issues examine relationships between theory, research, and classroom practice. Subscription: NCTE Subscription Service, 1111 W. Kenyon Road, Urbana, IL 61801-1086. Phone: 217-328-3870 or 877-369-6283 (http://www.ncte.org/).

Essentials of Children's Literature. 7th ed. Carol Lynch-Brown and Carl M. Tomlinson. Boston: Allyn & Bacon, 2011. ISBN 013704884X, ISBN 13 9780137048847.

Surveys children's literature, featuring genres, authors within the genre, and recommended titles. Includes a chapter on multicultural and international literature. Includes curriculum and teaching strategies for grades K-6. Combines lists, examples, figures and tables with clear, concise, and direct narrative.

Ethnic Book Awards: A Directory of Multicultural Literature for Young Readers. Sherry York. Worthington, OH: Linworth, 2005. ISBN 1586831879, ISBN 13 9781586831875.

Comprehensive listing of the award-winning titles of seven major multicultural awards: the Americas Award, the Asian Pacific American Award for Literature, the Carter G. Woodson Award, the Coretta Scott King Award, the Pura Belpré Award, the Sydney Taylor Book Award, and the Tomás Rivera Mexican American Children's Literature Award. Bibliographic information includes illustrator, translators, reading and interest levels, brief annotation for each title. Subject, author, editor, illustration, and translator indexes.

The Everyday Guide to Special Education Law: A Handbook for Parents, Teachers and Other Professionals. 2nd ed. Randy Chapman. Denver, CO: The Legal Center for People with Disabilities and Older People, 2008. ISBN 0977017931, ISBN 13 9780977017935.

Provides information from the IDEA regulations and court decisions dealing with special education. An excellent book to have in a professional collection for teachers and parents.

Exceptional Children. Arlington, VA: Council for Exceptional Children, 1934–. ISSN 00144029.

Four times a year (Fall, Winter, Spring, and Summer). Research-based articles. Reviews professional books. Publishes current articles on critical and controversial issues in special education, as well as credible articles on research and developments in the field. Subscribe call: 866-915-5000 (www.cec.sped.org).

Exceptional Parent: The Magazine for Families and Professionals Caring for People with Special Needs. River Edge, NJ: Exceptional Parent, 1971–. ISSN 00469157. Also *EP Magazine Online* at (www.eparentdigital.com).

Twelve issues per year. Provides practical advice, educational information and support for families with children with disabilities and the professionals who work with them. Subscription: EP Global Communications, Inc., 416 Main Street, Johnstown, PA 15901, Phone: 814-361-3860 or 800-372-7368 Fax: 814-361-3861 (http://www.eparent.com).

Exploring Science in the Library: Resources and Activities for Young People. Maria Sosa and Tracy Gath. Chicago: American Library Association, 2000. ISBN 0838907687 (pbk.), ISBN 13 9780838907689 (pbk.), ISBN 13 9780585311166 (electronic bk.), ISBN 0585311161 (electronic bk.).

Copublished with American Association for the Advancement of Science (AAAS). Includes supplemental activities for science instruction in the library, web references, a guide to selecting books, information about fundraising, and an annotated bibliography of science trade books.

Extreme Teens: Library Services for Nontraditional Young Adults. Sheila B. Anderson. Westport, CT: Libraries Unlimited, 2005. ISBN 1591581702, ISBN 13 9781591581703.

Provides tips on building a collection and providing library services to connect with nontraditional young people, including juvenile delinquents, pregnant teens, the homeless, home-schooled, dropouts, GLBTQ, and many others.

Fantasy Literature for Children and Young Adults: A Comprehensive Guide. 5th ed. Ruth Nadelman Lynn. Westport, CT: Libraries Unlimited, 2005. ISBN 1591580501, ISBN 13 9781591580508.

Comprehensive guide describing and categorizing fantasy novels and story collections published between 1900 and 2004 for readers grades 3–12. More than 7,500 titles. Organized in chapters based on fantasy subgenres and themes, including animal, alternate worlds, time travel, witchcraft, and sorcery. Complete bibliographic information, grade level, a brief annotation, and a list of review citations.

Fiction Catalog. 15th ed. John Greenfieldt. Bronx, NY: H.W. Wilson, 2006. ISBN 0824210557, ISBN 13 9780824210557.

Main edition plus annual supplements. Provides access by title, author, subject and theme, genre, and form or literary technique (http://www.hwwilson.com/news/news_4_10_06.cfm).

Fiction Core Collection. 16th ed. John Greenfieldt. New York: H.W. Wilson, 2010. ISBN 0824211030, ISBN 13 9780824211035.

Formerly known as *Fiction Catalog*. Features classic and contemporary works of fiction recommended for a general adult audience, written in or translated into English. Bibliographical information such as author, out-of-print status, title, reprint publication data, publisher, ISBN, date of publication, Library of Congress number, notes regarding sequels, illustration note, publication history, price, contents of story collections are provided. Lists works of fiction in alphabetical order by the last name of the author or by title, if it is the main entry. Includes title and subject index (www.hwwilson.com).

Fluent in Fantasy: The Next Generation. Diana Tixier Herald and Bonnie Kunzel. Westport, CT: Libraries Unlimited, 2008. ISBN 1591581982, ISBN 13 9781591581987.

A guide created as an update to *Fluent in Fantasy: A Guide to Reading Interests* (1999). Contains approximately 2,000 titles. All titles annotated. Includes author, title, and subject indexes.

For Younger Readers: Braille and Talking Books. Washington, DC: National Library Service for the Blind and Physically Handicapped (NLS), U.S. Library of Congress, 1967–. ISSN 00932825.

Biennial (every two years). Annotates Braille, disc, and cassette books announced in *Braille Book Review* and *Talking Books Topics*. Available in Braille, sound recording, and large type. Free to individuals who are visually impaired and/or physically handicapped. Large print available (http://www.loc.gov/nls/).

Free and Inexpensive Career Materials: A Resource Directory. 3rd ed. Elizabeth H. Oakes. Chicago: Ferguson, 2001. ISBN 0894343777, ISBN 13 9780894343773.

Contains over 800 free or inexpensive career material resources. Latest edition includes available websites and e-mail addresses for the resources.

Gay, Lesbian, Bisexual, Transgender and Questioning Teen Literature. Carlisle K. Webber. Santa Barbara, CA: Libraries Unlimited, 2010. ISBN 1591585066, ISBN 13 9781591585060.

Provides over 300 fiction and nonfiction titles, including poetry, drama, and graphic novels. Organized by genres and themes, with codes for the types of characters (G, L, B, T, and Q). Reading levels and titles that have video or audio versions are indicated.

Genreflecting: A Guide to Popular Reading Interests. 6th ed. Diana Tixier Herald and Wayne A. Wiegand. Englewood, CO: Libraries Unlimited, 2006. ISBN 1591582865, ISBN 13 9781591582861.

Updated classical text. Contains over 5,000 titles that are classified by genre, subgenre, and theme. Includes new chapters on Christian fiction and emerging genres as well as essays written by experts. Indexes are by subject or author and title.

Genreflecting: A Guide to Reading Interest in Genre Fiction. 6th ed. Diana Tixier Herald. Englewood, CO: Libraries Unlimited, 2005. ISBN 1591582245, ISBN 13 9781591582243, ISBN 1591582865 (pbk.), ISBN 13 9781591582861 (pbk.).

Describes nine fiction genres and subgenres, including historical fiction, romance, westerns, fantasy, crime, science fiction, horror, Christian fiction, and emerging genres such as Chick Lit and Women's Fiction. Includes a brief history of readers advisory and the reader's advisory interview.

Gifted Books, Gifted Readers: Literature Activities to Excite Young Minds. Nancy J. Polette. Westport, CT: Libraries Unlimited, 2000. ISBN 1563088223, ISBN 13 9781563088223 (teacher's edition).

Contains plot summaries for more than 200 children's books as well as activities meant to enhance the reading experience. The books are grouped in categories such as picture books, fantasy, and poetry.

Gifted Child Quarterly. Paula L. Olszewski-Kubilius, ed. Washington, DC: National Association for Gifted Children, 1957–. ISSN 00169862.

Quarterly. For educational researchers, administrators, teachers, and parents of gifted children. Publishes research and theoretical papers on the nature and needs of high-ability children. Supplies information on gifted and talented development (http://www.nagc.org).

Gifted Child Today Magazine: The Nation's Leading Resource for Nurturing Talented Children. Waco, TX: Prufrock Press, 1978–. ISSN 10762175.

Bimonthly. Features information about identifying gifted children, building effective gifted and talented programs, helping gifted children with learning disabilities, building effective gifted education in math, science, language arts, and social studies and designing quality learning activities for gifted children. Includes bibliographies, illustrations, book reviews designed to meet the needs of parents and teachers of gifted, creative, and talented youngsters (http://journals.prufrock.com/IJP/b/gifted-child-today).

GPO Access. U.S. Government Printing Office.

Free electronic access to information products produced by the Federal Government. Funded by the Federal Depository Library Program (http://www.gpoaccess.gov/about/index.html).

Graphic Novels for Young Readers: A Genre Guide for Ages 4–14. Nathan Herald. Santa Barbara, CA: Libraries Unlimited, 2011. ISBN 1598843958, ISBN 13 9781598843958.

Describes the growing number of graphic novels suitable for young readers. Organizes approximately 400 titles by genres, subgenres, and themes.

Great Web Sites for Kids Selection Criteria. Children and Technology Committee of the Association of Library Service to Children. Chicago, IL: American Library Association.

Helps parents, children, teachers, and librarians evaluate authorship or sponsorship, purpose, design, stability, and content. Recommends sites for children (http://www.ala.org/ala/alsc/greatwebsites/greatwebsitesforkids/greatwebsites.htm).

Guide to Microforms in Print: Author/Title. Munich, Germany: K.G. Saur, 1975–. ISSN 01640747.

Annual. Lists more than 225,000 publications available from around the world. Lists online titles and digitally scanned research material, made accessible to the user in electronic formats (http://www.saur.de). The website has an English option.

Guide to Reference Materials for School Library Media Centers. 6th ed. Barbara Ripp Safford. Santa Barbara, CA: Libraries Unlimited, 2010. ISBN 1591582776, ISBN 13 9781591582779.

Covers more than 2,000 titles including electronic resources with age and reading levels, presentation styles, strengths and weaknesses, comparison with other works, and citations to reviews. Includes resources recommended for use by school librarians.

Halliwell's Film Video and DVD Guide 2008. 23rd ed. John Walker, ed. London: HarperCollins Entertainment, 2007. ISBN 0007260806 (pbk.), ISBN 13 9780007260805 (pbk.).

Includes reviews for more than 24,000 movies. Provides country of origin, rating, format, year released, alternate title, brief description, quotes from reviews, and awards. Arranged alphabetically by title. Lists Academy Award winners, four-star reviews by title and by year, three-star reviews by title and year.

High/Low Handbook: Best Books and Web Sites for Reluctant Teen Readers. 4th ed. Ellen V. LiBretto and Catherine Barr. Westport, CT: Libraries Unlimited, 2002. ISBN 0313322767, ISBN 13 9780313322761.

A ready-reference resource to support the needs and interests of struggling or reluctant teen readers. Contains more than 500 book titles and URLs in subject categories such as fiction, subdivided by genre; biography and memoirs; health and fitness; history; science; and sports. Divided into two major sections: the first offers a core collection of fiction and nonfiction high or low titles, organized into broad topical areas that appeal to teens, such as careers, exploration, sports, disasters, and teen cultures. The second section presents YA books and magazine titles with descriptions and ordering information. Websites and graphic novels are also included. Appendixes include a publishers' list and web resources.

Historical Fiction for Teens: A Genre Guide. Melissa Rabey. Santa Barbara, CA: Libraries Unlimited, 2010. ISBN 1591588138, ISBN 13 9781591588139.

Organizes more than 300 titles by subgenres and themes. Provides annotations, subject lists, and reading levels.

The History Teacher. Long Beach, CA: Society for History Education, 1967–. ISSN 00182745.

Quarterly. Reviews books, textbooks, supplementary readers, and professional books. "Features informative and inspirational peer-reviewed analyses of traditional and innovative teaching techniques in the primary, secondary, and higher education classroom" (from website). Subscription: Society for History Education California State University, Long Beach 1250 Bellflower Boulevard, Long Beach, CA 90840-1601 (http://www.thehistoryteacher.org).

Hoagies' Gifted Education Page.

Consists of over 1,000 pages of information on gifted children and adults, including more than 550 pages of Hoagies' Page collection, plus more than 500 pages of ERIC Clearinghouse for Disabilities and Gifted Education (ERICEC). Provides information on topics such as Testing and Assessment, Academic Acceleration, and Differentiation of Instruction and Success Stories (http://www.hoagiesgifted.org/reading_lists.htm).

Hooked on Horror: A Guide to Reading Interests in Horror Fiction. 2nd ed. Anthony J. Fonseca and June Michele Pulliam. Englewood, CO: Libraries Unlimited, 2003. ISBN 1563089041, ISBN 13 9781563089046.

Describes contemporary and classic titles for English literature classes and horror fans. Focuses on widely available titles. Annotated bibliography of adult horror novels and films arranged by thirteen subgenres. History of the horror genre. Includes graphic novels, indications of audio, e-book, and large print formats. Identifies additional reading, sources for research on the subject of horror, and lists of award winners.

The Horn Book Magazine. Boston: Horn Book, 1924–. ISSN 00185078.

Six issues per year. Related work: *The Horn Book Guide to Children's and Young Adult Books*, 1989–. ISSN 1044405X. Two issues per year. Reviews and ratings for hardback and paperback books. Includes books in Spanish. The guide is published two times a year (April 1 and October 1). Subscription: The Horn Book, Attn: Circulation Dept. 7858 Industrial Parkway, Plain City, OH 43064. Phone 800-325-1170 (www.hbook.com/magazine/default.asp).

Huck's Children's Literature in the Elementary School. 9th ed. Charlotte S. Huck and Barbara Zulandt Kiefer. Boston: McGraw-Hill, 2006. ISBN 007312298X, ISBN 13 9780073122984.

Guides teachers and media specialists in the selection and use of all genres of literature with children. It helps the user to plan and evaluate children's understandings of literature. Related work: *Charlotte Huck's Children's Literature* and *Charlotte Huck's Children's Literature: A Brief Guide*.

Information Power: Building Partnerships for Learning. American Association of School Librarians and Association for Educational Communications and Technology. Chicago: American Library Association, 1998. ISBN 0838934706, ISBN 13 9780838934708.

Guidelines for school library media centers. Includes the national information literacy standards. Chapters discuss techniques and practices that support program development which enhances learning and teaching.

Informational Picture Books for Children. Patricia J. Cianciolo. Chicago: American Library Association, 2000. ISBN 0838907741, ISBN 13 9780838907740, ISBN 0585317534 (electronic bk.), ISBN 13 9780585317533 (electronic bk.).

Annotates 250 titles published between 1994 and 1999 for children from 6 months to 14 years. Titles grouped in eight categories, including the natural world, numbers, and arts and crafts. Wide bibliographic scope. Useful guidelines for evaluating other titles.

Instructional Technology and Media for Learning. 10th ed. Sharon E. Smaldino, James D. Russell, Robert Heinich, and Michael Molenda, Upper Saddle River, NJ: Prentice Hall, 2011. ISBN 0138008159, ISBN 13 9780138008154.

Discusses selection and use of media. Includes software package for teachers to use in creating, maintaining, printing, and evaluating lesson plans and the materials used in them. Incorporates technology and media to meet the needs of 21st-century learners and addresses concerns such as copyright, free and inexpensive media resources, learning theory, and instructional models. Updates technology use in schools. Includes educational resources and technology, teaching skills, and techniques.

Intellectual Freedom Manual. 8th ed. ALA Office of Intellectual Freedom. Chicago: American Library Association, 2010. ISBN 0838935907, ISBN 13 9780838935903.

Includes most up-to-date intellectual freedom guidelines, policies and their interpretations. Offers guidelines for developing policies and practices.

Internet Resource Directory for K–12 Teachers and Librarians. Elizabeth B. Miller. Englewood, CO: Libraries Unlimited, 2004. ISBN 0313009589 (electronic bk.), ISBN 13 9780313009587 (electronic bk.).

Describes selected resources on a wide range of subjects including resources to help teachers and media specialists, lesson plans, AUP, copyright, intellectual freedom, and selections. This Internet guide is curriculum organized and contains simple instructions.

Journal for the Education of the Gifted. Tracy Cross, ed. Waco, TX: Prufrock Press, 1978–. ISSN 01623532.

Quarterly. Reports on the latest research on topics such as the characteristics of gifted children, evaluating effective schools for gifted children, gifted children with learning disabilities, the history of gifted education, and building successful gifted and talented programs (http://journals.prufrock.com/).

Journal of Adolescent and Adult Literacy (JAAL). Newark, DE: International Reading Association, Inc., 1957–. ISSN 10813004.

Eight times a year (September to May; December/January combined). Classroom-tested ideas grounded in research and theory for published for teachers. Issues include practical ideas for instruction, reviews of student and teacher resources, and reflections on current literacy trends, issues and research (www.reading.org/General/Publications/Journals/jaal.aspx?mode=redirect).

Journal of Advanced Academics (JAA). Waco, TX: Proufrock Press, 2006–. ISSN 1932202X.

Quarterly. Formerly known as *Journal of Secondary Gifted Education.* This journal contains research programming ideas for gifted students.

Journal of Family and Consumer Sciences. Washington, DC: American Home Economics Association, 1909–. ISSN 10821651. (Formerly *Journal of Home Economics* ISSN 00221570.)

Quarterly. (Winter, Spring, Summer, and Fall). Reviews professional and trade books covering family relations, children, food and nutrition, household affairs, and teaching methods. Subscription: Mail to: AAFCS—Publications, P.O. Box 79377, Baltimore, MD 21279-0377, Phone: 800-424-8080 Fax: 703-706-4663 (www.aafcs.org/Resources/Journal.asp).

Journal of Geography. Macomb, IL: National Council for Geographic Education, 1902–. ISSN 00221341.

Bimonthly. Presents innovative approaches to geography research, teaching, and learning. Reviews textbooks and professional materials; has a column on free and inexpensive materials.

Subscription: Taylor & Francis Group, LLC 325 Chestnut Street, Philadelphia, PA 19106 Tel: 215-625-8900 Fax: 215-625-2940 http://www.ncge.org.

Journal of Physical Education, Recreation and Dance. Reston, VA: American Alliance for Health, Physical Education, Recreation, and Dance, 1896–. ISSN 07303084.

Monthly (nine/year). Index. Features bylined articles and short features on all aspects of physical education, recreation, dance, athletics, and safety education as taught in schools and colleges. Covers administration, curriculum methods, and equipment (http://www.aahperd.org/publications/journals/joped/index.cfm).

Journal of Secondary Gifted Education. Bonnie Cramond, ed. Waco, TX: Prufrock Press, 1993–2006. ISSN 10774610.

Quarterly. This journal contains research programming ideas for gifted students. Now known as: *Journal of Advanced Academics.*

Journal of Visual Impairment and Blindness (JVIB). Alan J Koenig, ed. New York: American Foundation for the Blind, 1977–. ISSN 0145482X.

Monthly. Articles pertaining to visual impairment and blindness. Available in regular print or in Braille. Available in microform, on audiocassette, and online at (http://www.afb.org). Subscription: (http://www.afb.org/Section.asp?SectionID=54).

Junior Genreflecting: A Guide to Good Reads and Series Fiction for Children. Bridget Dealy Volz, Lynda Blackburn Welborn, and Cheryl Perkins Scheer. Englewood, CO: Libraries Unlimited, 2000. ISBN 1563085569, ISBN 13 9781563085567, ISBN 0585333521 (electronic bk.). ISBN 13 9780585333526 (electronic bk).

Describes titles for children in grades 3–8. Provides a brief overview on fiction for children and library programs as well as provides tools and professional resources. Includes author/title and subject index.

Kids with Special Needs. Sheila Stewart and Camden Flath. Broomall, PA: Mason Crest, 2010–2011. ISBN 13 9781422217276 (hardback), ISBN 13 9781422219188 (paperback).

Eleven-volume book series written specifically for young people. Can be purchased as a set or as separate books. Available in hardback and paperback. Topics include: speech impairment, physical challenges, deaf and hard of hearing, intellectual disabilities, blindness and visual impairment, chronic illness, emotional disturbances, attention-deficit/hyperactivity disorder, autism, brain injury, and learning disabilities (http://www.masoncrest.com/catalog_series.asp?isbn=978–1-4222–1727–6).

Kirkus Reviews. New York: Kirkus Service, V N U Business Publications, 1933–. ISSN 00426598.

Semimonthly. Available online. Entries provide bibliographic or order information, paging, month and day of release, type of book, and grade level on more than 500 prepublication books. Subscription: Kirkusreviews.com or Kirkus Media LLC 6411 Burleson Road, Austin, TX 78744 or Phone: 877-441-3010 (http://www.kirkusreviews.com/).

Kliatt: Reviews of Selected Current Paperback Books, Hardcover Fiction, Audiobooks, and Educational Software. Wellesley, MA: Kliatt, 1978–. ISSN 10658602.

Six issues per year. Reviews software, paperbacks, and audiobooks for ages 12–19.

Language Arts. Urbana, IL: National Council of Teachers of English, 1924–. ISSN 03609170.

Bimonthly (September through July). Reviews children's books and professional materials. Issues discuss theory and classroom practice as well as examine current research. Subscription: National Council of Teachers of English, 1111 Kenyon Road, Urbana, IL 61801. Phone: 217-328-3870 or 877-369-6283 Fax: 217-328-9645 (http://www.ncte.org/journals/la).

Learning and Libraries in an Information Age: Principles and Practice. Barbara K. Stripling, ed. Englewood, CO: Libraries Unlimited, 1999. ISBN 1563086662, ISBN 13 9781563086663, ISBN 0585113955 (electronic bk.), ISBN 13 9780585113951 (electronic bk).

Blends latest research and theory with effective practices. Discusses the role of the media center in meeting informational and instructional needs and in establishing collaborative efforts with teachers.

Lesbian and Gay Voices: An Annotated Bibliography and Guide to Literature for Children and Young Adults. Frances Ann Day. Westport, CT: Greenwood, 2000. ISBN 0313311625, ISBN 13 9780313311628.

Thoughtful and thorough annotations of more than 275 titles featuring lesbian and gay characters appropriate for young readers, including picture books, fiction, short stories, nonfiction, biography, and autobiography. Suggested guidelines for evaluating books. Includes biographical information of 16 gay and lesbian authors.

Less is More: A Practical Guide to Weeding School Library Collections. Donna J. Baumbach and Linda L. Miller. Chicago: American Library Association, 2006. ISBN 0838909191, ISBN 13 9780838909195.

Practical guide outlining the steps for making weeding part of a library's ongoing procedures. Explains how to use automation tools. Includes web resources and weeding index.

Libraries, the First Amendment, and Cyberspace: What You Need to Know. Robert S. Peck. Chicago: American Library Association, 2000. ISBN 0838907733, ISBN 13 9780838907733.

Answers questions relating to censorship and access. Includes information on government authority, Internet use, free speech, and intellectual freedom. Appendices include important First Amendment documents.

Library Journal. New York: Reed Business Information, 1876–. ISSN 03630277. *Library Journal Digital* at (http://www.libraryjournal.com/).

Twenty times a year, semimonthly except monthly in January, July, August, and December, plus Buyer's Guide, 10 supplements and weekly review. Covers technology, management, policy, and other professional concerns. Available in microform. Reviews books, magazines, videos, CD-ROM, software, audiobooks, and systems that libraries buy. Monthly author index to reviews. Includes annual buyer's guide to hardware and equipment. Subscription: LIBRARY JOURNAL, PO Box 5881, Harlan, IA 51593-1381, Phone: 800-588–1030. E-mail: LJLcustserv@cdsfulfillment.com.

Library Media Connection: Magazine for Secondary School Library Media and Technology Specialists. Worthington, OH: Linworth, 2003–. ISSN 15424715 (*Library Talk* merged and incorporated into this publication).

Bimonthly. Blending practical information, professional development, and book and technology reviews by educators (http://www.librarymediaconnection.com/).

Literary Market Place: The Directory of the Book Publishing (LMP). Medford, NJ: Information Today, 1973–. ISSN 00001155. Also online at http://www.infotoday.com.

Annual. Lists publishing and publishing-related businesses from the United States and Canada, including distributors, literary agents, small presses, book producers, translators and interpreters, events, editorial and art devices, reference books and magazines, printers, binders and Literary Association, Societies and Awards. Also lists recent mergers and acquisitions and company reportage of publishers, that is, divisions, subsidiaries, and imprints.

Literary Market Place 2011. 71st ed. Medford, NJ: Information Today, 2010. ISBN 157387390X (set), ISBN 13 9781573873901(set), ISBN 1573873888 (v. 1), ISBN 13 9781573873888 (v. 1), ISBN 1573873896 (v. 2), ISBN 13 9781573873895 (v. 2).

Two volumes. Over 14,000 listings covering all aspects of the business. Fifty-four sections organize everyone and everything in the business including publishers, agents, ad agencies, associations, distributors, and events. Also features names and addresses, contact information, activities, specialists, and websites (http://www.infotoday.com).

Literature Lures: Using Picture Books and Novels to Motivate Middle School Readers. Nancy J. Polette and Joan Ebbesmeyer. Westport, CT: Libraries Unlimited, 2004. ISBN 0313010102 (electronic bk.), ISBN 13 9780313010101 (electronic bk.).

Tool for exploring important themes, basic components of literature and literary devices. Includes questions and writing prompts to motivate students to become involved in the literature experience. Titles carefully chosen, using as criteria the quality of the writing, the importance of its message, and how easily it could serve as a springboard to junior novels that explore the same theme. Grades 6–10.

Mathematics Teacher. Reston, VA: National Council of Teachers of Mathematics, 1908–. ISSN 00255769.

Nine times a year (monthly August through May, with a combined December/January issue). Features on the improvement of mathematics instruction in junior and senior high schools, two-year colleges, and teacher education colleges. The column "Reviewing and Viewing" covers teaching materials, including games, videotapes, workbooks, software, and books for teachers. About 100,000 mediagraphic items covered. Also provides a forum to link education research to practice and share activities and strategies. Related work: *Online Journal of School Mathematics (ON-Math).* Subscription: NCTM, 1906 Association Drive, Reston, VA 20191–1502. Phone: 800-235-7566.

Mathematics Teaching in the Middle School (MTMS). Reston, VA: National Council of Teachers of Mathematics, 1994–. ISSN 10720839.

Nine times a year (September to May, with a combined December/January issue and a yearly focus issue in February). A resource for middle school students, teachers, and teacher educators. The focus is on intuitive, exploratory investigations that use informal reasoning to help students develop a strong conceptual basis that leads to greater mathematical abstraction. Includes ideas for activities, lessons, strategies and practice problems (www.nctm.org).

Middle and Junior High School Core Collection. 10th ed. Anne Price, ed. Bronx, NY: H.W. Wilson, 2009. ISBN 0824211022, ISBN 13 9780824211028.

Quadrennial plus three annual supplements (2010, 2011, 2012). Formerly known as the *Middle and Junior High School Library Catalog.* Separate sections for nonfiction, fiction and short story collections. Contains entries for more than 10,000 books. Each book entry includes bibliographic description, suggested subject headings, an annotation, and an evaluation from a quoted source (when available). Multiple indexes included.

Middle and Junior High School Core Collection. 2010 supplement to the 10th edition. Anne Price, ed. Bronx, NY: H.W. Wilson, 2010.

Three annual supplements, for years 2010–2012, with over 4,000 titles listed.

Middle and Junior High School Library Catalog. 9th ed. Juliette Yaakov, ed. Bronx, NY: H.W. Wilson, 1965–. Available online at (http://www.hwwilson.com/print/mjhscat.cfm) and in book format. Bronx, NY: H.W. Wilson, 2006. ISBN 0824210530, ISBN 13 9780824210533.

Quinquennial plus four annual supplements. Comprehensive list of fiction and nonfiction books for young people in grades five through nine. Essential tool for curriculum support and collection development in school libraries, public libraries, and academic libraries. Special features include highly recommended web resources and a list of the most essential magazines and periodicals for middle and junior high school libraries. Recommends more than 4,200 fiction and nonfiction books in the main volume. Arranged by Abridged Dewey Decimal Classification. Indexes: author, title, subject, and analytics. As of 2009, the *Middle and Junior High School Library Catalog* became the *Middle and Junior High School Core Collection.*

Monthly Catalog of United States Government Publications. Washington, DC: U.S. Government Printing Office, 1895–. ISSN 03626830 and in print format, 2010. ISBN 1154790274, ISBN 13 9781154790276.

In print and online. Identifies publications by major branches, departments, and bureaus of the U.S. government. Provides depository and order information (http://catalog.gpo.gov/F?RN=583554046).

More Hot Links: Linking Literature with the Middle School Curriculum. Cora M. Wright. Greenwood Village, CO: Libraries Unlimited, 2002. ISBN 1563089424, ISBN 13 9781563089428.

Includes more than 300 additional fiction and nonfiction annotated titles chosen for recreational reading and curriculum connections for students from fifth to ninth grade. Sections on humor, series, and picture books for all ages. Recommends titles arranged by curriculum areas. Indicates high interest or low reading level titles. Titles chosen for quality of writing, interest level, appropriateness of illustrations, and current availability. Section highlighting best of newly published literature included.

Moving Library Collections: A Management Handbook. 2nd ed. Elizabeth Chamberlain Habich. Santa Barbara, CA: Libraries Unlimited, 2010. ISBN 1591586704, ISBN 13 9781591586708.

Offers suggestions for planning effective moves handled by staff or professional movers. This updated edition includes sections on electronic resources, space limitations, project management software, archival materials, and special guidelines for small libraries, supplemented by illustrations and charts. Includes an updated bibliography of over 230 resources.

Multicultural Children's Literature: Through the Eyes of Many Children. 3rd ed. Donna E. Norton. Upper Saddle River, NJ: Prentice Hall, 2009. ISBN 0135145287, ISBN 13 9780135145289.

Compact guide of selected high-quality examples of multicultural literature. Focuses on incorporating the best multicultural books into the classroom, honoring and respecting both the literature and the cultures in the classroom, and using literature to motivate and nurture a culturally responsive classroom. Includes annotated bibliography.

Multicultural Picturebooks: Art for Illuminating Our World. 2nd ed. Sylvia S. Marantz and Kenneth A. Marantz, eds. Lanham, MD: Scarecrow, 2005. ISBN 081084933X, ISBN 13 9780810849334.

Evaluates the quality and classroom appropriateness of picture books with a multicultural theme for grades K-4. Reviews storylines and special features, look and style of illustrations, design, and layout. Includes bibliographical references and index.

Multicultural Projects Index: Things to Make and Do to Celebrate Festivals, Cultures, and Holidays Around the World. 4th ed. Mary Anne Pilger. Medford, NJ: Libraries Unlimited, 2005. ISBN 1591582369, ISBN 13 9781591582366.

Index of multicultural projects that promote diversity and cross-cultural understanding in more than 1,700 books; indexed by subject and author. Also contains indexes to author and subject, educational games, crafts, activities. Grades K-8.

MultiCultural Review: Dedicated to a Better Understanding of Ethnic, Racial and Religious Diversity. Tampa, FL: Goldman Group, 1992–. ISSN 10589236.

Quarterly. Includes articles on current issues related to multiculturalism, bibliographic essays, articles on nonprofit resources, practical applications, and reviews of materials for juvenile and adult audiences. Official publication of EMIERT, the Ethnic and MultiCultural Information Exchange Round Table of the American Library Association. Available online. Subscription: (http://www.mcreview.com).

Neal-Schuman Authoritative Guide to Evaluating Information on the Internet. Alison Cooke. New York: Neal-Schuman, 1999. ISBN 1555703569, IBSN 13 9781555703561.

Discusses criteria for a range of sources including websites, electronic journals, newsgroups, databases, current awareness services, and FAQs. Includes tips for evaluating accuracy of information, as well as assessment guidelines, checklists, and a glossary. Order online at (http://www.neal-schuman.com).

Negotiating the Special Education Maze: A Guide for Parents and Teachers. 4th ed. Winifred Anderson, Stephan Chitwood, and Deidre Hayden. Bethesda, MD: Woodbine House, 2008. ISBN 1890627461, ISBN 13 9781890627461.

Covers changes in disability laws, reviews early intervention services for children from birth to age 3, and contains expanded information on transitioning young adults out of school. Presents an effective approach for obtaining appropriate instruction and therapy designed to meet the unique needs of every child with special needs and solving disagreements between families and schools. Process is explained, including eligibility, testing, evaluation, and the IEP. Includes bibliographic references and index.

The New Grove Dictionary of Music and Musicians. 2nd ed. rev. Stanley Sadie and John Tyrrell, eds. New York: Oxford University Press, 2004. ISBN 0195170679, ISBN 13 9780195170672. Also available online at (http://www.grovemusic.com).

First edition's 22,500 articles have been reviewed and revised, with many expanded. Thousands of new articles, topics, cross-references, and areas of scholarship. Previously neglected or under-represented areas are examined, explored, and explained. Articles cover more than 5,000 years of music history, instruments, composers, institutions, performers, and genres. Extensive, authoritative contributions on non-Western music. Valuable appendixes.

Newbery and Caldecott Awards: A Guide to the Medal and Honor Books. Chicago: American Library Association, 2011. ISBN 0838985696, ISBN 13 9780838985694.

Annual. Provides background information about the titles and their creators, including selection criteria. Bibliography and index included.

Newsletter on Intellectual Freedom. Judith F. Krug, ed. Chicago: Intellectual Freedom Committee of the American Library Association, 1952–. ISSN 00289485. Online at (http://www.ala.org).

Bimonthly (January, March, May, July, September, November). Reports events relating to intellectual freedom and censorship. Available online. Subscription: American Library Association, 50 E. Huron Street, Chicago, IL 60611 or email oif@ala.org (http://cs.ala.org/nif/subscribe.html).

Online Journal of School Mathematics (ON-Math). Reston, VA: National Council of Teachers of Mathematics, 2000–. ISSN 15346749.

Peer-reviewed journal developed and designed exclusively for the Internet. An interactive site with ideas for mathematics educators at all levels. Related work: *Mathematics Teacher.*

Online: The Magazine of Online Information Systems. Medford, NJ: Information Today, 1970–. ISSN 01465422. Available online at (http://www.infotoday.com/online/default.shtml).

Six times per year. Provides articles about online applications and in-depth evaluative reviews that deal with online information systems. Subscription: Information Today, 143 Old Marlton Pike, Medford, NJ 08055 (http://www.infotoday.com/).

Picture Books by Latino Writers: A Guide for Librarians, Teachers, Parents, and Students. Sherry York. Worthington, OH: Linworth, 2002. ISBN 158683052X, ISBN 13 9781586830526.

Features 65 picture books by Latino authors. Biographical information about authors, illustrators, and translators. Identifies literary awards won by the books; includes publisher and distributor information. Also has a bibliography of additional Latino-related picture books.

Popular Series Fiction for K-6 Readers: A Reading and Selection Guide. Catherine Barr and Rebecca L. Thomas. Westport, CT: Libraries Unlimited, 2009. ISBN 1591586593, ISBN 13 9781591586593.

Introduces best and most popular fiction series of today, appropriate for elementary readers. Annotations provide bibliographic information, as well as indicate series and titles accepted by some of the popular electronic reading programs (e.g., *Accelerated Reading, Reading First*). Appendixes include "Books for Boys," "Books for Girls," "for Reluctant Readers/ESL Students," and "Developing Series." Includes index.

Popular Series Fiction for Middle School and Teen Readers: A Reading and Selection Guide. Catherine Barr and Rebecca L Thomas. 2nd ed. Westport, CT: Libraries Unlimited, 2009. ISBN 1591586607, ISBN 13 9781591586609.

Introduces best and most popular fiction series of today, appropriate for middle school and teen readers. Annotations include bibliographic information and describe the series' appeal, lists characters, and location. Annotations also indicate series and titles accepted by some of the popular electronic reading programs (e.g., *Accelerated Reading*, Scholastic's *Reading Counts*). Appendixes include "Books for Boys," "Books for Girls," and "for Reluctant Readers/ESL Students." Includes index.

Preservation: Caring for Your Collections. Library of Congress. Online at http://www.loc.gov/preserv/careothr.html

Covers books, motion picture film, photographs, manuscripts, prints, posters, maps, audiorecordings, matting and framing, newspapers, documents, disc and tape care, damage from pollutants, and the drying of water-damaged materials.

Programming with Latino Children's Materials: A How-to-Do-It Manual for Librarians. Tim Wadham. New York: Neal-Schuman, 1999. ISBN 1555703526, ISBN 13 9781555703523.

Helps librarians understand Latino culture and literature. Provides background information on the Latino culture, book reviews, folktales, annotated bibliographies, suggestions for selection policies, and identifies acquisition sources. Includes the full text (in Spanish and English) for almost 100 fingerplays and nursery rhymes, and other programs. Special features include the Dewey Decimal Classification in Spanish, Latino holiday programs, a section on speaking Spanish, and ready-to-copy bilingual publicity materials.

Publishers, Distributors, and Wholesalers of the United States: A Directory of Publishers, Distributors, Associations, Wholesalers, Software Producers and Manufacturers Listing Editorial and Ordering Addresses, and an ISBN Publisher Prefix Index. New Providence, NJ: R.R. Bowker, 1979–. ISSN 0000–0671 and print; 32nd ed., rev. ISBN 1592376517, ISBN 13 9781592376513.

Annual, in two volumes. Lists publishers, wholesalers, distributors, software firms, and museum and association imprints. Access by name, imprint, subsidiaries, divisions, state, firms with toll-free numbers, ISBN prefix, and publisher's field of activity. Also includes discount schedule and return policies.

Publishers Weekly. New York: Reed Business Information, 1872–. ISSN 00000019.

Weekly. Reviews books and audiovisual materials. Discusses news and trends in the book industry, including author interviews, advance book reviews, marketing and book design, and manufacturing articles (http://www.publishersweekly.com/).

The Pura Belpré Awards: Celebrating Latino Authors and Illustrators. Rose Zertuche Trevino, ed. Chicago: American Library Association, 2006. ISBN 0838935621, ISBN 13 9780838935620.

Covers the first ten years of the Pura Belpré Awards. Annotates the award-winning titles and provides biographies of the authors and illustrators. Aids with collection development. Includes program ideas and activities.

Quill and Quire: Canada's Magazine of Book News and Reviews. Toronto: Key Publishers, 1935–. ISSN 00336491.

Ten times a year. Available online. Reviews books and has advertisements for tapes and records. Subscription: 111 Queen Street East, 3rd floor, Toronto, Ontario M5C 1S2, 416-364-333 or email: info@quillandquire.com (https://www.quillandquire.com).

Reaching Reluctant Young Adult Readers: A Handbook for Librarians and Teachers. Edward T. Sullivan. Lanham, MD: Scarecrow, 2002. ISBN 0810843439, ISBN 13 9780810843431.

Offers strategies, tools, and resources to entice reluctant readers with characters and themes that are appropriate on an intellectual and maturity level. Cultural relevance to Asian, Black, and

Latino students addressed. Includes fiction, comics, graphic novels, nonfiction, picture books, magazines, and audiobooks. Digitized: November 17, 2006.

Readers' Guide to Periodical Literature. Bronx, NY: H.W. Wilson, 1901–. ISSN 00340464.

Monthly. Available in print and online. Author and subject indexes to selected general interest periodicals of reference value in libraries, including book reviews. Related source: *Abridged Readers' Guide to Periodical Literature, Readers' Guide Full Text, Mega Edition* (online), *Readers' Guide Full Text, Select Edition* (online) (http://www.hwwilson.com/Databases/Readersg.htm).

Recommended Books in Spanish for Children and Young Adults: 2004–2008. Isabel Schon. Lanham, MD: Scarecrow, 2009. ISBN 0810863863, ISBN 13 9780810863866.

Critical annotations for more than 1,300 books in Spanish, including reference, nonfiction, and fiction. Section on publishers' series. Appendix of dealers. Indexes of authors, titles, and subjects.

Recommended Reference Books for Small and Medium-Sized Libraries. Bohdan S. Wynar, ed. Westport, CT: Libraries Unlimited, 1981–. ISSN 02775948.

Annual. Reviews coded to identify titles of interest to school library media centers.

Recommended Reference Books for Small and Medium-Sized Libraries and Media Centers. Vol. 30. Graff Hysell Shannon, ed. Westport, CT: Libraries Unlimited, 2010. ISBN 9781598845921; ISBN 13 9781598845921.

Based on *American Reference Books Annual*; written by over 200 subject specialists; identifies best, most affordable, and most appropriate new reference materials in any field.

Recommended Reference Books in Paperback. 3rd ed. Jovian P. Lang and Jack O'Gorman. Englewood, CO: Libraries Unlimited, 2000. ISBN 1563085836, IBSN 13 9781563085833, ISBN 0585325111 (electronic bk.), ISBN 13 9780585325118 (electronic bk.).

Annotates approximately 1,000 titles covering a wide range of subjects. Digitized: December 15, 2009.

Reference and Research Guide to Mystery and Detective Fiction. 2nd ed. Richard Bleiler. Englewood, CO: Libraries Unlimited, 2004. ISBN 1563089246, ISBN 13 9781563089244. Hardcover Edition: ISBN 9781563089244; ISBN 13 9781563089244.

Provides a comprehensive guide to mystery and detective titles for use as a reference and research tool and aid to collection development. Includes author index and website links.

Reference Sources for Small and Medium-Sized Libraries. 7th ed. Jack O'Gorman. Chicago: American Library Association, 2008. ISBN 0838909434, ISBN 13 9780838909430, ISBN 1441618929 (electronic bk.), ISBN 13 9781441618924 (electronic bk.)

Comprehensive buying guide. Describes reference sources recommended by the Reference Sources for Small and Medium-sized Libraries Editorial Committee, Collection Development and Evaluation Section, Reference and User Services Association of the American Library Association. Includes different types of affordable resources such as websites, CD-ROMs, electronic databases, and print. Titles are annotated and include bibliographic information.

Resources in Education (RIE). Kerri Nine, ed. U.S. Department of Education, Office of Educational Research and Improvement, National Library of Education, Educational Resources Information Center, Lanham, MD. ERIC Processing and Reference Facility, 1966–. ISSN 00980897.

Monthly. Also available from ERIC as part of a computer file, online sources, and CD-ROMs. Provides summaries of the documents and abstracts available from the ERIC Document Reproduction Service (EDRS). Distributor: U.S. Government Printing Office, Washington, DC 20402 (http://www.eric.ed.gov/).

Romance Fiction: A Guide to the Genre. Kristin Ramsdell. 2nd ed. Englewood, CO: Libraries Unlimited, 2011. ISBN 159158177X, ISBN 13 9781591581772.

Provides background information. Identifies selected titles for young adults. Updated edition includes new authors and titles as well as expanded literature categories.

S B & F (Science Books and Films). Washington, DC: American Association for the Advancement of Science, 1965–. ISSN 15335046. Also *S B & F Online* at http://www.sbfonline.com/.

Bimonthly. Reviews books, films, videos, and software. Lists Public Broadcasting System materials. Covers preschool through professional materials. Online-only format. Subscription: American Association for the Advancement of Science, 1200 New York Avenue, NW, Washington, DC 20005 (http://community.sbfonline.com/content/SubscribeToday.aspx).

Scholastic Reading Counts! Software Manual. New York: Scholastic Inc., 2006. ISBN 0439784840, ISBN 13 9780439784849.

Manages and motivates independent reading, grades K-12. Also available online at http://teacher.scholastic.com/products/independent_reading/scholastic_reading_counts/program_overview.htm.

School Libraries in Canada Online. Canadian Association for School Libraries, 1980–. ISSN 17108535. Free online at http://www.clatoolbox.ca/casl/slic/

Quarterly. Reviews books, films, videos, and CDs for grades K-12.

School Library Journal: The Magazine of Children, Young Adults, and School Librarians. New York: Reed Business Information, 1954–. ISSN 03628930.

Twelve issues per year. Reviews books (preschool through adult titles for young people, Spanish language, references), videos, recordings, CD-ROMs, and software. Includes checklists, pamphlets, posters, and free materials. Includes monthly index, annual author/title book review index, and audiovisual index (http://www.slj.com/).

School Talk. Urbana, IL: National Council of Teachers of English, 1995–. ISSN 10832939 (http://www.ncte.org/journals/st).

Quarterly. Each issue focuses on a theoretical or pedagogical topic of interest to elementary school teachers of English language arts.

Science. Washington, DC: American Association for the Advancement of Science, 1880–. ISSN 00368075.

Weekly. Scientific research and commentary (http://www.sciencemag.org/magazine).

Science and Children: The Journal for Elementary School Science Teachers. Washington, DC: National Science Teachers Association, 1963–. ISSN 00368148.

Nine times per year (September through May) and online at (http://www.nsta.org/pubs/sc/). Presents ideas and activities for science educators from preschool through middle school. Reviews software, curriculum materials, and children's books. Subscription: National Science Teachers Association (NSTA), 1840 Wilson Boulevard, Arlington VA 22201-3000 (http://www.nsta.org/membership/benefits.aspx?lid=ele).

Science Scope: A Journal for Middle-Junior High Science Teachers. Kenneth L. Roberts, ed. Arlington, VA: National Science Teachers Association, 1978–. ISSN 08872376.

Nine times a year. Ideas about how to teach science (http://www.nsta.org/middleschool/).

The Science Teacher. National Science Teachers Association, 1934–. ISSN 00368555. Available online at http://www.nsta.org/highschool#journal.

Nine times a year, (January, February, March, April, July, September, October, November, December). Reviews software, books for students, and professional books. Subscription: NSTA, 1840 Wilson Boulevard, Arlington VA 22201-3000 (www.nsta.org).

Science Through Children's Literature: An Integrated Approach. 2nd ed. Carol M. Butzow and John W. Butzow. Englewood, CO: Libraries Unlimited, 2000. ISBN 1563086514, ISBN 13 9781563086519, ISBN 0585252459 (electronic bk.), ISBN 13 9780585252452 (electronic bk.).

Features more than 30 instructional units and offers lesson ideas and activities. Identifies useful books with science in the storyline.

Selecting Books for the Elementary School Library Media Center: A Complete Guide. Phyllis Van Orden. New York: Neal-Schuman, 2000. ISBN 1555703682, ISBN 13 9781555703684.

Describes the selection process and identifies criteria for picture books, fiction, folk literature, poetry, information books, reference works, and professional books. Glossary.

Senior High School Library Catalog. 16th ed. Juliette Yaakov, ed. New York: H.W. Wilson, 2002. ISBN 0824210085, ISBN 13 9780824210083. Also available online at http://www.hwwilson.com/print/srhscat.htm.

Four annual supplements. Abridged Dewey Decimal Classification. Provides bibliographic and order information, availability of paperback editions, Sears subject headings, and descriptive or critical annotations. Index by author, title, subject, and analytics. Link directs to: "Senior High Core Collection: A Selection Guide."

Serving Boys Through Reading Advisory. Michael Sullivan. Chicago: American Library Association, 2009. ISBN 083891022X, 13 9780838910221.

Emphasizes nonfiction and boy-friendly categories of genre fiction. Includes lists of over 500 recommended books and suggestions for booktalks.

Serving LGBTIQ Library Archive Users: Essays on Outreach, Services, Collection and Access. Ellen Greenblatt, ed. Jefferson, NC: McFarland, 2011. ISBN 13 9780786448944.

Includes various essays about library services to LGBTIQ youth.

Social Education. Arlington, VA: National Council for the Social Studies, 1937–. ISSN 00377724.

Seven issues per year. Reviews books for children and young adults, and includes ideas for lessons, teaching techniques, and incorporating instructional technology. Subscription: National Council for the Social Studies, 8555 16th Street, Silver Spring, MD 20910 (http://www.socialstudies.org/publications/se/). Alternate Link: (http://www.socialstudies.org/socialeducation).

Social Studies and the Young Learner. Kristen Page, ed. Silver Spring, MD: National Council for the Social Studies, 1988–. ISSN 10560300.

Quarterly. Offers K-6 social studies educators practical tips in all aspects of social studies instruction (http://www.socialstudies.org/publications/ssyl).

Software and CD-ROM Reviews on File. New York: Facts on File, 1985–2006. ISSN 10876367.

Monthly. Reviews over 600 software programs per year. Indexes by subject and company. Provides publisher, address, price, and publisher's description. Condenses and cites reviews.

Software Encyclopedia: A Guide for Personal, Professional, and Business Users Including Application Software on CD-ROM. New Providence, NJ: R.R. Bowker, 2008. ISBN 0835249697, ISBN 13 9780835249690.

Annual. Provides annotated listings for over 44,600 software programs. Entries classified under 668 subject headings containing title, subtitle, version number, publication date, compatible system, memory, and application requirements.

Some of My Best Friends Are Books: Guiding Gifted Readers for Preschool to High School. 3rd ed. Judith Wynn Halsted. Scottsdale, AZ: Great Potential Press, 2009. ISBN 0910707960 ISBN 13 9780910707961.

Contains summaries of about 300 books and research on the reading needs of gifted students. Themes include achievement, imagination, perfectionism, relationships, and resiliency among others. Index of books organized by grade, subject, and author.

Special Education and the Law: A Guide for Practitioners. 2nd ed., updated with new IDEA regulations. Allan G. Osborne, Jr. and Charles J. Russo. Thousand Oaks, CA: Corwin Press, 2007. ISBN 1412926238, ISBN 13 9781412926232.

Information on every facet of special education law: federal mandates, statutes, regulations, and special education case law. Discusses rights to a free appropriate public education, related services, assistive technology, and transition services; due process procedures for evaluation, development of IEPs, and placement; student discipline, dispute resolution, remedies for failure to provide a free appropriate public education, conflict management, and IDEA compliance. Includes glossary, links to useful websites, and a listing of Special Education departments by state.

The Special Educator's Survival Guide. 2nd ed. Roger Pierangelo. Somerset, NJ: John Wiley & Sons, 2004. ISBN 0787970964, ISBN 13 9780787970963.

Practical guide covering current American laws and standards. Identifies various stages of the referral process, parent intakes and conferences, evaluation, interpretation, diagnosis, remediation, placement, individual education plans, classroom management, medication, educational law, and more. Offers essential tools including reproducible forms, checklists, and sample letters.

Subject Guide to Books in Print. See Books in Print.

Subject Guide to Children's Books in Print. See Children's Books in Print.

SUNLINK Weed of the Month Club. 1999–2005. Florida Department of Education. Archive available at http://www.wmrls.org/services/colldev/weeding.html.

Offers practical suggestions and criteria for weeding collections one subject at time. Recommends over 100 weeding subjects with suggested Dewey numbers and weeding criteria for each.

Talking Books Topics. Edmund O'Reilly, ed. Washington, DC: U.S. Library of Congress, National Library Service for the Blind and Physically Handicapped (NLS), 1935–. ISSN 00399183.

Bimonthly. Annotates magazines and books available through the cooperating libraries. Contains news of developments and activities in library services and announcements of new recorded books and magazines. Titles are available free to individuals with visual impairments and/or physical handicaps (http://www.loc.gov/nls/tbt/).

Teacher Librarian. David Loertscher and Elizabeth "Betty" Marcoux, eds. Blue Ridge Summit, PA: Scarecrow, 1973–. ISSN 14811782. (Formerly *Emergency Librarian.* ISSN 03158888).

Bimonthly. Available online. Reviews professional reading, magazines, paperbacks, software, videos, and websites. Subscription: Teacher Librarian, 15200 NBN Way, Blue Ridge Summit, PA 17214 (http://www.teacherlibrarian.com).

Teaching Children Mathematics. Editorial Panel. Reston, VA: The National Council of Teachers of Mathematics, 1994–. ISSN 10735836. (Formerly *Arithmetic Teacher.* ISSN 0004130X).

Monthly August—May. Includes articles on teaching mathematics to elementary-age children. Articles focus on intuitive and exploratory investigation. Subscription: included in membership dues in pre-K-8 section of The National Council of Teachers of Mathematics (http://www.nctm.org/publications/tcm.aspx).

Teaching Exceptional Children. Barbara Ludlow, ed. Reston, VA: The Council for Exceptional Children, 1968–. ISSN 00400599.

Six times a year. Articles deal with current issues and practical methods and materials for classroom use. Archives online 2001 to present. Subscription: Council for Exceptional Children, 2900 Crystal Drive, Suite 1000, Arlington, VA 22202-3557 (http://www.cec.sped.org/bk/abtec.htm).

The Teaching Librarian. Toronto: Ontario School Library Association, 1974–. ISSN 1188679X. (Formerly *The Reviewing Librarian.* ISSN 03180948).

Three times a year. Reviews books, audiovisual materials, government publications, and magazines. Ontario Library Association, 100 Lombard Street, Ste 303, Toronto, ON M5C 1M3, Canada.

Tech Trends: For Leaders in Education and Training. Association for Educational Communications and Technology, 1985–. New York: Springer. ISSN 87563894, ISSN 15597075 (online).

Six times a year. Included in membership dues "Copyright and You," a regular column. A forum for those in the educational communication and technology field focusing on application, training, and instruction. Subscription: AECT, 1800 North Stonelake Drive, Suite 2, Bloomington, IN 47404 (http://www.springer.com/education+%26+language/learning+%26+instruction/journal/11528).

Technology and Copyright Law: A Guidebook for the Library, Research, and Teaching Professions. 2nd ed. Arlene Bielefield and Lawrence Cheeseman. New York: Neal-Schuman, 2007. ISBN 1555705707, ISBN 13 9781555705701.

An exhaustive, scholarly examination of copyright history and law. Covers international developments in copyright law, judicial decisions, and congressional guidelines, offers examples of applying the law to real-life situations and discusses the electronic classroom.

Technology and Learning. New York: NewBay Media, 1980–. ISSN 10536728.

Ten issues a year. Reviews computer software and multimedia for elementary and secondary students. Provides hardware requirements, emphasis, grade level, publisher, description of software manuals and guides, rating, strengths, and weaknesses (www.techlearning.com).

Teen Chick Lit: A Guide to Reading Interests. Christine Meloni. Santa Barbara, CA: Libraries Unlimited, 2010. ISBN 13 9781591587569 (acid-free paper).

Describes and puts into categories more than 500 titles. Provides bibliographic information, recommended ages, book awards, media connections, keywords, and annotations.

Teen Genreflecting 3: A Guide to Reading Interests. Diana Tixier Herald. Santa Barbara, CA: Libraries Unlimited, 2011. ISBN 1591587298 (acid-free paper), 13 9781591587293 (acid-free paper), ISBN 1591587298 (hbk.), ISBN 13 9781591587293 (hbk.).

Guide covers nearly 1,300 titles (1,100 are new) and authors for popular teen genres of historical novels, science fiction, fantasy, mystery, suspense, horror adventure, sports, romance contemporary novels, contemporary realistic to fantasy, and graphic novels. In addition, each genre and subgenre is defined; current trends in publishing and teen interest, readers' advisory services to teens, and collection development are discussed.

Teen Legal Rights. Rev. ed. Kathleen Hempleman. Westport, Conn.: Greenwood Press, 2000. ISBN 031330968X (alk. paper), ISBN 13 9780313309687 (alk. paper).

Updated to include more information for the turn of the century. Includes driving, on the job, parents' divorce, alcohol and drug abuse, gay and lesbian teens, property rights, contracts, and how to find the law.

Teen Rights: A Legal Guide for Teens and the Adults in Their Lives. 2nd ed. Traci Truly. Naperville, Illinois: Sphinx Publishing (imprint of Sourcebooks), 2005. ISBN 1572485256, ISBN 13 9781572485259.

Legal responsibilities and rights of teens, what to do if rights are abused or revoked.

Teen Rights (and Responsibilities): A Legal Guide for Teens and the Adults in Their Lives. Kathleen A. Hempelman. PLACE: Paw Prints, 2008. ISBN 1435293770, ISBN 13 9781435293779.

Covers discrimination issues, freedom of expression, school libraries, and school newspapers.

Television Production: A Classroom Approach. 2nd ed. Keith Kyker and Christopher Curchy. Santa Barbara, CA: ABC-CLIO, 2004. ISBN 156308774X (instructor ed.), ISBN 13 9781563087745 (instructor ed.).

Reflects advances in television production in the past 10 years, including digital imaging and equipment, equipment use, project planning instruction, news gathering methodology, studio production, and movie production. The teacher's guide has instructional notes, answer sheets, instructional ideas, and evaluation notes.

Thematic Guide to Popular Nonfiction. Lynda G. Adamson. Westport, CT: Greenwood Press, 2006. ISBN 0313328552, ISBN 13 9780313328558.

Identifies popular works of nonfiction related to particular themes. Included are alphabetically arranged entries on 50 prevalent themes, such as animals, exploration, genocide, immigrants, poverty, and race relations. Lists of additional nonfiction for further reading, additional themes, and related works, bibliography of works on popular nonfiction.

Through Indian Eyes: The Native Experience in Books for Children. 5th ed. Beverly Slapin and Doris Seale, eds. Berkeley, CA: Oyate, 2006. ISBN 0962517593, ISBN 13 9780962517594.

Expands on earlier editions of *Books Without Bias: Through Indian Eyes*. Critically evaluates and offers guidelines for selection of books on Native Americans. Gives book reviews and history and criticism. Includes bibliographical references and index.

Through the Eyes of a Child: An Introduction to Children's Literature. 8th ed. Donna E. Norton and Saundra E. Norton. Upper Saddle River, NJ: Prentice Hall, 2010. ISBN 9780137074013, ISBN 13 9780137074013 (with MyEducationKit), ISBN 013702875X (hbk.), ISBN 13 9780137028757 (hbk.)

Prepares reader to evaluate, choose, and share quality literature with children. Focus on classroom-tested teaching strategies and new teaching ideas. Treats multicultural literature as a separate chapter as well as integrated throughout. Updated edition expands coverage of biography, informational books, and integrated technology, as well as author insights.

TV Guide.

Provides a daily listing of television programs (http://www.tvguide.com).

University Press Books Selected for Public and Secondary School Libraries. Association of American University Presses, 1991–. ISSN 10554173. Online at http://aaupnet.org/librarybooks/.

Annual. Selections rated by a committee from the AASL and the Public Library Association (PLA). Rates books in terms of general audience, regional interest, and in-depth collections for students in grades 6–12. For publishers listed, see website for the AAUP On-Line Catalog (http://aaupnet.org/librarybooks/). Members of AASL and PLA automatically receive copies. Librarians can obtain a free copy of the bibliography by writing on their school's stationery to the Association of American University Presses Marketing Department, 28–30 West 36th Street, Suite 602, New York, NY 10018.

U.S. Government Books. U.S. Government Printing Office (formerly *U.S. Government Book: Publications for Sale by the Government Printing Office*. ISSN 07342764). Now online at http://www.gpoaccess.gov/index.html.

Lists available books. A free service of the U.S. Government Printing Office. Information can be used without restriction, unless specifically noted.

U.S. Government on the Web: Getting the Information You Need, 3rd ed. Peter Hernon, Robert E. Dugan, and John A. Shuler. Westport, CT: Libraries Unlimited, 2003. ISBN 1591580862, ISBN 13 9781591580867.

Serves as a directory, as a map to the government's structure, and as a playbook outlining strategies for locating information. Describes issues, types of publications, search engines, and websites. Includes a chapter about websites for children. Indexes by government body, title, and author.

Venture into Cultures: A Resource Book of Multicultural Materials and Programs, 2nd. ed. Olga R. Kuharets. Chicago: American Library Association, 2001. ISBN 0838935133, ISBN 13 9780838935132.

Rich stories, illustrations, traditions, and music from around the world, including African, Caribbean, Indian, Jewish-American, Korean, Latin American, Middle Eastern, Native American, and Russian items. Recommends books, websites, videos, audiotapes, and directions for programming materials. Includes bibliographical references and index.

Vertical File Index: Guide to Pamphlets and References to Current Topics. New York: H.W. Wilson, 1955–. ISSN 0042–4439.

Monthly (except August). Provides order information for over 3,000 sources of free and inexpensive materials including reading lists, charts, posters, maps, and government publications. Arranged by subject with title index. Subscription: H.W. Wilson, 950 University Avenue, Bronx, NY 10452 (http://www.hwwilson.com/).

The Video Librarian: Video Review Guide for Libraries. Randy Pitman, ed. Seabeck, WA: Video Librarian, 1986–. ISSN 08876851.

Bimonthly. Reviews nearly 200 videos for public, school, and university libraries. The magazine's supplement is available online at http://www.videolibrarian.com/. Subscription: *Video Librarian,* 8705 Honeycomb Court NW, Seabeck, WA 98380 (http://www.videolibrarian.com).

Video Source Book. Jim Craddock, ed. Farmington Hills, MI: Gale Group, 1979-. ISSN 07480881.

Annual. Covers prerecorded video programs currently available on videocassette, videodisc, and videotape. Provides date of release, running time, major plot, theme, closed captions, or signing for individuals with a hearing impairment, and availability. Order from: Gale Group, 27500 Drake Road, Farmington, MI 48331 (http://www.gale.com).

The Video Source Book: A Guide to Programs Currently Available on Video in the Areas of: Movies/Entertainment, General Interest/Education, Sports/Recreation, Fine Arts, Health/Science, Business/Industry, Children/Juvenile, How to/Instruction. 46th ed. Farmington Hills, MI: Thomson Gale, 2011. ISBN 13 9781414448442 (v. 01: A-B), ISBN 13 9781414448459 (v. 02: C-E), ISBN 13 9781414448466 (v. 03: F-I), ISBN 13 9781414474991 (v. 04: J-M), ISBN 13 9781414475004 (v. 05: N-R), ISBN 13 9781414475011 (v. 06: S-T), ISBN 13 9781414475028 (v. 07: U-Z), ISBN 13 9781414475035 (v. 08: Subject index), ISBN 139781414475042 (v. 09: Credits index).

Comprehensive coverage of video offerings with listings for more than 130,000 complete programs, encompassing more than 160,000 videos. All titles arranged alphabetically with bibliographic information included. Multiple indexes (www.gale.cengage.com).

VOYA: Voice of Youth Advocates. Metuchen, NJ: Scarecrow, 1978–. ISSN 01604201. Available online.

Bimonthly. Reviews books (trade, paperbacks, reprints, professional), reference titles, and media of materials for or about adolescents (http://www.voya.com).

Weaving the Literacy Web: Creating Curriculum Based on Books Children Love. Hope Vestergaard. St. Paul, MN: Redleaf Press, 2005. ISBN 192961070X, ISBN 13 9781929610709.

Introduction to book-based webbing and ideas for activity planning, as well as helpful tips for observing children's interests and evaluating books for the classroom library.

Web Braille. Library of Congress, National Library Service for the Blind and Physically Handicapped (NLS).

Provides information on how to access electronic Braille books (http://www.loc.gov/nls/reference/factsheets/webbraille.html).

Weeding Library Collections: Library Weeding Methods. 4th ed. Stanley J. Slote. Boulder, CO.: NetLibrary, 2000. ISBN 0585202672 (electronic bk.), ISBN 13 9780585202679 (electronic bk.).

Discusses the policies and practices used in weeding collections.

The World of Work Through Children's Literature: An Integrated Approach. Carol M. Butzow and John W. Butzow. Greenwood Village, CO: Teacher Ideas Press, 2002. ISBN 1563088142, ISBN 13 9781563088148.

Features lessons, activities, and ideas based on a variety of themes about work, including local economy, work skills, work communities. Explores skills needed to succeed, including teamwork and cooperative learning.

The World Through Children's Books. Susan Stan. Lanham, MD: Scarecrow, 2002. ISBN 0810841983, ISBN 13 9780810841987.

Annotated bibliography organized geographically by world region and country, and containing nearly 700 books representing over 70 countries. Titles published between 1996 and 2000. Companion volume to Carl M. Tomlinson's *Children's Books from Other Countries,* focused on titles published between 1950 and 1996.

WWW Evaluation Guide. Tana Hudak. Takoma Park, MD: Takoma Park Maryland Library (http://www.studyplans.com/Evaluatingwebsites.htm).

Evaluation guide listed under "School Resources." Helps the evaluator assess the identifying factors for the site, analyze content and sources, and evaluate visuals.

Youth with Special Needs. Mason Crest Publishers. 15-volume set (from Mason Crest Web site): ISBN 13 9781590847275.

Fictional stories that contain factual information having to do with the realities of life for youth with special needs (http://www.masoncrest.com/catalog_series.asp?sid=6D6B3A11-D1E6).

Index

About the Author

KAY BISHOP, PhD, is associate professor and director of the Online MLS Program at the University at Buffalo. She has a bachelor's degree from Florida State University, a Master of Arts from the University at South Florida, a Master of Education from Washington State University, and a Ph.D. from Florida State University. Her most recent books include *Positive Classroom Management Skills for School Librarians* (2012) and *Connecting Libraries with Classrooms: The Curricular Roles of the Media Specialist, Second Edition* (2011).

CPSIA information can be obtained at www.ICGtesting.com
Printed in the USA
LVOW09s0747310816

502442LV00001B/1/P